Breaking Barriers

Rayden Foster

Published by Rayden Foster, 2024.

While every precaution has been taken in the preparation of this book, the publisher assumes no responsibility for errors or omissions, or for damages resulting from the use of the information contained herein.

BREAKING BARRIERS

First edition. September 30, 2024.

Copyright © 2024 Rayden Foster.

ISBN: 979-8227889751

Written by Rayden Foster.

Table of Contents

Dedicated to all Black British pioneers, past present and future at all levels of society. It is recognition of all the struggles and tribulations that Black trailblazers, heroes and heroines have had to, or will endure and how this has contributed to British society.

Breaking Barriers

Black British Pioneers

Rayden Foster

Acknowledgement

Massive thanks are due to my family, particularly my wife and son, for putting up with me while I was setting this up. I am grateful to all the people who have provided the information and naturally grateful to and appreciate all the people mentioned.

It has been painful at times discovering all the injustices, hardships and obstacle that people had to endure just to be able to exist and do the things they were more than capable of doing. Each and every one of them has helped to improve British society. The perversity of racism means that despite these pioneers proving their capability, it did not always lead to acceptance of other black people who would have been just as capable.

Introduction

In 2019 Michael Fuller wrote a book called "Kill the Black one First". It is a book which relates his experiences as a police officer He was the first (and so far only) ethnic minority chief constable in the United Kingdom and the first black officer of chief constable-equivalent rank. The book highlights his trials and tribulations encountered in trying to work and succeed to the best of his ability.

Reading the book led me to consider all the other Black Firsts. Seeing Black people in particular positions seems common place now but there was clearly a period when Black people were not accepted or welcome in various positions. There is a significant amount that they had to endure in striving to achieve in their chosen area.

For centuries, black individuals have brought a wealth of contribution into the fabric of British society, helping to shape and transform it in profound and inspiring ways.

This book seeks to provide a summary of some of the remarkable contributions, accomplishments, and milestones of Black Britons throughout history. It is a celebration of the enduring spirit, resilience, ingenuity and triumph that has propelled generations forward, in spite of adversity and marginalization.

I have embarked on a captivating journey, exploring various spheres of British society discovering stories of trailblazers, visionaries, and change-makers who defied the limitations imposed upon them, challenging societal norms and redefining what it means to be British.

From pioneers such as Ignatius Sancho, whose literary brilliance and activism inspired generations, to the remarkable achievements of Mary Seacole, whose indomitable spirit led her to the battlefields of the Crimean War, Black Britons have consistently left an indelible mark on their nation's history. The likes of Sir Lewis Hamilton, Michael Fuller, and Walter Tull, whose unwavering determination shattered barriers and paved the way for future generations.

This book is not just about the past; it is also a testament to the present and a beacon for the future. It celebrates contemporary Black British luminaries, including artists, entrepreneurs, scientists, and community leaders, who continue to shape the ever-evolving landscape of modern Britain. Their stories, aspirations, and achievements stand as a testament to the unyielding human spirit and the boundless potential that lies within each of us.

It is crucial to recognize that Black British achievement is not separate from the broader British narrative. Rather, it is an integral part of the nation's identity, interwoven with its triumphs and challenges. By acknowledging and honouring the contributions of Black Britons, we enrich our collective understanding of history and pave the way for a more inclusive and equitable future.

The aim is to inspire, educate, and instil pride and act as a testament to the fact that greatness knows no boundaries, that the human spirit is relentless, and that the power to change the world resides within each and every one of us.

These stories and deserve to be heard, cherished, and celebrated and the achievements deserve to be unveiled. The fact is that throughout British society there have been a lot of Black firsts, whether it is the first Black person to be engaged in a particular company or achieve a particular position. I also owe a big apology to all the people in this book. I have not written their life stories but given a summary. To limit their life stories to a few pages does them a disservice. So please see this as a start to go further and identify and understand even more about these truly remarkable people.

A Time Line of Black People in Britain

AD 43 - The Roman conquest of Britain begins with soldiers drawn from all over North Africa and Europe.

668 - African-born Abbot Hadrian becomes abbot of St Augustine's Abbey, Canterbury.

1241 - The earliest known drawing of a black Briton is made in the Domesday Book.

1507 - John Blanke became one of the court trumpeters for Henry VII. He performs at both Henry VII's funeral and Henry VIII's coronation in 1509.

1508 - A poem written by William Dunbar called Of Ane Black-Moir, tells us there were black people in Britain at that time.

1555 - A group of African people are brought to Britain to learn English so they can act as interpreters for English traders.

1562 – Britain enters the Atlantic slave trade as John Hawkins leads the first slaving expedition to Sierra Leone. Over three million Africans are transported to British colonies over the next two centuries.

1672 - The Royal African Company is created in England to manage the slave trade.

1700s - The population of black and Asian slaves, servants and seamen increases.

1760s - 20,000 black people live in Britain, including up to 15,000 in London. Black people are often shown and written about as less than human.

1765 - The campaign for the freedom of slaves begins in Britain.

1772 - A decline in slavery begins in England.

1775-1783 - African American slave soldiers who fought for Britain in the American Revolutionary War arrive in London but have no money and are forced to beg on the streets.

1781 - 132 sick Africans thrown off the British slaving ship, Zong. Their murder is authorised by the ship's captain, Luke Collingwood, to claim insurance money. The event sparks the movement against the slave trade.

1792-1815 - Black soldiers and seamen settle in London after fighting in the Napoleonic Wars.

1807 - The Slave Trade Act was passed prohibiting the slave trade in the British Empire. It did not abolish the practice of slavery. It took effect on 1st May after 18 years of trying to pass an abolition bill. Slavery on English soil was unsupported in English law but it remained legal in most of the British Empire.

1833 - The Slavery Abolition Act was passed providing for the gradual abolition of slavery in most parts of the British Empire. It expanded the jurisdiction of the 1807 Slave Trade Act and made the purchase or ownership of slaves illegal within the British Empire, with the exception of "the Territories in the Possession of the East India Company", Ceylon (now Sri Lanka), and Saint Helena. The Act was repealed in 1998 as a part of wider rationalisation of English statute law; however, later anti-slavery legislation remains in force.

1834 - There is a decline in the black population due to restrictions on immigration from Africa.

1880s - New black communities are formed in Liverpool and Cardiff.

20th Century - Britain sees an increase in African students, professionals, businesspeople and athletes.

1914 - 1918 - The First World War brings an influx of Black people from different countries around the world fighting for and serving Britain. Despite volunteering and fighting for Britain they met racial prejudice and discrimination.

1919 - January to August, Race riots in London, Glasgow, Liverpool, Cardiff, Salford, Hull, South Shields, Newport, Barry.

1939 - 1945 - World War Two. People from the Caribbean and West Africa arrive as wartime workers and servicemen in the army, navy and air force, again meeting racial prejudice and discrimination.

1948 – Empire Windrush ship arrives at Tilbury Docks in Essex on 21st June with 1027 passengers. After WWII, the British government encouraged mass immigration from the former countries of the British Empire and Commonwealth to fill shortages in the labour market.

The British Nationality Act 1948 gave Citizenship of the UK and Colonies to all people living in the United Kingdom and its colonies, and the right of entry and settlement in the UK. Many West Indians were attracted by better prospects in what was often referred to as the mother country. As a result, Afro-Caribbean immigration to Britain increased

1950s-1960s - There is a huge migration of people from all over the Caribbean to work in hospitals and on transport and railway networks. They often struggle with racial prejudice.

1958 – Race riots in St Ann's, Nottingham and Notting Hill, London

1963 – Bristol bus boycott over refusal to employ black people.

1965 - The Race Relations Act, the first legislation in the United Kingdom to address racial discrimination. It outlawed discrimination on the grounds of colour, race, or ethnic or national origins in public places in Great Britain. This led to the creation of the Race Relations Board in 1966 to consider complaints under the Act.

1966 - First Notting Hill Carnival

1968 - The Race Relations Act made it illegal to refuse housing, employment, or public services to a person on the grounds of colour, race, ethnic or national origins in Great Britain (not in Northern Ireland, which had its own parliament. It also created the Community Relations Commission to promote harmonious community relations. The Act made amendments to the Race Relations Act 1965. It was superseded by the Race Relations Act 1976.

Many Asian people are expelled from Kenya and settle in Britain.

Enoch Powell makes his Rivers of Blood racist speech, 20th April 1968

1970 - During a peaceful protest against the unfair police targeting of The Mangrove Caribbean restaurant in Notting Hill, the 'Mangrove 9' were arrested for causing a riot. The subsequent trial lasted 55 days before a judge ruled against the police and found the activists not guilty.

1971 - The Immigration Act of 1971 passed, stripping Commonwealth citizens' right to remain in the UK and further restricting immigration.

1976 - The Race Relations Act is passed and the Commission for Racial Equality is established to prevent discrimination on the grounds of race. This included discrimination on the grounds of race, colour, and nationality, ethnic and national origin in the fields of employment, the provision of goods and services, education and public functions.

British Asian people from Malawi settle in Britain.

1980s - Somali refugees arrive in Britain.

1981 - New Cross house fire. On 18th January 13 Black young people killed. 20,000 people march on Parliament for racial justice on 2nd March.

1985 – Shooting of Cherry Groce on 28th September leading to Brixton riots. The death of Cynthia Jarrett of a heart attack after police searched her house looking for her son Floyd on 5th October leading to the Broadwater Farm riot in Tottenham on 6th October. Police Officer Keith Blakelock was murdered during the riot.

1987 - The first black members of parliament are elected. Diane Abbot, Bernie Grant, Paul Boateng along with Asian Keith Vaz.

1993 - The Asylum and Immigration Appeals Act is passed.

Stephen Lawrence murdered on 22nd April in Eltham after a racially motivated attack.

1999 – McPherson inquiry following the Stephen Lawrence murder concluded that the Metropolitan Police's murder investigation had been marred by a combination of professional incompetence, institutional racism and a failure of leadership by senior officers.

2000 - The Race Relations (Amendment) Act 2000 passed, an extension of the Race Relations Act 1976, requiring the police and other public authorities such as colleges and universities to take action to promote race equality.

Killing of Damilola Taylor in Peckham, highlighting issue of youth violence and stabbing.

2001 - The Race Relations Amendment Act states all public services must actively promote racial equality.

2006 - The Racial and Religious Hatred Act makes it illegal to stir up hatred against someone because of their race or religion.

2010 - The Equality Act consolidated previous anti-discrimination Acts and Regulations, including the Equal Pay Act 1970, the Sex Discrimination Act 1975, the Race Relations Act 1976, the Disability Discrimination Act 1995 and three major statutory instruments protecting discrimination in employment on grounds of religion or belief, sexual orientation and age. It also followed four major EU Equal Treatment Directives.

It protects citizens against discrimination based on nationality and citizenship and also extending individuals' rights in the workplace, in religion or belief, disability, age, sex, sexual orientation and gender reassignment.

2011 - 1,904,684 people (3% of the population) record they were 'Black, African, Caribbean or Black British' in the UK census.

2016 – UK votes to leave the European Union following a referendum by 52% votes to 48%.

First Black Lives Matter protest in the UK

2017 - On 14 June a fire broke out in the 24-storey Grenfell Tower block of flats in North Kensington, West London, burning for 60 hours. Seventy people died at the scene, and two people died later in hospital. Over 70 were injured with 223 escaping. It was the worst UK residential fire since the German Bombings of World War II.

2018 - The Windrush scandal was a British political scandal concerning people who were wrongly detained, denied legal rights, threatened with deportation, and in at least 83 cases wrongly deported from the UK by the Home Office. Many of those affected had been born British subjects and had arrived in the UK before 1973, particularly from Caribbean countries, as members of the Windrush generation.

Many were detained, lost their jobs or homes, had their passports confiscated, or were denied benefits or medical care to which they were entitled. A number of long-term UK residents were refused re-entry to the UK; a larger number were threatened with immediate deportation by the Home Office. This was created by the hostile environment policy instituted by Theresa May during her time as Home Secretary, the scandal led to the resignation of Amber Rudd as Home Secretary in April 2018 and the appointment of Sajid Javid as her successor. The scandal also prompted a wider debate about British immigration policy and Home Office practice.

Meghan Markle married Prince Harry. Media and commentators engage in blatantly racist and deeply offensive campaign against her, from the time their meeting was announced, because she had a black mother and white father.

2020 - UK officially leaves the European Union

World Health Organisation (WHO) declared Covid-19 as a pandemic with most of the world going into lockdown to contain the virus. Black British population particularly hard-hit by the virus with studies indicating they are at greater risk of catching and dying from the infection. Numerous reports suggest that the high prevalence is due to racial inequality in employment and housing.

Following the brutal killing of George Floyd by policemen in America, Black Lives Matter protests sweep the world. Demonstrations in the UK about racism and questions are raised about Britain's colonial past and its role within the slave industry. Demonstrators in Bristol topple a statue of slave trader Edward Colston.

2021 - The Welsh government become the first UK nation to make the teaching of Black, Asian and minority ethnic histories and experiences mandatory.

2024 - On 29 July 2024, 17 year old Axel Rudakubana killed three children and injured ten others at a Taylor Swift–themed dance workshop attended by 26 children in Southport Merseyside.

Following social media claims he was a Muslim asylum seeker there were days of mass anti-immigration protests and riots nationwide. It transpired Axel was a Christian born in Wales, though this did not change the attitude of the rioters and far-right supporters.

On 2 November 2024 Kemi Badenoch was elected the new leader of the Conservative party, the first Black leader to hold this role and the fourth woman after Margaret Thatcher, Theresa May and Liz Truss.

First Black male police officer in Britain

John Kent – (1805-1886)

John Kent was born in 1805 and he is considered to be the first black police officer in Britain. His father, Thomas Kent, was a victim of the slave trade, arriving in Whitehaven, England, as a slave in the 18th century. After about seven years, Thomas gained his freedom and became a sailor. He later returned to Carlisle, married a local woman from Cumbria, and they had 10 children, one of whom was John Kent, born at their family home in Low Hesket, Carlisle. He attended Hesket School.

John Kent married Mary Bell, a woman from Longtown, Cumbria, and they settled on Botchergate Street, Longtown as recorded in the 1841 national census. They had three children, William, Mary and Jane. He was known as a quiet, unassuming, yet strong and powerful man. Before joining the police force, he worked for the local authority, laying paving slabs.

His police career started in 1835 as a constable in Maryport, Carlisle. In August 1837 he joined Carlisle City Police force becoming a full Constable. Despite facing racial prejudice, he was known for his capable service and earned respect in the community, where he was referred to as "Black Kent." His presence was so notable that parents used the phrase "Black Kent's coming" to discipline misbehaving children, although he was known for his kindness towards children.

One of his notable achievements was the arrest of two counterfeiters. After apprehending the first suspect, John handcuffed him to his own fireplace and left an unloaded pistol with his wife, instructing her to use it if he tried to escape. He then successfully arrested the second suspect.

His career faced a setback in 1844 when he arrived drunk for duty. A new Chief Constable had implemented strict rules against officers being drunk on duty. Consequently, he was disciplined and dismissed from the police force on 12 December 1844.

After his dismissal, he worked as a court bailiff and later as a parish constable in the Eskdale ward. He eventually returned to Carlisle to work for the London and North Western Railway Companies, serving as an attendant in the waiting rooms at Citadel station.

John Kent passed away at the age of 81 on July 20, 1886, at his home in Henry Street, Carlisle. He was a significant and notable figure in Carlisle's history.

A plaque to commemorate his life was placed where Maryport jailhouse was located.

First Black police officer to join the London Metropolitan Police

Robert Branford – (1820-1869)

Robert Branford is believed to be the first black police officer in the London Metropolitan Police. Sadly there are few details about his life and no photographs. However it has been established that he was born in 1820 in Stoke-by-Nayland to a white mother called Hannah Branford and a Black father of whom little is known.

Robert Branford joined the Metropolitan Police in 1838 apparently lying on his form that he was born in 1817 and not 1820. He spent his entire career serving the Borough and Bermondsey, stationed at Stone's End Police Station near Borough High Street in London. His dedication and skill quickly earned him promotions. He became a Sergeant in 1846, an Inspector in 1851, and by 1856, he was appointed Superintendent of M Division, overseeing the Southwark area.

His achievements were recorded in a book written in 1893 by Timothy Cavanagh called "Scotland Yard Past and Present," where he is described as "half-caste" and praised for his extensive knowledge of police work, despite not being formally educated. Cavanagh remarked that he was probably the only superintendent of mixed race the Metropolitan Police ever had at that time.

However, Cavanagh also reported the racism he would have faced, saying that some colleagues referred to him as the N word behind his back. Living and working in the Victorian era, he undoubtedly faced significant prejudice and discrimination. His rise through the ranks is a testament to his resilience and capability. Unfortunately, his accomplishments were not widely recognized or celebrated during his lifetime, but his legacy as a pioneering figure in law enforcement endures.

Despite the obstacles he must have faced he was clearly a talented and highly-respected leader. On his retirement in 1866, The South London Journal reported that a very large meeting of officers and local tradesmen gathered on Kennington Lane to celebrate his tenure. Amid enthusiastic cheers he was given a gift of a silver inkstand liberally subscribed for by all members of the force. By perseverance he had raised himself to the highest post in his division.

He went on to enjoy his retirement with his wife Sarah who he had married at the Trinity Church near Newington Causeway in 1841. They had no children.

Despite spending his career in the hustle and bustle of inner London, it seems he was always attracted by the rural life of his childhood. He moved to Little Waldingfield where he died from kidney failure in 1869, just three years after retiring.

First Black police officer to be employed in Plymouth

Cecil Wilberforce Rodgers – (1899-1966)

Cecil Wilberforce Rodgers was employed by Plymouth City police as a special constable the first Black police officer in Plymouth and is believed to be Britain's first Black Special Constable. He was born on 16 January 1899, in South Milton near Salcombe,

His father, John, arrived in England in the late 19th century, accompanying the son of a Jamaican plantation owner for education. John Rodgers became a talented cabinet maker and musician. He was well-educated and active in the Methodist community and the Salvation Army. His mother, Susan Bessie Jarvis, was a seamstress from Kingsbridge.

Cecil was one of seven children and he was educated at Salcombe School.

During World War I, Cecil served in the 2nd Battalion of the British West Indies Regiment, which was composed primarily of Black soldiers from the Caribbean and the UK. The regiment experienced significant racial discrimination, culminating in the Taranto Revolt due to poor conditions and unequal treatment compared to white soldiers. Cecil was court-martialed but successfully appealed, maintaining an unblemished military record and his service medals.

After the war, he moved to Plymouth, where he married Frances Alice Lamble in 1922 and had four children. He also became a Special Constable with 'D' Sub-Division of the Plymouth City Police. He was designated Special Constable 295. There is not much record of his actual duties, as very few records were held of special constables; however, there are many photographs of him with his fellow officers at the Plymouth City Police during and after World War 2.

During the war, the police station in Greenbank was bombed. He was part of the team to help evacuate people, and he stayed for the duration of the war to further protect the city which faced bombing due to Plymouth's strategic naval base and dockyard.

Despite the challenges, he felt that there was no resentment toward him due to his race from either colleagues or the public. He was awarded a police long service medal, along with the British War Medal and the Victory Medal from his military service. He also sang as a first tenor in the Plymouth Clarion Choir, performing nationwide.

He passed away on 17 May 1966, at the age of 67, leaving behind a legacy of service and breaking racial barriers in both the military and police force.

The photograph below shows Cecil Wilberforce Rodgers on the left receiving a police long service medal.

First Black Special Police Officer in Gloucestershire

Astley Lloyd Blair – (1937-????)

Before he moved to England in July 1961, Astley Lloyd Blair worked for five years as a full-time policeman in Rae Town, East Kingston, Jamaica. He decided to move as he saw limited opportunities for advancement in the Jamaican Police Force. Hence he moved to England with his wife Bernice. They were initially welcomed by Bernice's brother, Sylvester Grant, who already lived in England.

At that time, the British police force was predominantly white, so Astley doubted his chances of being accepted despite his prior experience as a Jamaican police officer. He found work at the British Nylon Spinners factory, where a Welsh co-worker encouraged him to apply to the police force. Surprisingly, he was accepted.

In 1964, at the age of 27, Astley became a Special Constable in Gloucestershire, making him the first Black Special Police Officer in Gloucestershire. He expected his duties would be to handle traffic mainly in the summer, but his time as an officer wasn't easy due to discrimination and prejudice.

One notable incident involved stopping two cars with missing headlights. The first driver, known to Astley's fellow officer, received a warning. However, when they stopped a black driver for the same issue, Astley's colleague wanted to prosecute him. Astley was unwilling to accept this double standard and threatened to testify in court if the case proceeded, leading the officer to back down.

Despite such challenges, he continued his police career. In 1972, he joined the Metropolitan Police Force, where he served until his retirement in 1988. Sadly there is no documentary evidence of when he died.

His story is one of resilience and determination. He faced adversity and discrimination but remained dedicated to justice and making a positive impact on his community.

First Black woman police officer in Britain

Fay Allen — (1938-2021)

Sislin Fay Allen, known as Fay Allen, made history as the first Black woman police constable in the United Kingdom. She was born in Jamaica on 20March 1938. She moved to the UK in the early 1960s, initially working as a nurse at Queen's Hospital in Croydon. In 1968, she decided to explore a career in the police force after seeing a newspaper advertisement for prospective female police officers in the Metropolitan Police in London. Despite there being no Black female officers in Britain at the time, she applied and was accepted, starting her police career at Croydon's Fell Road Police Station.

She faced significant challenges, including negative attitudes from her own community and general prejudices within society. However, she found support among her colleagues in Croydon. Her first day on patrol was marked by curiosity and attention, with many people staring at her but also offering congratulations. She did not realize she was making history; she simply wanted a new career path and to do her job well.

Throughout her time as a police constable, she received some hate mail, but her superiors protected her from the worst of it. She stayed committed to her work, eventually transferring to the Missing Persons Bureau at Scotland Yard before returning to active duty at Norbury police station near Croydon.

In 1972, she left the Metropolitan Police due to family commitments and returned to Jamaica, joining the Jamaican Constabulary Force. She received a welcoming letter from the Jamaican Prime Minister, Michael Manley. She moved back to England in 2015, living in South London. In 2020, she was honoured with a lifetime achievement award from the National Black Police Association for her groundbreaking achievements.

She returned to Jamaica and passed away in Ocho Rios in July 2021 at the age of 83. Her story is a testament to her determination and courage in breaking barriers as a pioneering Black female police officer. Her contributions to law enforcement have left a lasting impact on the history of policing in the UK.

First Black police officer to join the London Metropolitan Police

Norwell Roberts QPM – (1946-)

Norwell Lionel Roberts QPM is renowned as the first black police officer to join the London Metropolitan Police in the 20th century, eventually reaching the rank of Detective Sergeant.

He was born Norwell Lionel Gumbs on 23 October 1946, in Anguilla, West Indies. Law enforcement ran in his family as his grandfather and three uncles served as high-ranking police officers. One uncle even received the Colonial Police Medal.

His early life was challenging due to the death of his father. His mother moved to England hoping for a better life while leaving him with his strict, preacher grandparents. He joined his mother in England at the age of nine, where he faced significant racial prejudice and discrimination. His mother had run several neighbourhood shops back in Anguilla, but in London she took any domestic jobs she could get. The family eventually settled in Bromley, Kent.

He excelled at school, but he was denied the opportunity to attend grammar school due to racism because he was black. He had to attend a secondary modern school where he endured severe bullying. The older sixth form students dropped him head first to the ground in order to see the colour of his blood. He still carries the scar on his forehead, but never once complained to his mother as he felt she would be powerless to do anything.

He started his working career as a scientific laboratory technician before joining the Metropolitan Police in 1967, inspired by an advert in the Daily Mirror newspaper seeking black candidates to become police officers. He applied as a joke not believing he would get in. However he discovered he was successful in a newspaper article stating a coloured man was on way to join police force. They did not bother to inform him first. He officially joined the Metropolitan Police on 3 April 1967.

Despite facing systemic racism and hostility from colleagues, he persevered. After putting up with the constant misspelling of his name "Gumbs", he changed his name in 1968 by deed poll, taking his mother's maiden name of Roberts.

After he completed his training, he served at various police stations, often encountering racial abuse and sabotage. He faced ostracism and harassment, but found support within the community he served. His resilience was tested numerous times, yet he remained committed to his duty. He eventually became a Detective Constable in 1977 and continued to serve in various roles until his retirement in 1997.

His contributions to improving relations between black and white communities were recognized with three police commendations and the Queen's Police Medal in 1995. Post-retirement, he remains active in advising other officers on dealing with racism and is a member of the Freemasons.

His story is a powerful testament to courage and perseverance. Despite ongoing challenges highlighted by reports like the Baroness Casey Review in 2023, his legacy as a trailblazer in the Metropolitan Police endures, inspiring future generations to continue the fight for equality and justice.

First Black chief constable in the United Kingdom

Michael Fuller QPM – (1959-)

In 2004, Michael Fuller made history, becoming the first black man to hold the title of Chief Constable of Kent Police and Chief Inspector of the Crown Prosecution Service.

Michael Fuller was born in 1959. His parents were part of the Windrush Generation of Black Caribbean's who arrived on the promise of a better life in Britain. Sadly they separated when he was young. His mum struggled to look after him and he was taken into care. He was raised in Surrey by a lady he called Auntie Margaret.

He grew up in the era of TV programmes like Alf Garnett and the influence of far right racist groups like the National Front. When he faced racism and discrimination in and out of school, Auntie Margaret told him to "stop, think and decide how to react". This advice served him well both as a child and an adult.

He had a childhood dream of becoming a police officer, despite the reservations of those around him. He realised this dream in 1975, aged 16, by joining the Metropolitan Police as a cadet. He served in uniformed and CID positions throughout London, including several postings at New Scotland Yard.

In the streets the reaction to him was a mix of curiosity and hostility. The black community were split as he received abuse from being seen as a sell-out or traitor for joining the police. Alternatively there was friendliness from black people who thought it was wonderful to see a black officer.

He also faced the constant stream of racist jokes from colleagues who claimed it was just banter and did not mean anything, despite the obvious connotations. It was difficult leading him to question if it was worth staying.

Fortunately he had allies to help support him, though these were few and far between compared to the barrage of negativity he had to endure.

He became popular by taking on jobs which were unpopular, such as searching dead bodies or dealing with domestic incidents and his passion for policing shone through. As a result he rose through the ranks, working on some of the most challenging policing working on race relations.

He was the founding chair of the Met Black Police Association, which meant that for the first time Black and Asian colleagues had a safe space to share experiences and meet other officers like them. He made a point of listening to the community to air their grievances and issues. For example, following reports of police brutality, he led the move to get CCTV installed in police custody cells. He also noted that it was a fact that if you were a black victim of crime, your crime had less chance of being solved than if you were white.

He devised an innovative burglary control programme whilst a detective chief inspector stationed at Shepherd's Bush and Hammersmith, which successfully reduced burglary. This was a forerunner to the London-wide Operation Bumblebee. As a DCI at Paddington, he devised innovative covert techniques which successfully reduced street robbery under the Operation Eagle Eye initiative.

As a detective superintendent he worked as a specialist staff officer seconded to Her Majesty's Inspectorate of Constabulary based at the Home Office. He gave specialist advice on crime and terrorism issues and carried out inspections of police force Special Branches in relation to counterterrorism. He also gave regular advice to the Chief HMI, Ministers, and the Home Secretary.

In 1998, he helped set up the Racial and Violent Crime Task Force in response to criticism of the Metropolitan Police arising from the murder of Stephen Lawrence and the subsequent Macpherson Inquiry. Following this he served as a uniformed superintendent in Lambeth and was the chief superintendent in charge of Battersea, where he was successful in reducing street crime.

In January 2000, as a commander, he took command of West Area Serious Crime Group. As well as overseeing murder investigations, he set up Operation Trident to tackle gun crime within black communities in London. He was highly successful in securing the confidence and support of minority communities recognising that there was an issue with the way crimes were being dealt with in black communities, often being labelled "black on black crime", and as a result largely ignored. This helped lead to the arrest and imprisonment of some of the most dangerous violent criminals involved in gun crime in London.

In 2001, he won the G2 'Man of the Year Award' in recognition of his personal achievements and contribution to policing in London. In February 2002, he was promoted to deputy assistant commissioner. As well as heading the Metropolitan Police Drugs Directorate, he was the Director of Intelligence, as part of a newly formed Specialist Crime Directorate.

On 5 January 2004 he took up his role as Chief Constable of Kent. During his time amongst other achievements, he increased the representation of female officers and ethnic minority officers within Kent Police

He has successfully completed the Cabinet Office's Top Management Programme and was awarded the Queen's Police Medal for distinguished police service in July 2004.

On 26 July 2007, he was called to the Bar at Lincoln's Inn.

He retired from his role in Kent in 2010, by which time the force was deemed one of the five most improved forces in England and Wales. He started a new role as Her Majesty's Chief Inspector of the Crown Prosecution Service Inspectorate. He retired from this post in 2015.

In 2019, he published his memoirs about his experiences in policing in a book entitled, "Kill the Black One First": A Memoir of Hope and Justice. He was also awarded an honorary doctorate by Arden University for his long-standing commitment to mentoring black officers and community support work.

As well as holding a Bachelor of Arts Honours Degree in Social Psychology, he has attained a Masters Degree in Business Administration from Brunel University and holds separate postgraduate diplomas in law, marketing and criminology. He was awarded Honorary Doctorates of Laws from both Sussex University and the University of East London. He is a companion of the Institute of Management and a fellow of the Royal Society of Arts.

When asked about what mark he would like to leave on the world of policing, he said,

"I'd like to go down in history as somebody who made a positive difference to policing and the police service, who carried out his role as the Chief Constable with humility.

I was passionate about joining the police. It was something I really wanted to do. I felt I could make a positive difference and I feel I have done. I've reached the highest levels of the police service. So that's something I'm really proud of."

The level of work and influence that he has made to British policing as a human being has been staggering. He has shown considerable resilience and fortitude not to give up given all his adversities.

First Black British barrister and first graduate of the University of Oxford

Christian Cole – (1852-1885)

Christian Frederick Cole was a Sierra Leone Creole lawyer and the first African barrister to practice in the English courts. His achievement was groundbreaking, especially during a time when racial barriers were formidable. He was also the first black graduate of the University of Oxford, an impressive feat that showcased his intellectual prowess despite societal prejudices.

Born in 1852, he was educated at Fourah Bay College in Freetown, Sierra Leone, which was then a British colony. He came from humble beginnings as the grandson of a slave and was adopted by Reverend James Cole of Waterloo.

In 1873 he enrolled at Oxford to study classics as a non-collegiate student and later attended University College. His peers included notable figures like Cecil Rhodes and Oscar Wilde. Despite facing financial difficulties, he was determined to succeed. He supported himself by teaching Responsions, a qualifying exam for Oxford degrees, and giving music lessons. When his funds ran out his fellow students helped to raise money to help him continue his studies.

Biographer Michèle Mendelssohn noted that American abolitionist Col. Thomas Wentworth Higginson described Cole as "a very black youth from Africa" in a B.A. gown at Oxford, where he was affectionately nicknamed King Cole by undergraduates. Despite not being formally attached to a college, he graduated in 1876 with a fourth-class honours degree. He later became a member of University College, actively participating in college life and speaking at the Oxford Union. Throughout his time at Oxford, he confronted racism and stereotypes, using his writings to advocate for anti-racism.

He returned to Sierra Leone in 1880 but was unable to find employment. He then returned to England, trained as a barrister, and in 1883 became the first black African to practice in the English courts after being accepted by the Inner Temple. He eventually moved to Zanzibar to continue his legal career.

Tragically he died from smallpox in 1885 at the age of 33. His legacy was revived by Pamela Roberts, founder and director of Black Oxford Untold Stories, who brought his achievements to the attention of Ivor Crewe, Master of University College. On October 14, 2017, they unveiled a plaque in Cole's honour at University College.

Apart from his legal career, he was passionate about education. He delivered lectures on education in Freetown, published in 1880, and authored two pamphlets in 1879. One pamphlet, What Do Men Say about Negroes?, addressed racial prejudice, while the other, Reflections on the Zulu War, By a Negro, BA, of University College, Oxford, and the Inner Temple, offered insights on the Anglo-Zulu war. In 2006, University College alumni raised over a thousand pounds to purchase a copy of this pamphlet, which includes two poems, for the college's library.

First Black woman to be appointed a Queen's Council

Baroness Patricia Scotland of Asthal PC QC – (1955-)

Patricia Scotland, Baroness Scotland of Asthal PC QC, is a prominent British lawyer, politician, and international leader. She has served in many high-profile roles, such as Attorney General for England and Wales, a Member of Parliament, and Secretary-General of the Commonwealth of Nations.

Patricia Janet Scotland was born on 19 August 1955, to parents from Antigua and Dominica. She moved to the UK with her family at the age of two. She grew up in Walthamstow, London, as the 10th of 12 children in a Roman Catholic family. She attended Chapel End Secondary School and Walthamstow School for Girls, before studying law at the University of London through Mid Essex Technical College. She was called to the bar in 1977, specializing in family law. She was called to the Dominican bar in 1978.

In 1991 she made history as the first black woman to become a Queen's Counsel (QC), and at 35, she was the youngest woman ever appointed to this prestigious legal position. She founded the 1 Gray's Inn Square barristers' chambers and was involved in various legal reforms and initiatives, including the International Criminal Court Bill and the Pro Bono Lawyers Panel.

Her political career began in earnest when she received a life peerage in 1997, becoming Baroness Scotland of Asthal. She held significant positions in the Foreign and Commonwealth Office and the Lord Chancellor's Department, where she played key roles in legal reforms, including the Land Registration Act 2002 and the creation of the Corporate Alliance Against Domestic Violence.

In 2007 she became the first woman and first black person to serve as Attorney General for England and Wales. She advised the government on legal matters and represented it in court. Following the devolution of justice powers to Northern Ireland, she briefly served as Advocate General for Northern Ireland.

After the Labour Party's loss in 2010, she became Shadow Attorney General. In 2012, she was appointed Prime Ministerial Trade Envoy to South Africa, and in 2014, she was elected as Alderman for the ward of Bishopsgate in the City of London and appointed Chancellor of the University of Greenwich.

In 2016 she became the first woman to serve as Secretary-General of the Commonwealth of Nations, a position she was re-elected to in 2022. As Secretary-General, she has championed democracy, human rights, gender equality, climate change action, and peace among member countries.

Throughout her career, she has received numerous awards and honours for her contributions to law and public service. She is an advocate for social justice, women's rights, and diversity, and has been recognized as Peer of the Year and Parliamentarian of the Year, among other accolades. She has also supported various charities and organizations, furthering her impact on society.

Her achievements serve as an inspiration, especially to women and minorities, demonstrating the significant impact of dedication and service in the legal and political arenas.

First Black Head of a major Barristers Chambers. First Black Deputy Circuit Judge in the UK

Tunji Sowande – (1912-1996)

Tunji Sowande was born in Nigeria. Coming to Britain in 1945 he pursued a legal career and was called to the Bar in 1952. Despite the racial barriers of the time, he was offered a tenancy at 3 Kings Bench Walk chambers. He specialised in criminal law, handling many complex cases and built a respected reputation at the Bar. His career progressed so that by 1968 he became the first Black Head of a major Barristers' Chambers. 10 years later, in 1978, he was appointed as the first Black Deputy Circuit Judge in the UK. He sat at various Crown Courts, including Inner London and Croydon. He was later made a Bencher of the Inner Temple and retired as a Recorder in the late 1980s.

Tunji Sowande was born in Lagos, Nigeria, in 1912 to an affluent and very musical family. His father, Emmanuel, was an Anglican priest and a pioneer of church music in Lagos. His brother, Fela, became a renowned classical composer and organist, who was awarded an MBE in 1955 for his services as the musical director of the Nigerian Broadcasting Service.

Tunji and Fela both attended CMS Anglican Grammar School and Yaba Higher College in Lagos. Tunji earned a diploma in pharmacy in 1940 and worked with Lagos' Public Health Department as a dispensing pharmacist. He later went into private pharmacy with his contemporary Adeyinka Oyekan, who became the Oba or Leader of Lagos from 1965 to 2003.

He was also an extremely talented musician and a talented baritone singer. He could play the organ, drums and saxophone. He decided to move to the UK in 1945 to develop his music skills. He also decided to pursue a career in law, in order to help him to live and fund his music career.

He studied law at King's College London and passed the Bar Finals at Lincoln's Inn. His legal studies were balanced with a vibrant music career, focusing on jazz, classical and choral music, while also collaborating on live sets with contemporary musicians like Johnny Dankworth, Paul Robeson, Ambrose Campbell, Edumondo Ros, Rita Cann and Ronnie Scott. He became part of a circle of Black intellectuals and musicians who met regularly at the Regents Park flat of African-American musician, John Payne.

He was called to the Bar in 1952 and, despite the prevailing racial barriers of the time, was offered a tenancy at 3 Kings Bench Walk Chambers. He was somewhat shocked as tenancies in these prestigious chambers had not previously been permitted to Black Barristers because of racist restrictions. He initially refused it as his passion was his music career, but he was eventually persuaded by his Pupil Master who claimed that his exceptional intellect would serve him well in a career at the Bar.

Specializing in criminal law, he handled many complex criminal matters, gaining the respect of his peers, and rose to Head of Chambers in 1968. This made him the first Black Head of a major Barrister's Chambers set.

Ten years later, in 1978, his hard work earned him the title of the first Black Deputy Judge in Snaresbrook, and eventually in the crown courts of Croydon, Inner London and Knightsbridge. It was then that he was promoted further to a Recorder of the Crown Court, or in other terms, the first black judge.

He held a lot of power in his position and used it well realising that he was in a place of authority and experience. He helped promote and support the careers of a number of successful lawyers from BAME backgrounds.

He was later made a Bencher of the Inner Temple and retired as a Recorder in the late 1980s.

Sadly, he was not exempt from blatant and constant racism and discrimination during his career. During an interview in a barrister's chambers, the interviewer had the audacity to say to him that he should return to "bongo-bongo land." Here, in a professional environment, as an established barrister with a wide range of professional experience, he was treated appallingly because of the colour of his skin.

He was socially active, a member of the Hurlingham Club, Justice, and several theatrical societies, as well as a lifelong supporter of Marylebone Cricket Club and Crystal Palace Football Club.

His musical legacy includes live performances, compositions, and recordings, such as the Afro-Caribbean tracks "Ihin Rere" and "Igi T'Olorun". A lot of the music he did make throughout his life was for charitable purposes, including entertaining elderly audiences often performing as a duo with Rita Cann a famous Black singer and pianist.

Tunji Sowande passed away in 1996 at the age of 84.

In 2017, actor and playwright Tayo Aluko commemorated his life in the play Just an Ordinary Lawyer, celebrating his remarkable journey and contributions to both law and music.

First Black man to become a Queen's Counsel in England and Wales.

Dr John Anthony Roberts QC CBE – (1928-2016)

Dr John Anthony Roberts had a variety of careers from accounts to joining the Royal Air Force before turning to law. In 1988 he made history by becoming the first Black man to be appointed a Queen's Counsel at the English Bar. He was also called to the Bars of 10 other countries.

John Anthony Roberts was born on 17 May 1928 in Sierra Leone. His great grandfather, Joseph Jenkins Roberts, was the first President of Liberia. His father, John Anthony Roberts Jnr., was a Brazilian, and his mother, who was born in Freetown, Sierra Leone, was descended from liberated Africans, who chose to return to Africa after the Slave Trade.

By the 1940s he worked as a Costs Clerk for Taylor Woodrow in Sierra Leone and then as a Civil Servant. He was a keen pianist, organist, guitarist and choir singer, who was passionate about helping people.

He was fascinated by airplanes, having seen members of the Royal Air Force (RAF) in Sierra Leone during World War II. He went to the UK in 1952 to join the RAF, qualifying initially as an accountant, and later, he was selected for aircrew duties. He served in the RAF until 1962 in Europe, the Near East, the Far East and the South Pacific.

He married his wife, Eulette, a Jamaican in 1961, and the couple had a son, Tony. When not on duty, he was an avid boxer and sprinter.

After his service in the RAF, he was invited to serve in the Sierra Leone Civil Aviation Service by the then Prime Minister of Sierra Leone, where he worked in the Air Traffic Control Services Department until 1964.

In 1964 he returned to England with his wife and son. From 1964 to 1969 he worked as a civil servant. He began to read law part-time, as well as working, at the Inns of Court School of Law in 1966, because he wanted to help people. He was called to the Gray's Inn Bar in 1969, becoming a Master of Bench in 1996. In 1972 he also became a Member of Lincoln's Inn.

In 1970 he helped set up Chambers at 9 Stone Buildings, Lincoln's Inn. In 1975 he left these to set up his own Chambers at 2 Stone Buildings. He made sure that his set of Chambers was fully representative, mixed and diverse with Asian, white and African and Caribbean members. He also became the first Head of Chambers to accept seven female barristers simultaneously, a groundbreaking move at that time or ever.

He was made an Assistant Recorder, essentially a part-time judge of the Crown Court in 1983 and became a Recorder in 1987. In 1988, he made history by becoming the first Black man to be appointed a Queen's Counsel at the English Bar.

Apart from the English Bar, he was also called to the Bars of 10 other countries: Jamaica (1973), Sierra Leone (1975), Trinidad & Tobago (1978), Bahamas (1984), St Kitts & Nevis (1988), Antigua (2002), Barbados (2002), Bermuda (2003), Anguilla (2006) and Grenada (2007). This may well be a record.

His judicial career extended overseas when, in 1992, he left 2 Stone Buildings as he was appointed High Court Judge in the Supreme Courts of the British Virgin Islands and Anguilla, becoming the first individual of African descent to hold such a post in a British-dependent territory. He tried many high profile cases, including homicide.

From 1990 to 1992, he tutored advocacy at the Inns of Court School of Law and served as a Bencher of the Council of Legal Education in Sierra Leone.

Apart from his legal work, he served as the President of the British West Indian Ex-Servicemen and Ex-Service Women's Association along with serving as a joint President of the British Caribbean Association. He also served as a fellow of the Chartered Institute of Arbitrators and sat as an arbitrator and a door tenant at Warwick Court Chambers for some years.

In 1991 he was made an Honorary Citizen of Atlanta, Georgia, USA. He became a Freeman of the City of London, and was awarded an Honorary Doctorate at City University in 1996.

In 1998, aged 70, he retired from the Bench as a Recorder.

In 2000, he was made an Honorary Citizen of the British Virgin Islands.

In the 2011 New Year Honours, he was awarded a Commander of the British Empire (CBE) for his services to administration of justice, diversity, and equal opportunities

Dr John Roberts passed away on 26 June 2016, aged 88. He was survived by his wife Eulette, son Tony, grandchildren, Lauren and James and great granddaughter, Amelia.

In his memory, the Descendants charity in Ealing established the annual Dr John Roberts QC CBE Achievement Awards, celebrating outstanding young people of African and Caribbean heritage in areas such as education, sports, and the arts. This ceremony continues to inspire and promote excellence across generations.

First Black nurse practitioner

Mary Seacole – (1805-1881)

Mary Seacole was a trailblazing nurse and healer who defied societal expectations to care for those in need. She was born Mary Jane Grant on 23 November 1805, in Kingston, Jamaica and she grew up in a community of free black people. Her father, James Grant, was a Scottish Lieutenant in the British Army, and her mother, known as "The Doctress," was a healer who used traditional Caribbean and African herbal medicines.

On 10 November 1836 she married Edwin Horatio Hamilton Seacole, believed to be the illegitimate son of Lord Nelson and Emma Hamilton. Edwin was a merchant, but he sadly passed away in October 1844.

Inspired by her mother's practice of herbal medicine, Mary developed a deep interest in healing and began assisting her mother, gaining valuable knowledge about medicinal plants and traditional treatments. Her curiosity and passion for medicine led her to travel extensively to countries like England, Cuba, and the Bahamas, where she learned about diverse medical practices.

When the Crimean War started in October 1853, she travelled to England in 1855, hoping to join Florence Nightingale's nursing team. Unfortunately, due to racial prejudice, her offers were rejected. Undeterred, she travelled independently to Crimea and established her own medical facility.

She set up the British Hotel in Balaclava, near the frontlines, providing a safe haven for wounded soldiers. The hotel served as a sanctuary where soldiers received care, nourishment, and emotional support, as well as a resource centre for medical supplies and rest. Her exceptional nursing skills and compassionate nature earned her immense respect from both soldiers and officers. She tirelessly tended to the wounded, using her herbal remedies and traditional healing methods when modern medicine failed.

Despite her significant contributions, she faced many challenges, including financial difficulties and racial discrimination. These obstacles, coupled with her own health issues, made her work even more challenging. However, her unwavering determination and spirit allowed her to continue her life-saving efforts.

After the war ended, she returned to England, where her heroic actions were celebrated. In 1857, she published her autobiography, "Wonderful Adventures of Mrs. Seacole in Many Lands", detailing her remarkable experiences. The book received critical acclaim, solidifying her place in history.

Her legacy extends far beyond her lifetime. Her relentless pursuit of equality and dedication to helping others make her a true pioneer. Today, she is celebrated as a symbol of diversity, resilience, and the triumph of the human spirit. Statues and memorials have been erected in her honour, ensuring that her extraordinary life and achievements will always be remembered.

First Black British fireman

Frank Bailey – (1925-2015)

Frank Arthur Bailey achieved renown as one of the earliest black firefighters in the UK. He was born on 26 November 1925, in British Guiana, and was educated in church schools. After school, he initially trained as an engineering apprentice and then he found work as a coal trimmer on a German trade ship. After that he worked as a medical assistant in a New York hospital, where he notably protested against racial segregation.

In 1953 he moved to London, where he encountered discrimination firsthand at a Trades Union Congress conference. Refusing to accept the notion that black individuals were deemed unfit for firefighting roles due to lack of education or physical prowess, he challenged this bias by applying to become a firefighter.

He successfully joined the West Ham Fire Brigade in 1955 becoming London's first full-time black firefighter, though there were earlier reports of black firefighters active during World War II.

Despite his groundbreaking role, he faced systemic barriers to advancement within the fire service, leading to his departure in 1965. Undeterred, he transitioned to a career in social work, becoming one of the first black mental welfare officers and psychiatric social workers in the Royal Borough of Kensington and Chelsea. He also served as a legal advisor and volunteer warden, actively engaging in community service and advocacy.

His commitment to equality extended beyond his professional endeavours. He was politically active, advocating for the rights of black individuals and studying the impact of colonialism on the Caribbean Diaspora. An outspoken communist, he championed the cause of working people throughout his life.

Despite personal challenges, including three marriages ending in divorce, his legacy as a pioneer in firefighting and social work endured. He passed away on 2 December 2015, leaving behind three daughters. His contributions were honoured posthumously, with over 80 firefighters paying respects at his funeral in January 2016. Google UK commemorated his 95th birthday in 2020 with a Doodle.

First Black British Bus Driver

Joe Clough – (1910-1976)

Joe Clough moved to England from Jamaica and in 1910 became the first Black bus driver of a London motorbus.

Joseph Alan Clough was born in Kingston, Jamaica on 10 November 1885. He faced adversity from an early age when both his parents passed away, leaving him an orphan.

After moving to England in 1906, he worked as a servant and companion to a Scottish doctor, Dr. R. C. White. His initial duties were to care for the doctor's polo ponies. However, as time passed he soon adapted by learning to drive motorcars, eventually becoming the doctor's chauffeur. Despite prevalent racial attitudes, Dr. White treated him as an equal, creating a positive environment for him.

In 1910, after a stint working as a roller skate fitter at Hackney roller skating rink he applied to work at London General Omnibus Company the largest bus operation in London. He trained at Shepherds Bush garage and after passing his bus driving test, he became a spare driver, driving different routes when needed. He then became a regular driver on bus route 11, operating between Liverpool Street and Wormwood Scrubs. This made him the first Black London bus driver. He was also among the very first drivers of motor buses in London, as petrol engines began to replace horse-drawn transport.

Throughout his career, he faced discrimination, including a wrongful suspension for speeding by a racist company official. However, his outstanding driving record and character led to his swift reinstatement. Despite such challenges, he persevered, supported by his wife Margaret Millicent, a Scottish domestic servant, whom he married in 1911.

His dedication extended beyond his professional life. During World War I, despite racial barriers preventing him from active service, he volunteered as an ambulance driver, serving in the Army Service Corps from 1915 to 1919 in France and Belgium.

After the war, he continued his career in the transportation industry, eventually settling in Bedfordshire with his family. He became a beloved figure in the community, known for his positive demeanour and resilience against racial prejudice, working as a taxi driver until his retirement in 1968. Despite facing racial abuse, he remained resilient and garnered widespread respect.

In recognition of his contributions, he was featured in various media outlets notably in a book called The Un-melting Pot, highlighting Bedford's immigrant communities. He became a symbol of resilience and progress for immigrant communities. His legacy as a trailblazer for Black individuals, especially during the Windrush migration era, continues to inspire generations.

He passed away on 27 December 1976, leaving behind a legacy of courage, resilience, and pioneering spirit.

First Black British Train Driver

Wilston Samuel Jackson – (1927-2018)

Wilston Samuel Jackson moved from Jamaica to Britain as part of the Windrush generation in 1952. Through sheer determination he worked his way up to becoming Britain's first black train driver.

Wilston Samuel Jackson was born on 17 May 1927, in Portland, Jamaica. He was all set to become a dentist, but his plans changed at the age of 17 with the death of his father. In 1952, responding to Britain's call for workers to aid in post-World War II reconstruction, he joined the Windrush generation and immigrated to London, encountering racism and discrimination despite the invitation extended to people of colour.

Throughout British society there an official and unofficial colour bar that reserved certain positions for white individuals only. In his case there were no Black train drivers. There was an unspoken rule that the driver's job was reserved for whites only. Black railway workers came to believe that it was not possible for a Black man to become a driver and as a result many quit their rail jobs because of the lack of prospects.

Wilston had an ambition to become a train driver. Undeterred by the lack of prospects and rampant discrimination, he embarked on a journey that led him from a cleaner to a fireman, enduring gruelling conditions while pursuing his dream. In 1962, through unwavering determination and diligent study, he passed his exams with flying colours to achieve his goal of becoming Britain's first black train driver.

Nevertheless, his triumph was met with resistance from his white colleagues, who organized against him, initially refusing to work alongside him. Despite facing ongoing resentment and challenges, he fulfilled his dream, navigating trains like the iconic Flying Scotsman and Mallard from King's Cross station.

However tragedy struck in 1964 when a signalman mistakenly gave a green light near Finsbury Park, north London. His train ploughed into the back of a stationary goods train. He told his fireman to jump, which he did and was saved. Unfortunately, Wilston himself was crushed breaking both his legs and had to be cut from the wreckage. Despite the prognosis of permanent disability, his perseverance and resilience saw him through months of painful rehabilitation, eventually allowing him to return to work.

In 1966, he seized an opportunity to share his expertise by travelling to Zambia with his family to train local train drivers. Upon his return to Britain, he continued his career until his passing. Despite his immense contributions, he faced further challenges, including illness, before his death on 15 September 2018, at the age of 91, following a stroke.

In recognition of his groundbreaking achievement, a commemorative blue plaque was unveiled at Kings Cross station the year before his passing, though he sadly never had the opportunity to see it due to his declining health. His legacy endures as a testament to his perseverance, courage, and trailblazing spirit in the face of adversity.

First Black British Army Officer

Walter Tull – (1888-1918)

Walter Tull was a trailblazer in both football and the military. He went from amateur football to playing for Tottenham Hotspur in 1909 and during World War 1 he was commissioned as a second lieutenant becoming one of the first mixed-heritage infantry officers in a regular British Army.

Walter Tull was born in 1888 in Folkestone, Kent. He faced adversity from a young age after losing his parents and being raised in an orphanage. Growing up he excelled academically and athletically. His football career began with amateur club Clapton, where he achieved considerable success before becoming the first black British professional outfield footballer with Tottenham Hotspur in 1909.

His time at Tottenham was marked by both athletic achievement and racial abuse from fans. Despite this, his talent and character were undeniable, earning him respect from teammates and observers alike. In 1911, he moved to Northampton Town, where he continued to excel on the field.

After the First World War broke out in August 1914, he was the first Northampton Town player to enlist in the British Army, in December of that year. He served in the 17th and 23rd Football Battalions of the Duke of Cambridge's Own (Middlesex) Regiment, and also in the 5th Battalion. He was promoted to a sergeant due to the recognition of his leadership skills and courage. He fought in the Battle of the Somme in 1916.

His leadership skills and courage were evident on the battlefield. He did encounter racial prejudice and discrimination from some of his comrades, however, his skills as a soldier earned him the respect of his fellow officers and men. In the midst of the chaos and horror of war, he displayed exceptional bravery and cool-headedness. He was known for leading his troops fearlessly into battle, showing a dedication to duty inspiring those around him.

On 30 May 1917 he was commissioned as a second lieutenant becoming one of the first mixed-heritage infantry officers in a regular British Army regiment, following his attendance at officer training school at Gailes, Scotland. This was despite the fact that the 1914 Manual of Military Law excluded soldiers that were not "natural born or naturalised British subjects of pure European descent" from becoming commissioned officers in the Special Reserve. However the army was desperately short of officers and he had demonstrated that he was a natural leader and cool under pressure, gaining the respect of his unit's officers and men.

His 23rd Battalion fought on the Italian Front from 30th November 1917 to early March 1918 and he received praise for his gallantry and coolness under fire. The 23rd Battalion returned to northern France on 8th March 1918 and sadly he was killed in action near the village of Favreuil in the Pas-de-Calais in March 1918, while leading an attack. His body was never recovered.

Despite his untimely death, his legacy endures. He has been commemorated through various mediums, including memorials, coins, stamps, and even a painted post box. His story serves as an inspiration, highlighting his courage, resilience, and determination to overcome barriers in pursuit of excellence.

First Black British Pilot

William Robinson Clarke – (1895-1981)

During World War 1, William Robinson Clarke, a Jamaican native, undertook a remarkable journey to Britain, aiming to contribute to the war effort as a pilot despite facing racial barriers. Initially employed as a mechanic due to discriminatory practices, he persevered and eventually became the first and only Black pilot in World War 1. Unfortunately, his flying career was cut short when he sustained a spinal injury during a photography mission.

William Robinson Clarke was born on 4 October 1895 in Jamaica. With the outbreak of World War 1 in 1914, he paid £150 in 1915 to travel from Kingston, Jamaica, to England so that he could learn how to fly and support the war effort. However, there were barriers in place against people from certain ethnic groups joining Britain's Armed Forces. The attitude was expressed by Colonel Sir Garnet Wolseley in the 19th century who thought that Africans were an objectionable animal who should become the white man's servant. These were one of his least objectionable thoughts.

The Manual of Military Law in 1914 made it clear that people who were considered "alien", a man or woman who was not a British citizen, were allowed to enlist but there were restrictions that inevitably reminded them they were considered second class citizens, with restricted rights and opportunities in Britain's Armed Forces. This colour bar prevented people who were not white from having the equal rights as white people. Only men of "pure European descent" could qualify for a commission into the armed forces.

However, as the casualties of war increased, reducing manpower, these barriers began to dissolve, allowing black individuals to serve. So, although initially labelled as "alien" and restricted in rank, Clarke and others were granted equal privileges while serving, highlighting the significant role they played in the war.

He joined the Royal Flying Corps (RFC) in July 1915 as an air mechanic. In October 1915, he was posted to France as a driver with an observation balloon company. However, his real ambition was to fly and, in December 1916, he was selected to undergo pilot training in England. He qualified on 26 April 1917, receiving Royal Aero Club (RAeC) Aviators' Certificate No. 4837. His RAeC photograph is held in the RAF Museum's Archive with an accompanying index card that describes his nationality as British.

On 29 May 1917 he was promoted to sergeant, joining No. 4 Squadron RFC at Abeele in Belgium. The squadron was engaged on artillery observation and reconnaissance duties. He began flying over the Western Front just before the opening of the Battle of Messines in June 1917.

On the morning of 28 July, along with his observer, he was flying on a photographic mission when they were attacked by enemy fighters. He suffered a bullet through his spine but managed to pilot his plane back to the aerodrome. His observer escaped without any injury.

He was treated at a field hospital in Dannes-Camiers but, needing further rehabilitation, was transported to England and hospitalised at Lichfield until November 1917. When he had recovered he returned for duty with an RFC Reserve Depot, and then as a mechanic in Devon.

He returned to Jamaica in 1919, working in the building trade. He was appointed Life President of the Jamaican branch of the Royal Air Forces Association.

He passed away on 26 April 1981, leaving behind a legacy of courage and determination that continues to inspire.

His legacy, along with other Caribbean pilots, was commemorated in 2014 with an exhibition at the RAF Museum in London, shedding light on the contributions of Black personnel in the Royal Air Force and their often overlooked achievements during World War 1.

First Black woman to join the British Armed Forces

Lilian Bader – (1918-2015)

When World War II broke out in 1939, Lilian Bader wanted to do her bit for the war effort. She found a job in a NAAFI canteen, serving food and drink to servicemen but after seven weeks she was dismissed as her father hadn't been born in the UK and was black. Later she discovered that West Indian men had been accepted into the RAF, so she applied to the WAAF (Women's Auxiliary Air Force) and was accepted in March, 1941, becoming the first black woman in the Air Force and the British Armed Forces as a whole.

Lilian Bader was born on 18 February 1918 in Liverpool to a Barbadian-born father and Irish mother. When she was seven years old, she moved to Hull with her father and two older brothers, following the break-up of her parents' marriage. However things did not work out and soon after their arrival in Hull, the three children were placed in a children's home. Her brothers remained in Hull, but later she was sent on to a children's home in Middlesbrough.

She was then raised in a convent where she remained until she was 20, because due to racism, no one would employ her until she got a job in domestic service. Following the outbreak of World War II she joined the Navy, Army and Air Force Institutes (NAAFI) at Catterick Camp, Yorkshire, serving food and drink to servicemen. However, she was asked to leave after seven weeks when her father's Caribbean heritage was discovered. It is suggested that the District Manager had toyed with the decision for several weeks, sympathizing with her Irish and Roman Catholic backgrounds as he himself was Irish and Roman Catholic.

Upon leaving the NAAFI, she found work on a farm near RAF Topcliffe, which she subsequently left to work as a domestic servant. In 1941 she heard a radio interview where West Indians were saying they had been rejected by the Army but accepted by the RAF. Seeing an opportunity here, she applied and was accepted into the Women's Auxiliary Air Force (WAAF) on 28 March, 1941 and was sent to York for training. She was one of the first black women to join the WAAF, facing discrimination and prejudice from some of her white colleagues.

Unfortunately two weeks into her training, she discovered her brother had been lost at sea while serving as a Merchant Seaman. She was allowed compassionate leave and on returning she went on a twelve-week training course, qualifying her as an Instrument repairer. This was a relatively new job that had been made available to women in 1940 due to men being unavailable because of the war.

Her academic prowess and personable nature once again shone through and after passing several exams, she graduated as a First Class Airwoman with her pay doubled from twenty two shillings a fortnight, to forty four. She went to Shropshire where she was promoted to Corporal and leading Aircraftwoman and by the time she left the service she had been promoted to Acting Corporal.

As servicewomen, the role played by women like her was limited to running routine repairs and replacing sensitive equipment. However, the sheer scale of the work these women undertook was significant and critical to the war effort.

She was one of the first groups of women to be allowed on to planes to check for leaks in their vital pipes. The WAAF uniform skirt was not suitable for clambering around inside twin-engined light bombers, so her group were the first women in the WAAF to be issued with more practical overalls and battle dress.

During her time in the WAAF, she met her husband, Ramsay Bader, a tank driver serving in the 147th Essex Yeomanry Field Regiment, Royal Artillery. The couple married in 1943 and in 1944 she was given compassionate discharge from her position when she became pregnant with her first son. The couple went on to have two children, Geoffrey and Adrian.

After she had raised her two sons, she went back into education as a mature student. She achieved the necessary 'O' and 'A' levels to gain entry into London University where she successfully secured an external BA from London University, after which she became a teacher of languages. After retiring, she continued teaching private pupils and U3A classes well into her eighties.

In 1989, her memoir, Together – Lilian Bader: Wartime Memoirs of a WAAF 1939-1944, was published by the Imperial War Museum.

She fought hard against racism and prejudice all her life, often writing letters to the media and politicians. She told her story, and the stories of six other members of her family of African descent who had fought for Britain during two world wars to the Imperial War Museum and to journalists. She also appeared on several television programmes. She was determined that the contribution made by Black and Asian Britons to the country's defence should be recognised and remembered, so it is fitting that she was invited to meet the Queen at the inauguration of the Commonwealth Memorial Gates in Hyde Park in 2002.

In the 2003 Queen's Birthday Honours list, she was awarded a Member of the Most Excellent Order of the British Empire (MBE) in recognition of her pioneering role in the Armed Forces and her contributions to education.

On 13 March 2015 she passed away at the age of 97. She was a courageous and inspirational woman who broke down barriers and paved the way for future generations.

First Black male bishop in the Church of England

Wilfred Wood KA – (1936-)

Wilfred Wood KA, a Barbadian-British Anglican, served as the Bishop of Croydon from 1985 to 2003, making history as the first black bishop in the Church of England.

Wilfred Denniston Wood was born on 15 June 1936, in Barbados to Barbadian parents. He initially intended a career in Barbados politics but felt a calling to priesthood, leading him to attend Codrington College in St John, Barbados.

He was ordained as a deacon in Barbados and later as a priest in England at St Paul's Cathedral, London, in 1962. He began his ministry as a curate at St Stephen's Church, Shepherd's Bush.

He married Ina Smith in 1966. The couple had five children.

A staunch advocate for racial justice, he championed anti-racist activism throughout his career. Notably, in 1968, he co-submitted proposals known as the Wood Proposals, aiming to replace the National Committee for Commonwealth Immigrants with a more inclusive Community Relations Commission. He played a pivotal role in establishing the UK's Martin Luther King Fund and Foundation.

Throughout the 1970s and 1980s, he held various positions within the Church of England, including president of the Institute of Race Relations and Moderator of the World Council of Churches' Programme to Combat Racism. In 1985, he became the area Bishop of Croydon, overseeing 102 parishes and becoming the Church of England's first black bishop.

He continued his advocacy beyond the church, serving on numerous boards and commissions focused on racial equality, housing, and youth welfare.

His efforts earned him recognition, including being named an Honorary Freeman of the London Borough of Croydon in 2002.

On 30 November 2000 which happened to be Barbados Independence Day, he was appointed as a Knight of St Andrew by Queen Elizabeth II. This was the highest class award within the Order of Barbados. It was given "for his contribution to race relations in the United Kingdom and general contribution to the welfare of Barbadians living here".

He retired as Bishop of Croydon in September 2002 and returned with his wife to their native Barbados. Sadly, he lost his sight in 2004.

First Black Archbishop in the Church of England

John Sentamu, Baron Sentamu PC – (1949-)

John Sentamu, Baron Sentamu, PC, is a retired Anglican bishop and life peer. Notably, in 2005, he became the first Black Archbishop in the Church of England when he was appointed to the office of Archbishop of York.

John Tucker Mugabi Sentam was born on 10 June 1949, in Masooli village, Gayaza near Kampala in Uganda. He was the sixth of thirteen children. Despite being born prematurely and weighing just four pounds, he survived and enjoyed a happy childhood. He pursued higher education at Makerere University, obtaining a degree in law in 1971 before practicing as an advocate of the High Court of Uganda and briefly serving as a High Court judge.

In 1973, he married his wife Margaret.

He was outspoken in his opinions against Ugandan President Idi Amin, which led to his imprisonment for 90 days. He was beaten almost to death in prison, but was released to spend several months under house arrest.

In 1974 he left Uganda to travel to and settle in Britain.

He studied theology at Selwyn College, Cambridge, where he received a BA degree in 1976, then an MA in 1979, and a PhD degree in Theology in 1984. He trained for the priesthood at Ridley Hall, Cambridge, being ordained a priest in 1979. He worked as assistant chaplain at Selwyn College, as chaplain at a remand centre and as curate and vicar in a series of parish appointments.

His career in the Church saw him consecrated as a bishop in 1996, serving in various capacities, including as Bishop of Birmingham. Throughout his career, he faced racial discrimination, including physical assault in 2002. On his way home from St Paul's Cathedral after celebrating the Queen's golden jubilee, a man spat at him, hurling abuse and pushed him down a escalator for which he was hospitalised.

On 21 July 2005 he was formally elected by the chapter of York Minster and legally confirmed as archbishop at St Mary-le-Bow, London on 5 October, and enthroned at York Minster on 30 November 2005, at a ceremony with African singing and dancing and contemporary music, where he played African drums during the service. As Archbishop of York, he sat in the House of Lords and was admitted, to the Privy Council of the United Kingdom. He was the first black archbishop in the Church of England.

He was confirmed as Lord Archbishop of York, Primate of England and Metropolitan. It is the second highest position in the entire Anglican Church, second only to the prestigious position of Archbishop of Canterbury, who is in charge of the well-being of the entire world-wide Anglican Church. His appointment was made by the Queen on the recommendation of Prime Minister Tony Blair.

His tenure was marked by activism and advocacy on various social issues, including human rights abuses and conflicts abroad. He received numerous honours and awards for his contributions to academia and society, including honorary degrees from several universities and titles such as Yorkshireman of the Year. However, his later years were not without controversy, as he faced criticism for his handling of reports of clerical child abuse.

In 2018 he announced his retirement, scheduled for June 2020. In 2019 he ordained his wife as a deacon.

Following the 2020 Political Honours list he was made a life peer.

On 27 April 2021 he became Baron Sentamu, of Lindisfarne in the County of Northumberland and of Masooli in the Republic of Uganda. He took his seat among the lords temporal on 25 May, the last life peer to be introduced by Thomas Woodcock as Garter King of Arms.

He moved with his wife to Berwick and, on 14 June 2021 was licensed an honorary assistant bishop of the Diocese of Newcastle.

In 2023 he was asked to step down from his position as an assistant bishop in the Diocese of Newcastle after an independent review criticised his failure to act regarding a claim of abuse.

He has two grown-up children, Grace and Geoffrey with his wife, Margaret. His interests are said to include music, cooking, reading, athletics, rugby and football.

First Black female bishop in the Church of England

Rose Hudson-Wilkin MBE QHC – (1961-)

Rose Hudson-Wilkin, MBE, QHC is a British Anglican bishop, who has been suffragan Bishop of Dover in the diocese of Canterbury, deputising for the Archbishop, since 2019. She is the first black woman to become a Church of England bishop. A suffragan is a bishop appointed to help a diocesan bishop where a diocese is a district under the pastoral care of a bishop.

Rose Josephine Hudson-Wilkin was born on 19 January 1961 in Montego Bay, Jamaica. She was raised by her father and aunt Pet, as her mother had left for England when she was born. She was educated at Montego Bay High School, which was an all-girls secondary school in Montego Bay. At the age of 14 she decided to join the ministry.

In 1982 she travelled to the UK to train at the Church Army College in the West Midlands She later trained at the West Midlands Ministerial Training Course in preparation for ordained ministry.

On 30 June 1991 she was made a deacon in the Church of England by Keith Sutton, Bishop of Lichfield, at Lichfield Cathedral.

From 1991 to 1994, she served as the Deacon of St Matthew's Church, Wolverhampton. She was ordained a priest

On 23rd April 1994 she was ordained as a priest, serving her curacy at St Matthews Church from 1994 to 1995.

From 1995 to 1998 she was assistant curate of St Andrew's Church, West Bromwich. She also worked with the Committee on Black Anglican Concern which was designed to combat racism in the Church of England. This Committee has since been replaced by the Committee for Minority Ethnic Anglican Concerns.

In 1998 she took the role as vicar of Holy Trinity Church, Dalston, and All Saints Church, Haggerston, which is an inner-city parish in Hackney, London.

In 2008 she became the first black female to be appointed a Chaplain to the Queen.

In 2010 she was appointed as Chaplain to the Speaker of the House of Commons in addition to her parish work. Some people alleged that this was an act of political correctness on the part of the Speaker John Bercow. Eventually the role was split in two with Hudson-Wilkin remaining in her Hackney parish and attending to the Commons via daily prayers and services in St Mary Undercroft, while Andrew Tremlett took up the post of Canon of Westminster and Rector of St Margaret's, Westminster.

In an interview after her appointment to the Commons, she commented that she would like to see a more civil attitude among MPs. She also criticised what she felt was the institutional racism within the church.

In March 2013 she was installed as a Prebendary of St Paul's Cathedral in recognition of her service to the Church, community and as Chaplain to the Speaker of the House of Commons. A prebendary is a member of the Roman Catholic or Anglican clergy, a form of canon with a role in the administration of a cathedral or collegiate church.

In October 2014 she became priest-in-charge of St Mary-at-Hill, City of London. She moved to her new parish in November 2014, while doing her other work. She held this post until late 2019 along with the roles of Chaplain to the Speaker of the House of Commons; priest vicar at Westminster Abbey and a Chaplain to the Queen.

On 19 May 2018 she was one of several religious leaders to lead prayers at the wedding of Prince Harry and Meghan Markle.

On 28 June 2019 she was announced as the next Bishop of Dover, to run the Diocese of Canterbury on behalf of the Archbishop of Canterbury, additionally she was to become Bishop suffragan of Dover. As a suffragan bishop, the Bishop of Dover has authority delegated by the Archbishop of Canterbury to oversee the Diocese of Canterbury as if the diocesan bishop.

On 19 November 2019 she was consecrated as a bishop by Archbishop Justin Welby at St Paul's Cathedral. She was installed as Bishop of Dover during a service at Canterbury Cathedral on 30 November 2019 which made her the first black woman to become a Church of England bishop. Incidentally, Guli Francis-Dehqani who was born in Iran was the first ethnic minority woman to become a bishop, in 2017.

In 2020 she was awarded an MBE - Member of the Order of the British Empire for services to young people and the Church.

In February 2023 she was appointed an Honorary Bencher of Lincoln's Inn and in May 2023 she was one of three female bishops to take part in the coronation of King Charles III and his wife Camilla.

During an interview on Desert Island Discs, she was asked about the proposed ordination of women as bishops and said: "I believe that we hold certain prejudices about certain things and we believe them to be true ... What I want is for people to be open to the possibilities that their minds might be changed." She added: "I think the church has been the poorer actually for not having the gifts of women – men and women – in its leadership."

She met her husband, the Revd Kenneth Wilkin, when she was training at the Church Army College. He serves as chaplain to HM Prison Downview near Banstead in Surrey. The couple have two daughters and a son.

First Black Chief Midwifery Officer

Jacqueline Dunkley-Bent OBE – (1964-)

Professor Jacqueline Dunkley-Bent OBE is England's first black Chief Midwifery Officer and Professor of Midwifery at King's College London and London South Bank University.

Jacqueline Dunkley-Bent was born in February 1964 to Caribbean parents and she started her career as a general nurse, but decided to move to midwifery seeing it as a natural career progression. After midwifery training she worked in all areas of maternity but particularly enjoyed supporting a personal caseload of women through the antenatal, labour and postnatal period. She received her diploma in midwifery at the Royal College of Midwives.

She also felt drawn to education having mentored a lot of students when she was a junior midwife. So, after completing an advanced diploma in midwifery at the Royal College of Midwives and a post-graduate teaching certificate (PGCEA) at Surrey University, she became a lecturer, then a senior lecturer, and then curriculum leader, at Middlesex University.

She gained a Master's degree in health promotion, and authored a book on health promotion in midwifery. She expanded her career by roles as a consultant midwife and head of midwifery and women's services at Guy's and St. Thomas' NHS Trust, and eventually the positions of honorary clinical director at NHS London and the director of midwifery and divisional director of nursing at Imperial College Healthcare NHS Trust.

In 2015 she won the Health Services Journal BME Pioneers award.

In the 2018 New Years honours list, she received an Order of the British Empire (OBE) award for services to Midwifery.

In 2019 she became the most senior midwife in England when was appointed the Chief Midwifery Officer in the NHS, becoming the first black Chief Midwifery Officer.

As Chief Midwifery Officer she provided professional, strategic and clinical leadership to colleagues working across the country. She was responsible for measures that upgrade support for new and growing families, including greater digital access to "red book" medical records, better access to physiotherapy for mums recovering after labour and improved care for critically ill new-borns.

By simultaneously working as a midwife, educator, and manager for most of her career, she gained a unique and critical perspective making her stand out from her peers. Alongside her roles as head of Maternity, Children and Young People at NHS England and maternity safety champion for the Department of Health, she was a visiting professor of midwifery at both King's College London and London South Bank University and a practising midwife. She holds honorary doctorates from Worcester and Winchester Universities

Throughout all her positions in education and management, she remained a practising midwife as it allowed her to advise on maternity matters and contribute to policy development from an experiential practice perspective. She felt it was important to be able to shape strategy and policy by reflecting the views of maternity services, using empirical evidence.

She offered support and advice wherever possible, mentoring many healthcare professionals from diverse backgrounds and different professions. She is a member of the 'Women of the Year' management committee and works as midwifery advisor for the Wellbeing Foundation Africa, contributing to the reduction in maternal mortality across the African continent, as well as sitting on the Tommy's charity pregnancy advisory board.

In May 2023, she stepped down from her role as Chief Midwifery Officer for England following her appointment as the first chief midwife with the

International Confederation of Midwives (ICM). She will represent the interests of midwives around the world, and lead initiatives deemed essential to the growth of midwifery globally. She has relocated to the Netherlands to work at the ICM's head office in The Hague.

First Black Guard at Euston Station

Asquith Xavier – (1920-1980)

Asquith Xavier was a West Indian-born Briton who ended a colour bar at British Railways in London by fighting to become the first non-white train guard at Euston railway station in 1966.

Asquith Camile Xavier was born on 18 July 1920, on the island of Dominica in the West Indies. He married Agnes Disney St John in Dominica and they had seven children. He is thought to have worked as a policeman.

After World War II, like many Caribbean's, he answered the call of the British government asking for people to travel to Britain to help rebuild the country. As a result he boarded the TN Ascania in Roseau, the capital of Dominica and docked in Southampton on 16 April 1958, accompanied by his wife and four of their children.

Settling in Paddington, West London, he worked for British Rail as a porter before progressing to becoming a guard at Marylebone depot.

In 1966 Britain's railways were changing. British Railways launched a new fast and frequent electric train service between London's Euston station and Manchester and a new Euston station was being constructed. The railway was modernising in parts, but also contracting. Large sections of the former Great Central Railway route linking Nottingham and Sheffield to London's Marylebone station were closed leading to redundancies amongst Marylebone's train guards. Hence, he applied for a transfer to London Euston station.

He was unsuccessful in his application. A letter from a staff committee at Euston, which was dominated by members of the National Union of Railwaymen, explained that the rejection was because of his colour. Unions and management had informally agreed in the 1950s to ban non-white people from jobs at Euston involving contact with the public. They could be cleaners and labourers, but not guards or ticket collectors

One of his colleagues at Marylebone, Tony Donaghey, a future President of the Rail, Maritime and Transport Union, saw him as a semi-father figure. Donaghey, who came from Donegal, Ireland, was also on the Marylebone redundancy list and had faced discrimination himself when he was rejected for a position at Paddington because he was Irish. He had also witnessed the "no Blacks, no dogs, no Irish" signs. Donegal successfully applied for a job at Euston only to turn it down in solidarity when he realised that this was the very post Asquith Xavier had been rejected from.

Dissatisfied with this decision to reject him, Asquith campaigned to end the racial discrimination practiced by British Rail.

In 1965, the first Race Relations Act had been passed which made it illegal to discriminate on the grounds of colour, race, ethnic or national origins in public places. But the railways were not considered public. Asquith gained support from a number of colleagues, particularly Jimmy Prendergast, Marylebone's NUR branch secretary. Prendergast had served in the International Brigade during the Spanish Civil War and as an RAF rear gunner in the Second World War. He was a formidable figure and leaked the story of Asquith Xavier's rejection to the press.

Asquith received further support from the West Indian Standing Conference and the Campaign against Racial Discrimination. His case was then raised in Parliament by two Labour MPs, William Hamling and Lena Jeger. However, his family and friends recalled that the stress he was under probably contributed to him being admitted to hospital suffering from an ulcer.

Whilst he was in hospital, Barbara Castle, the Labour Secretary of State for Transport, progressed matters with the British Railways Board, reporting back to Parliament on 15th July 1966;

"The [British Railways] Board are at one with the Government in being strongly opposed to discrimination on grounds of colour in any circumstances.... The Board tell me that they have re-emphasised to all concerned ... the need for vigilance to prevent discrimination and for using every endeavour to resolve these difficulties when they do arise, as in the case which has recently received so much publicity".

On the same day that Castle addressed Parliament, Asquith's rejection was overturned and on 15 August 1966 he finally took up his post at Euston becoming the first non-white guard to be employed at Euston Station. He refused to accept discrimination and his quiet determination not only ended in him securing the job, but his pay was backdated to when he had first applied for the position. His case helped with the creation of the Commission for Racial Equality. His campaign also led to the strengthening of the Race Relations Act in 1968 which made it illegal to refuse housing, employment or public services to people because of their ethnic background.

On the day he started at Euston, station manager Ernest Drinnan said: "We expect Mr Xavier to fit in very well here... His record at Marylebone was exceptionally good and we know everyone here will take to him."

However, this was no ordinary working day as he needed police protection due to the threats to his life and race hate letters he had received. The Daily Express quoted one of those threats, "When you have finished at Euston we will send you back to the jungle."

In 1972 he moved with his family moved from London to Chatham, Kent, where he commuted daily by train to work at Euston, but his career was curtailed when ill health forced him to leave the railway in the early 1970s. He died in 1980 aged only 59.

In 2016 during Black History Month, Network Rail revealed a plaque in honour of him at Euston Station. Another plaque was unveiled in September 2020 at Chatham station, in Kent which had become his home town.

First Black leader of a major British trade union

William Morris, Baron Morris of Handsworth, OJ, DL – (1938-)

William (Bill) Morris, Baron Morris of Handsworth, OJ, DL is a former British trade union leader. He was General Secretary of the Transport and General Workers' Union from 1992 to 2003, and the first black leader of a major British trade union.

William Manuel Morris was born on 19 October 1938, in Manchester Parish, Jamaica. Following the death of his father, William, a part-time policeman, his mother, Una, emigrated to England to find work settling in Handsworth, Birmingham. He joined her as a 16 year old in 1954 and got his first job in local car parts manufacturer, Hardy Spicer Engineering Ltd.

William who was known as Bill Morris married his wife Minetta in 1957 and sadly she died in 1990. They had two sons.

Working at Hardy Spicer, he showed his potential for representing workers' concerns. On an occasion, his colleagues put him forward to meet managers and challenge them over the workers need to be protective gloves. He won a precursor for his battles on workers' rights.

In 1958 he joined the Transport and General Workers' Union (TGWU), becoming a shop steward in 1962. After serving on the TGWU General Executive Council (GEC) from 1972 to 1973, he joined the union as a full-time official. He served as district officer of the Nottingham District from 1973 to 1976 and district secretary of the Northampton District from 1976 to 1979.

In 1979 he became national secretary of the Passenger Services Trade Group, which was responsible for staff working for bus and coach companies. He was elected deputy general secretary on the 18 September 1985, working under general secretary Ron Todd. As deputy general secretary he was responsible for managing union activities in four transport sectors, in the energy sector, in engineering, as well as representing many white collar workers.

In 1988 he became a member of the TUC General Council and Executive Committee, a post he held until 2003.

In 1992 when Ron Todd retired, he was elected as general secretary of the Transport and General Workers Union making him the first black leader of a British trade union. He referred to himself not as the black candidate, but the candidate who happened to be black. He was re-elected in 1995 and remained in post until his retirement on his 65th birthday the 19 October 2003.

In 1998 he became a non-executive director of the Bank of England, a remarkable achievement for a first-generation immigrant with almost no formal education beyond the age of 16. His reputation as a skilled negotiator with the ability to grasp complex issues and express them in a fair and balanced way led to him being appointed to the Economic and Social Affairs Committee of the European Union

From 1999 to 2000 he was a member of the Royal Commission on the Reform of the House of Lords from 1999. He is a member of the Board of Governors of London South Bank University, a Trustee of the Open University Foundation, and the member of the Courts of the University of Northampton and the University of Bedfordshire.

In 1999 he was appointed as the first Chancellor of the University of Technology, Jamaica and in 2004 he was appointed Chancellor of Staffordshire University.

He has been a member of the advisory councils of the BBC and IBA and a Commissioner of the Commission for Racial Equality and in 2004 he chaired the Morris Inquiry into professional standards in the Metropolitan Police. He sits as a member of the Employment Appeal Tribunal. He is also a patron of the Refugee Council.

He is an independent non-executive Director of the England and Wales Cricket Board.

In 2002 he was awarded the Order of Jamaica, the fifth order in precedence in Jamaica. It is awarded to any Jamaican citizen of outstanding distinction.

In 2003 he received a knighthood in the Queen's Birthday Honours list.

In 2006 he took a seat in the House of Lords as a working life peer, and he was gazetted as Baron Morris of Handsworth in the County of West Midlands serving on the Parliamentary Joint Committee on Human Rights. He sat in the House of Lords, under the Labour Party whip, from 2006 to 2020.

He retired from the House of Lords on 21 July 2020.

From humble beginnings he rose to the highest level of a British institution conducting himself with a quietly spoken determination, fighting for the rights and justice of all workers.

First Black person to vote in a British general election

Charles Sancho – (1729-1780)

Charles Sancho was a British abolitionist, writer and composer. He was also a black man. In 1700s Britain only rich men who owned property were allowed to vote or stand for election to parliament. Sancho, a former black slave, owned a house and grocery shop, which made him legally qualified to vote, which he did in 1774 and 1780, making him the first known Black person to have voted in Britain as officially recorded in the British Library.

Charles Ignatius Sancho was born in 1729 on a slave ship in the Atlantic Ocean during the Middle Passage in the slave trade. When the ship docked he was sold into slavery in the Spanish colony of New Granada which formed parts of the countries known today as Colombia, Ecuador, Panama and Venezuela. His mother passed away soon after arriving in New Granada and it is thought his father committed suicide rather than live as a slave. After his parents died, Sancho's owner took the two-year-old orphan to Britain and presented him to three unmarried sisters in Greenwich as a slave. He lived with them from 1731 to 1749.

The Duke of Montagu regularly visited the sisters and became impressed by Sancho's intellect, frankness, and amiability. The Duke encouraged him to read, lending him books from his library. This heightened Sancho's resentment at being treated as a slave and led to him running away to Montagu House, Blackheath in 1749. He worked as a butler for the Duchess of Montagu, immersing himself in reading, writing, poetry and music

In 1751, two years later, the Duchess died and upon her death Sancho received an annuity of £30. He also received a year's salary.

On 17 December 1758 he married a West Indian woman named Anne Osborne. They had seven children: Frances Joanna, Ann Alice, Elizabeth

Bruce, Jonathan William, Lydia, Katherine Margaret, and William Leach Osborne.

Around the time of the birth of their third child, he became a valet to George Montagu, the son-in-law of the Duke of Montagu, a position he maintained until 1773.

In 1774 with help from Montagu, and despite suffering from ill health with gout, he opened a grocery shop, offering merchandise such as tobacco, sugar and tea, at 19 Charles Street in London's Mayfair, Westminster. These were goods which were mostly produced by slaves in the West Indies.

As a black man and former slave, he was highly motivated to be involved in the British abolitionist movement, whose aim was to outlaw the slave trade and the institution of slavery itself. He became one of the movements most devoted supporters and a symbol of the humanity of Africans and the immorality of the slave trade and slavery. He wrote many letters to papers and interested parties on the subject.

In Britain in the1700s politics and democracy was very limited for the running of the country. Women were not allowed to vote at all. Only rich men who owned some property were allowed to vote or stand for election to parliament. Another limiting factor was the fact that members of parliament were not paid, so only the wealthy could afford to stand for election. Hence Sancho, a former black slave, as an independent male property owner with a house and grocery shop, was legally qualified to vote in a general election, which he did in 1774 and 1780, making him the first known Black Briton to have voted in Britain. This was officially recorded in the British Library

In spite of his status, he still suffered racial discrimination, insults and abuse for being a black man. Despite this, he had many visitors to his shop and managed to find time to socialise, correspond with his many friends, and share his enjoyment of literature, He was a prolific writer of words and music. He also wrote letters and in newspapers, under his own name and under the pseudonym "Africanus". His correspondence included domestic issues, slavery and abolition as well as politics and literature

He died from the effects of gout on 14 December 1780 and was buried in the churchyard of St Margaret's, Westminster. There is no memorial at the church, as the gravestones in the churchyard, which were flat and became covered over with grass in 1880 and no inscription can be found for him. However, he does have the distinction of being the first person of African descent known to be given an obituary in the British press.

In 1782 Frances Crewe, one of his correspondents, arranged for 160 of his letters to be published in two volumes entitled The Letters of the Late Ignatius Sancho, an African. Joseph Jekyll, a British Whig MP for Caine added a memoir for Sancho. The book sold very well and four more editions had been issued by 1803. This was one of the earliest accounts of African slavery written in English from a first-hand experience.

Sancho's son, William Leach Osborne Sancho, inherited the grocery shop on Charles Street, Mayfair, and transformed it into a printing and book-selling business. In 1803 at this shop he printed a fifth edition of Letters of the Late Ignatius Sancho with Memoirs of His Life by Joseph Jekyll.

On 19 December 2023 a stone memorial was unveiled at St Margaret's Church, Westminster, where Charles Ignatius and Ann Sancho were married in 1758

First Black British MP in Scotland

Peter McLagan – (1823-1900)

Peter McLagan was a British Liberal Party politician who sat in the House of Commons from 1865 to 1893. He was Scotland's first non-White and first Black MP.

Peter McLagan was born on 1 January 1823 in Demerara in British Guiana on the north coast of South America. His father was also called Peter and his mother was an unknown black woman. His father co-owned a sugar plantation with Samuel Sandbach. The UK Government passed the Act of Parliament to abolish the slave trade in 1807. However slaves in the colonies were not freed until 1838 when the slave-owners, not the slaves, received compensation for loss of earnings. As co-owners of the plantation, the father McLagan and Sandbach received compensation to the equivalent of millions of pounds in today's money. McLagan used his share to help purchase an estate called Pumpherston in West Lothian

The McLagans left British Guiana while the son was still a child to live in Scotland. The child Peter Mclagan was educated in Tilicoultry and Peebles in Scotland before attending the University of Edinburgh.

In 1846 he married Elizabeth Ann Taylor.

In 1860 his father passed away due to a heart disease

In 1865 at the general election he was elected unopposed as the Member of Parliament for Linlithgowshire, a Scottish county which became West Lothian. He was re-elected at the next six general elections. He resigned his seat after a business partnership to mine shale oil on his land, which he inherited from his father, led to bankruptcy and his withdrawal from public duties in 1893.

In 1876 he married Elizabeth Ann Taylor.

As an MP, he won favour as being willing to actually talk to his constituents to explain his views on issues. He supported Home Rule for Ireland and the need for women doctors. In the 1800s this was controversial as it meant Scottish universities would have to be open to women wishing to train as doctors. He also supported women's suffrage as he believed that women should be able to vote, which was still exclusively for men.

However, he was also a product of times in that he was a firm believer in the Empire and had no problem with the use of force to help preserve it. He was also in favour of Temperance, essentially the limiting or even banning the consumption of alcohol. Alcohol was seen as leading to bad health effects. It was also blamed for causing issues such as domestic abuse, public disorder, and financial ruin generally leading to moral decay. This view tended to be held by the upper and middle classes and targeted at the lower classes.

He died at Marylebone in London and he was buried with his wife in the churchyard of Kirk of Calder in Mid Calder, West Lothian. He was reportedly an upright, an honourable and an honest man.

First Black woman elected to the British Parliament

Diane Abbott – (1953-)

Diane Julie Abbott is a trailblazing British politician. In 1987 she became the first black woman and one of the first three black Members of Parliament, along with Bernie Grant and Paul Boateng. Representing Hackney North and Stoke Newington since 1987, she is also the longest-serving black MP in the House of Commons. A dedicated socialist and member of the Labour Party, she served as Shadow Home Secretary from 2016 to 2020 under Jeremy Corbyn.

Diane Julie Abbott was born on 27 September 1953 in Paddington, London, to Jamaican parents. Her father worked as a welder and her mother as a nurse. She excelled academically, attending Harrow County Grammar School and then Newnham College, Cambridge, where she earned a Master's degree in history.

Her working career began in public service and journalism before transitioning to politics. She was a Home Office Civil Servant, a Race Relations Officer, and worked in media as a reporter and press officer. Her political journey started in 1982 as a Councillor on Westminster City Council. Although she lost a bid to become the Labour candidate for Brent East in 1985, she continued her public service career.

In the 1987 general election, she was elected as MP for Hackney North and Stoke Newington, making history as one of the first black MPs alongside Bernie Grant and Paul Boateng. She was also the first black female MP. She has been known for her strong socialist views and opposition to many of Tony Blair's policies, including the Iraq War and ID cards. Throughout her parliamentary career, she served on various committees focusing on social and international issues.

Despite facing significant challenges, including being a single mother and dealing with systemic racism and misogyny, she has remained a dedicated public servant.

She married David P. Ayensu-Thompson in 1991, though they divorced in 1993. They had a son, a year before the House of Commons introduced a crèche. The archaic male-dominated nature of Parliament was demonstrated by the fact that she did not have maternity leave and had to attend Parliament and vote throughout her pregnancy. Having given birth on a Monday, she was made to work until the Thursday before, and returned to parliament eight days later, navigating the demands of motherhood without maternity leave.

Her contributions to public health and her support for the Labour Party's left-wing platform are notable. She ran for Labour Party leadership in 2010, later serving as Shadow Minister for Public Health. During her career, she has been a vocal advocate for pro-choice policies and has consistently opposed renewing Britain's Trident nuclear weapons.

In 2016 she was appointed Shadow Home Secretary, a high profile position leading to heavy scrutiny, more than her peers.

On 2 October 2019 she became the first black MP at the dispatch box at Prime Minister's Questions. She served as a temporary stand-in for Jeremy Corbyn, the Leader of the Opposition, while Dominic Raab, First Secretary of State stood in for Prime Minister Boris Johnson.

Following the 2019 general election, she left the Shadow Cabinet, remaining in the House of Commons as a backbencher. In 2020 she stood down as Shadow Home Secretary and leaving the frontbench upon the election of a new Labour leader.

As a black woman she has faced a constant stream of obstacles due to blatant misogyny and racism, while just trying to do her job. In a Guardian article in February 2017, she wrote about receiving racist and sexist abuse online every day, such as threats of rape. An Amnesty International report found that she was the subject of almost half of all abusive tweets about female MPs on

Twitter during the 2017 election campaign, receiving ten times more abuse than any other MP. The abuse has increased in subsequent years.

In April 2023, she faced controversy for comments on racism and subsequently had the Labour whip withdrawn, meaning she sat as an independent MP. Despite apologizing and clarifying her remarks, the whip was not reinstated until 2024.

In March 2024 The Guardian newspaper alleged that businessman and Tory party donor Frank Hester had said in 2019 that she made him "want to hate all black women" and that "she should be shot". Hester wrote a disingenuous apology to her on social media site X, after the allegations were published, stating that his comments were "rude" and had "nothing to do with her gender nor colour of skin". The Tory government refused to really condemn him for his remarks leading to the opposition parties calling on the Tory party to return his £10 million donation, which they had no intention of doing. She described his remarks as frightening and reported him to the Metropolitan Police's parliamentary liaison and investigations team.

On 13 March 2024 she criticised the Speaker of the House of Commons for failing to allow her to speak during Prime Ministers Questions which was dominated by the race row surrounding her. During a 35 minute period she up 46 times to speak and was ignored.

She received cross party support as the comments are racist, misogynistic and disgusting, but Hester has not apologised properly. He remains a major donor to the Tory party.

In July 2025 she was suspended from the Labour party again after reconfirming her comments made in 2024.

Her career exemplifies perseverance and dedication to public service. She remains a prominent figure in British politics, advocating for educational initiatives and standing firm against racism and sexism. Her legacy as the longest-serving black MP is a testament to her remarkable strength and commitment.

First Black British Cabinet Minister

The Right Honorable Paul Boateng CVO, PC, DL – (1951-)

The Right Honorable Paul Boateng CVO, PC, DL is a British Labour Party politician who in 1987 along with Bernie Grant and Diane Abbott became the first black Members of Parliament. He was the Member of Parliament for Brent South from 1987 to 2005. He became the UK's first Black Cabinet Minister in May 2002, when he was appointed as Chief Secretary to the Treasury.

Paul Yaw Boateng was born on 14 June 1851in Hackney, London in 1951 to a Ghanaian father and a Scottish mother. His father was a lawyer and Cabinet Minister during Kwame Nkrumah's regime. When he was four, the family moved to Ghana, He attended Ghana International School and the Accra Academy, a high school in Ghana.

His life changed in 1966 when his father was imprisoned for 4 years without trial following a military coup overthrowing the Ghanaian government. His mother fled to Britain with him and his sister, settling in Hemel Hempstead.

He attended Apsley Grammar School and later studied law at the University of Bristol. Following that he began a career as a solicitor and then retrained as a barrister, focusing on social and community cases. He gained recognition for his work on civil rights issues, including advocating for women's rights and challenging police misconduct.

His political journey began in 1981 when he was elected to represent Walthamstow on the Greater London Council. He unsuccessfully stood as a parliamentary candidate for Hertfordshire West in 1953.

In the 1987 general election he was successfully elected as the MP for Brent South becoming one of the first three Black British MPs, elected alongside fellow Labour Party Black Sections members Bernie Grant, Diane Abbott. Keith Vaz was also elected at the same time to become Britain's first British Asian MP since the 1920s.

In 1989 he became a junior Treasury spokesman and then the first Black person to join the front bench as a party spokesperson covering economics, industrial strategies and corporate responsibility.

In 1992 he became shadow minister for the Lord Chancellor's Department, a post he held until the 1997 general election, where he was a strong advocate for increasing pro bono legal services among UK law firms.

In 1997 following Labour's landslide general election victory he became the UK's first black government minister as Parliamentary Under-Secretary for Health. He was responsible for social services, mental health and disabled people and published guidelines to end the denial of adoptions purely based on race.

In 1998 he became a Minister of State at the Home Office and in 1999 he was made a Privy Councillor. He gained a reputation for being tough on crime, particularly aggressive begging on the streets. He also worked with Eric Holder, then United States Deputy Attorney-General, and Louis Freeh, then Director of the FBI, on issues related to international drug trafficking and interdiction.

In 2000 he became the first Minister for Young People, with a remit to listen to and be a voice for Britain's youth.

In 2001 he was made Financial Secretary to the Treasury, and in May 2002 he was promoted to the Chief Secretary to the Treasury making him Britain's first black cabinet minister. He was quoted as saying "My colour is part of me but I do not choose to be defined by my colour." His appointment was greeted with praise by civil rights activists stating that it gave hope to young black youths and would inspire them to become involved in politics.

He had a leading role in coordinating the Every Child Matters policy paper, calling for the reform of children's services, including greater accountability and coordination among government agencies.

He was passionate in advocating for increased development aid to Africa and the developing nations making a number of trips to Africa, meeting with business and government leaders.

In March 2005 he decided not to stand for re-election as an MP at the general election. He was successfully replaced by Dawn Butler. He then became High Commissioner to South Africa from 2005 to 2009 making him the first black ambassador in British history. This move was praised by many Africans who saw it as a symbolic break from Britain's colonial past.

He proved to be a successful advocate for Africa on the world stage.

On 27 June 2010 he was created Baron Boateng, of Akyem in the Republic of Ghana and of Wembley in the London Borough of Brent and joined the House of Lords on 1 July 2010.

In 2011 he was a non-executive Director of Aegis Defence Services, a private security, military and risk management company.

He is an active Methodist and lay preacher. He served as a Methodist delegate to the World Council of Churches and as Vice-Moderator of its program to combat racism. During the 1994 South African General Elections ending apartheid, he was a member of the delegation sent by the Association of Western European Parliamentarians Against Apartheid to monitor the elections.

Outside of politics, from 1984 to 1997, he served on the board of the English National Opera and from 1993 to 1997, the English Touring Opera. He has been active in charity work and served on the boards of organizations like the English National Opera and BookAid International. He also holds positions in academia, serving as Chancellor of the University of Greenwich since 2019.

His achievements have been recognized both nationally and internationally. He received honours such as the Dr. Martin Luther King Jr. Award from the Southern Christian Leadership Conference.

He received honorary Doctor of Law degrees from Lincoln University (Pennsylvania) in 2004, the University of Bristol in 2007 and West London University in 2018.

He married his wife Janet, a former councillor in Lambeth, in 1980. The couple have two sons and three daughters.

First Black British MP – One of 3

Bernie Grant – (1944-2000)

Bernie Grant was a British Labour party politician. In 1987, along with Paul Boateng and Diane Abbott, the three of them became the first black Members of Parliament.

Bernard Alexander Montgomery Grant was born on 17 February 1944 in Georgetown, Guyana. His parents, Eric and Lily were schoolteachers, and he attended a Jesuit-run secondary school called St Stanislaus College. The family arrived in England in 1963 like a lot of West Indian families seeking a better life. He attended Tottenham technical college then went on to do a degree course in mining engineering at Heriot Watt University in Edinburgh.

In the mid-1960s, he joined the Socialist Labour League which became known as the Workers Revolutionary Party. He became a trade union official and moved into politics. He challenged and fought against racism and injustice at all levels. He became a full-time official for the National Union of Public Employees.

Aside from his leftwing trade union background, he was also an anti-apartheid campaigner, a supporter of revolutionary governments, feminist causes, black studies and a multi-racial school curriculum.

In 1978 he became a Labour councillor in the London Borough of Haringey. The borough had a growing ethnic population which was being confronted by blatantly racist organisations.

In 1985 he became the leader of the Borough. He gained notoriety during the Broadwater Farm riot where PC Keith Blakelock was murdered. He actually stated, "The youths around here believe the police were to blame for what happened on Sunday and what they got was a bloody good hiding." This was reported him saying, "What the police got was a bloody good hiding." As a result, he was pilloried by the media, government and his own

Labour party. He stated that his words were taken out of context and offered an apology to the family of PC Blakelock. He added that he was merely explaining to a wider audience what the feeling on the estate was like.

Despite this he was successfully elected as the MP for Tottenham at the 1987 general election, due mainly to the respect and affection that large segments of the local electorate felt for him. He became one of the UK's first Black British MPs along with Diane Abbott and Paul Boateng. They were all members of the Labour Party Black Sections movement. Keith Vaz was also elected at the same time to become Britain's first British Asian MP since the 1920s. Grant showed his individuality by entering Parliament dressed in African robes.

In 1989, he developed and chaired the Parliamentary Black Caucus which was modelled after the Congressional Black Caucus of the United States. The remit was to help advance the opportunities of Britain's ethnic minority communities.

In 1993 he co-founded and chaired the African Reparations Movement (ARM UK) campaigning for reparations and the moral debt owed to Africans to compensate for the evils of slavery and racism.

He was associated with the Socialist Campaign Group and spoke out against police racism.

He married three times, living with his third wife in Muswell Hill.

Unfortunately he suffered from chronic diabetes later in his life. This began to disable him and reduced his ability to attend the House of Commons.

He died from a heart attack at Middlesex Hospital on 8 April 2000, aged 56.

He was survived by his three children from his first marriage and by his third wife Sharon.

He was characterised as being his own man and people who felt he was occasionally rash and hasty acknowledged that he was likeable, charming, generous to friends and enemies, and relentlessly honest. Never one to just toe the party line he had a passionate devotion to an ideal of justice, and he believed that politics was about these notions.

His views were often strongly opposed by political allies and enemies alike, but he had become a highly respected figure, and while he faced plenty of criticism, it was muted by the respect and affection in which he was generally held.

In September 2007 Haringey Council opened the Bernie Grant Arts Centre in Tottenham, named after him in recognition of what he had done for the borough.

In October 2012 a blue plaque in tribute to him was unveiled at Tottenham Old Town Hall. This was organised by the Nubian Jak Community Trust, was unveiled at Tottenham Old Town Hall in tribute to Grant.

In March 2019 the Labour Party launched the Bernie Grant Leadership programme, which was designed to train and equip BAME Labour members.

First Black woman to become a Cabinet Minister, first black leader of the House of Lords, first black leader of a university and first black Companion to the Garter in the United Kingdom

Baroness Valerie Amos LG, CH, PC – (1954-)

Valerie Amos, Baroness Amos is a British Labour Party politician who on appointment as the Secretary of State for International Development on 12th May 2003, became the first black woman o serve as a Cabinet Minister. She was also the first black leader of the House of Lords

Valerie Ann Amos was born in 1954 in British Guiana in South America. She moved to Britain with the family in 1963. She went to Bexley Technical High School for Girls, which has now become Townley Grammar School in Bexleyheath. She became the first black deputy head girl. She went on to complete a degree in Sociology at the University of Warwick, an MA in cultural studies at the University of Birmingham and further studies in education at the University of East Anglia.

She began her career working in Equal Opportunities, Training and Management Services in local government for the London boroughs of Lambeth, Camden and Hackney. She became Chief Executive of the Equal Opportunities Commission in 1989, leaving the position in 1994.

From 1990 to 1998 she was also Deputy Chair of the Runnymede Trust, a Trustee of the Institute for Public Policy Research, a non-executive Director of the University College London Hospitals Trust, a Trustee of Voluntary Service Overseas, Chair of the Afiya Trust, Member of the board of the Sierra Leone Titanium Resources Group, a director of Hampstead Theatre and chair of the Board of Governors of the Royal College of Nursing Institute.

In 1995 she co-founded a consultancy firm called Amos Fraser Bernard for which she was an adviser to the South African government on public service reform, human rights and employment equity. The same year she was awarded an Honorary Professorship at Thames Valley University in recognition of her work on equality and social justice.

In August 1997 she received a peerage as Baroness Amos, of Brondesbury in the London Borough of Brent. In the House of Lords she became a co-opted member of the Select Committee on European Communities Sub-Committee F (Social Affairs, Education and Home Affairs) from 1997 to 1998.

From 1998 to 2001 she was a Government Whip and spokesperson on Social Security, International Development and Women's Issues as well as one of the Government's spokespersons in the House of Lords on Foreign and Commonwealth Affairs.

On 11 June 2001 she was appointed Parliamentary Under-Secretary for Foreign & Commonwealth Affairs, with responsibility for Africa; Commonwealth; Caribbean; Overseas Territories; Consular Issues and FCO Personnel.

Having threatened to resign as International Development Secretary in the lead-up to the 2003 invasion of Iraq, Labour MP Clare Short stood down in May 2003 over a draft UN resolution that she felt failed to give "the UN its promised central role in rebuilding Iraq". Baroness Amos was serving as Foreign Office minister and as a spokesperson in the Lords for International Development at the time. She was drafted in as Short's replacement. This appointment made her first black woman cabinet minister Britain. It was also an unusual step for a government department to be headed by a member of the House of Lords.

On 6 October she became Leader of the House of Lords following the unexpected death of the existing leader Lord Williams of Mostyn. This meant her time as Secretary of State for International Development lasted less than six months.

In June 2007 she left the cabinet when Gordon Brown replaced Tony Blair as Prime Minister, taking up a directorship with Travant Capital, a Nigerian private equity fund.

In 2009 she was appointed British High Commissioner to Australia.

In 2010 she was appointed the United Nations Under-Secretary-General for Humanitarian Affairs and Emergency Relief Coordinator. She left the post in May 2015.

In September 2015 she became the ninth director of SOAS University of London. This made her the first black woman to be the director of a university in the United Kingdom.

In 2015 Margaret Chan, the Director General of World Health Organization (WHO), appointed her as a member of the Advisory Group on Reform of WHO's Work in Outbreaks and Emergencies with Health and Humanitarian Consequences.

In 2019 she co-led a report by Universities (UUK) and the National Union of Students (NUS) addressing the disparity between the proportions of "top degrees" (first or 2:1 degrees) achieved by white and black, Asian and minority ethnic (BAME) students.

From 2019 she served on the Centre for Strategic & International Studies' (CSIS) Task Force on Humanitarian Access, co-chaired by Cory Booker and Todd Young.

In January 2021 she left her position at SOAS to become Master of University College, Oxford, which made her the first female appointed to that post and the first black head of any Oxford college.

On 1 July 2010 she received an honorary doctorate from the University of Stirling in recognition of her "outstanding service to our society and her role as a model of leadership and success for women today." She has also been awarded the honorary degrees of Doctor of Laws from the University of Warwick in 2000 and the University of Leicester in 2006.

The Guild of Students at the University of Birmingham, where she studied as an undergraduate, named one of the committee rooms "The Amos Room" after her, in acknowledgement of her services to society.

In 2013 she was made an honorary Doctor of Civil Law at Durham University.

In the 2016 Birthday Honours list she was appointed a Companion of the Order of the Companions of Honour (CH) for services to the United Nations and emergency relief.

In 2017 she was awarded an honorary degree at Middlesex University, thereby "recognising achievement at the highest level as well as dedication to public duty and making a difference to others' lives."

In July 2018 she received an honorary Doctor of Laws degree from the University of Bristol. In December 2018 she was awarded an honorary Doctor of Literature by the University of the Witwatersrand.

She was elected to the American Academy of Arts and Sciences as an International Honorary Member in 2019.

On 1 January 2022 the Queen appointed her a Lady Companion of the Order of the Garter. This is the most senior order of knighthood in the British honours system.

Membership of the Order, founded in 1348, is an honour reserved for royalty (domestic and overseas), former prime ministers and highly-esteemed individuals, including judges, generals and public servants. Her banner of arms was erected at St George's Chapel, Windsor on 13 June, making her the first black "knight or lady companion" member of the order since its foundation, excluding the Emperor of Ethiopia Haile Selassie, who as a foreign monarch was a stranger knight companion of the order.

In November 2022 she was awarded an honorary fellowship of the University of London.

In May 2023 she took part in the Coronation of Charles III, representing the Order of the Garter.

In November 2023 she was conferred with an Honorary Doctor of Law degree from the University of Guyana

Looking at what she has done and achieved, it is clear that her decades of public service, as a former government minister, long-term leader of the House of Lords, UN under-secretary general, former British High Commissioner to Australia, former head of SOAS and Master of University, have been recognised.

First Black woman leader of the Conservative Party

Kemi Badenoch – (1980-)

After the 2024 Conservative election defeat, former Prime Minister Rishi Sunak decided to step down as leader of the Conservative party. Following three MP ballots and subsequent Members vote Kemi Badenoch defeated Robert Jenrick thus becoming the first Black Leader of the Conservative Party, a major UK political party, Leader of the Opposition, and the fourth woman to lead the Conservative Party, after Margaret Thatcher, Theresa May and Liz Truss.

Olukemi Olufunto Kemi Adegoke was born on 2 January 1980. Her father Femi was a general practitioner, founder of a publishing company in Nigeria and an activist for the rights of the Yoruba people. Her mother Feyi was a professor of physiology at the University of Lagos. Feyi travelled from Nigeria to Britain for medical treatment, and gave birth to Olukemi (Kemi) in St Teresa's Maternity Hospital, Wimbledon. She was among the last to benefit from the automatic birthright citizenship rules which her heroine, Margaret Thatcher, abolished in the 1981 British Nationality Act. Feyi returned to Nigeria shortly after Kemi was born.

Kemi spent her childhood in Lagos, Nigeria, and in the United States, where her mother lectured. Her family lived in the middle class neighbourhood of Surulere, Nigeria studying at the private International School of Lagos. She had a middle-class background though her family went through periods of poverty. As a result of the deteriorating political and economic situation in Nigeria, she returned to the UK aged 16 to live with a friend of her mother's.

She studied A Levels at Phoenix College, Further Education College in Morden, south London, achieving a B in biology, a B in chemistry and a D in maths, claiming that she was not pushed to fulfil her potential despite being a straight A student in Nigeria. She felt let down by the British education system and this formed part of her decision to lean politically towards the conservatives. Among other jobs she worked for McDonald's claiming this made her working class. She studied Computer Systems Engineering at the University of Sussex, completing a Master of Engineering (MEng) degree in 2003.

She worked in IT as a software engineer at Logica from 2003 to 2006. While working there she read Law part-time at Birkbeck, University of London, graduating as Bachelor of Laws (LLB) in 2009. She became a Fellow of Birkbeck in 2018.

She started work as a systems analyst at the Royal Bank of Scotland Group, before going to a career in consultancy and financial services, working as an associate director at private bank and wealth manager Coutts from 2006 to 2013 and later a digital director for The Spectator from 2015 to 2016.

She joined the Conservative Party in 2005 aged 25. At the 2010 general election, she contested the Dulwich and West Norwood constituency coming third, behind the Labour Party incumbent MP Tessa Jowell.

In 2012 she married to banker Hamish Badenoch, whom she met at a local Conservative association in 2009, and they have three children.

She also stood for the Conservatives in the London Assembly election, in 2012, but failed being placed fifth on the London-wide list. In 2015 she successfully became an Assembly member and retained her seat in the 2016 election.

In 2017 she was shortlisted to be the Conservative Party candidate for the marginal Hampstead and Kilburn constituency but was unsuccessful. She was subsequently selected for the same election as the Conservative candidate for Saffron Walden, a safe seat which she won.

In her maiden speech as an MP on 19 July 2017, she described Brexit as "the greatest ever vote of confidence in the project of the United Kingdom" and cited her personal heroes as the Conservative politicians Winston Churchill, Airey Neave and Margaret Thatcher.

In the same month, she was selected to join the 1922 Executive Committee. In September, she was appointed to the parliamentary Justice Select Committee. She was appointed as the Conservative Party's Vice Chair for Candidates in January 2018.

In the run-up to the 2019 Conservative Party leadership election, she was tipped as a possible contender though she supported the campaign of Michael Gove. In the December 2019 general election, she was re-elected with an increased majority.

In July 2019, she was appointed Parliamentary Under-Secretary of State for Children and Families by Boris Johnson. In February 2020, she was appointed Exchequer Secretary to the Treasury and Parliamentary Under-Secretary of State (Minister for Equalities) in the Department for International Trade.

In a Cabinet reshuffle in September 2021, she was promoted to Minister of State for Equalities and appointed Minister of State for Housing, Communities and Local Government. Within days of her appointments, the latter title was renamed Minister of State for Levelling Up Communities. In July 2022, along with a number of Conservative MPs, she resigned from the government, blaming Prime Minister Johnson's handling of the Chris Pincher scandal.

Following Johnson's subsequent resignation, she joined the race to succeed him, but was eliminated in the fourth round of voting.

In September 2022, after Liz Truss became prime minister, she was made the cabinet Secretary of State for International Trade. When Liz Truss resigned the next month, she supported Rishi Sunak who became Prime Minister. Sunak retained her as Secretary of State for International Trade. She also became Minister for Women & Equalities.

In a February 2023 Cabinet reshuffle, she was appointed as the first Secretary of State at the newly created Department for Business and Trade, with continued responsibility for equalities.

Due to a review of Westminster constituencies, in 2023, her constituency of Saffron Walden was abolished, and replaced with North West Essex. At the 2024 general election, she was elected to Parliament as MP for North West Essex.

Following the Conservative defeat at the general election, she was appointed Shadow Secretary of State for Housing, Communities and Local Government. She publicly criticised Rishi Sunak and Home Secretary Suella Braverman.

In July 2024, at least three officials reported her for bullying in the Department for Business and Trade stating that she had created an intimidating atmosphere. She denied these claims, describing them as smears from former staff and accusing them of covering up their own failures and general gross incompetence, claiming it was also politically motivated. There were no formal complaints or investigations into her alleged behaviour.

Following the 2024 Conservative election defeat and decision of former Prime Minister Rishi Sunak to step down she ran to be elected as the new Tory leader.

She was considered the frontrunner but in the first and second MP ballots, she came second to Robert Jenrick. She came third in the third MP's ballot, with 30 votes, but topped the final vote of MPs with 42, one ahead of Robert Jenrick and five clear of James Cleverly who was eliminated. In the Member's vote, she defeated Jenrick, thus becoming the first Black Leader of the Conservative Party, a major UK political party, and the fourth woman to lead the Conservative Party, after Margaret Thatcher, Theresa May and Liz Truss.

Her election as leader is a remarkably historic political and personal achievement. In her 2017 Commons maiden speech she declared that "To all intents and purposes, I am a first-generation immigrant." She vowed to renew the party claiming it had two responsibilities, to hold the Labour Government to account and to prepare for government.

She stated that Winston Churchill, Airey Neave and Margaret Thatcher were her political heroes.

She said the public had rejected the Conservative Party as it was not trusted and did not deliver. She dismissed concerns that her approach of not having specific policy positions would leave a vacuum that could be filled by Reform UK, acknowledging that the forthcoming 2025 United Kingdom local elections would be difficult for her party. She criticised past party actions on issues such as delivering Brexit and lowering immigration, admitting that they had told the public what they wanted to hear first and then tried to work it out later.

In the May 2025 local elections the Conservatives and Labour lost about two-thirds of the council seats held. All 16 councils where the Conservatives had a majority were lost to Reform UK or the Liberal Democrats, or no party had a majority. She apologised to all unseated councillors, describing the result as a bloodbath. In the Runcorn and Helsby by-election for an MP held on the same day, the Conservative Party won 7% of the vote, coming third behind Reform and Labour on 39% each.

She is considered to be on the right wing of the Conservative Party, though she describes herself as being on the liberal wing of the Conservative Party, though not really left-leaning on anything, insisting that the left do not have a monopoly on caring issues. She was also pro-Brexit. She has been characterised as a social conservative and anti-woke politician. She has described herself as a net zero sceptic and has generally voted against measures to reduce greenhouse gas emissions in Parliament.

She has said that being a very angry young person got her involved in politics and helped push her towards the right of centre, by feeling patronised by careers advisers and development campaigners who did not value African voices. She claimed her Conservative views were formed from her experience at college among snotty, middle-class north Londoners who talked of helping Africans, while not knowing what they were talking about.

She felt that skin colour was no more relevant than hair colour but the identity politics that she uses sound much more colour conscious than that, claiming, "I am Labour's worst nightmare, they can't paint me as prejudiced".

Her position on immigration has hardened since 2018. Then, she welcomed the Conservative government's proposal to relax restrictions on visas for skilled migrants. But as net migration has trebled since Brexit, she has changed her mind. She argued that numbers matter but culture matters more, and that the most important fact was who came to Britain and what their values and aspirations were.

First Black UK peer

Learie Constantine, Baron Constantine, Kt, MBE – (1901-1971)

Learie Constantine, Baron Constantine, Kt, MBE was a West Indian cricketer, lawyer and politician who served as Trinidad and Tobago's High Commissioner to the United Kingdom and became the UK's first black peer.

Learie Nicholas Constantine was born on 21 September 1901 in Petit Valley, a village close to Diego Martin in north-west Trinidad. He was the second child of the family and the eldest of three brothers. His father, Lebrun Constantine, was the grandchild of slaves. Lebrun was the overseer on a cocoa estate in Cascade, near Maraval, where the family moved in 1906. Lebrun was also a famous cricketer representing Trinidad and Tobago and twice touring England with a West Indian team.

Constantine's mother, Anaise Pascall, was the daughter of slaves, and her brother Victor, was also a Trinidad and Tobago and West Indian first-class cricketer; a third family member, His brother Elias, later represented Trinidad and Tobago. Unsurprisingly, he enjoyed cricket from an early age.

He went to the St Ann's Government School in Port of Spain, and then attended St Ann's Roman Catholic School until 1917. He showed more sports than academically ability. He captained the cricket team with a reputation as an attacking batsman, a good fast-medium bowler and an excellent fielder. His father banned him from playing competitive club cricket until 1920 for fear of premature exposure to top-class opposition at a young age.

He left school taking a job as a clerk to solicitors in Port of Spain though as a black man he would not be allowed to progress far. At this time few black Trinidadians were allowed to become solicitors, and he faced many social restrictions owing to his colour.

In 1927 he married his wife Norma Agatha Cox. Initially she had little interest in cricket, though this inevitably grew. They had a daughter called Gloria born in April 1928.

Due to the lack of opportunities for black people in Trinidad and Tobago, he decided to pursue a career as a professional cricketer in England, and during the 1928 tour was awarded a contract with the Lancashire League club Nelson Cricket Club. His fielding, fast bowling batting skills made him famous. In a mediocre team he stood out as an exceptional cricketer. He was a great attraction on the grounds he visited. He played eighteen Tests in his career for the West Indies, whilst also playing for Nelson C.C. and for Trinidad and Tobago. He became a prolific cricketer locally and internationally.

Despite his successes on the pitch he suffered from racial discrimination at all levels, within society and institutionally within the structure of cricket. The rules, roles and systems were stacked heavily against black people.

From the outbreak of the Second World War in 1939, while continuing his cricket career, he worked as a billeting officer at Nelson. In 1941 he was appointed as a welfare officer under the Ministry of Labour to look after a large number of West African workers in the Liverpool area.

During the war, the British government asked him make radio broadcasts to the West Indies, reporting on the involvement of West Indians in the war effort. He was also asked to speak on BBC radio about his life in England. His radio performances met with critical acclaim, and he became a frequent guest on radio panel shows. He also took part in a film documentary, West Indies calling, in 1943.

However he still met with racism. In a dance hall he was accosted by a man in an American Air Force officers' uniform who aggressively yelled at him to 'get out,' shouting that 'where we are' they did not allow Black people to mix with white. However, it was the aggressor who had to get out.

That was not the only incident of racial discrimination he faced during the Second World War, or throughout his stay in the United Kingdom.

In 1943 the manager of the Imperial Hotel in Russell Square refused to accommodate him and his family on the grounds of their race in an instance of the UK colour bar. He successfully sued the hotel, though he was only awarded £5 5s, the cost of the room. Nothing for the distress and humiliation the family suffered. However this coverage of the racism he faced as a prominent public figure in Britain highlighted the endemic racism and racial discrimination within the country, and the case was seen as a milestone in British racial equality.

In the 1946 New Years Honours list he was awarded a Member of the Order of the British Empire (MBE) for his welfare work during the Second World War.

In 1947 he was appointed coach to Leinster and Dublin University clubs. The same year he had become Chairman of the League of Coloured Peoples, to help affect real change in race relations. He held this until the League was discontinued in 1951.

In 1954, he published a book entitled Colour Bar, which contained the following:

"I am black. My grandfather and grandmother were the children of slaves born into slavery. I am neither proud nor ashamed of these things...Black or white – it appears to be what we call an accident of birth. But it is a fact, and one which has inevitable economic, social and political results."

The book addressed race relations in Britain and the racism he had experienced. It also discussed worldwide racial oppression and how the lives of black people could be improved. This included him being prevented from playing for Lancashire County Cricket Club. It was apparent there was some unpleasant disagreement because of his colour even though the customers and most members of the committee would have welcomed him

Racism did not just affect him. In the book Colour Bar, he related an incident when his wife and daughter had booked a sleeper train to take them from London to Edinburgh, to attend his daughter Gloria's graduation at St. Andrew's University. When they entered the sleeper train to deposit their things, a white woman called out "Steward, what does these mean?" protesting that she would not sleep alongside Black people. To add further insult to this appalling display, a white girl who his daughter knew quite well, added her complaint in similar terms, though previously she had never offered the slightest objection. This scene so upset his wife and daughter that they refused to travel down in a sleeping compartment.

The book allowed him to give a voice to Britain's growing Black population. He called out difficult truths, which were reported in the newspapers. As a famous sportsman, broadcaster, and now writer, he became a spokesperson for Britain's Black community, a position that he embraced.

In 1954 he was asked to solve an issue at a great powder factory in the North-West, employing some 30,000 people including Black employees. The workers were put up at various hostels. Some of the workers objected to the Black workers being so housed. To help promote understanding between the workers, he took a private room in one of the hostels and lived there for a time. He hoped that the white workers would see that he was an ordinary sort of person like themselves and then they might be willing to try seeing the other black people similarly. This proved to be quite successful.

In amongst his other task such as writing books, broadcasting, and coaching, he had been studying law to take his career in a new direction. As a result he became a qualified barrister.

Having spent 25 years in the country, he decided to leave Britain to help shape the future of Trinidad. He recognised that he had arrived in Britain as an inexperienced boy, and he was leaving as a qualified barrister-at-law, able to use his legal knowledge for the benefit of his own people and for the improvement of relationships between white and black.

In a newspaper article in 1954 writing about his experiences in Britain from the warmth of the reception he received, to the appalling discrimination he faced. He wrote:

"It hasn't always been easy. There were times when life seemed to hold champagne to my lips – as thousands of generous English spectators applauded a century I had hit or some bowling or fielding feat I had done. There was also a time when – at the wicket – somebody nearby spoke of my colour in terms which would have cost him dear in a more private place."

In 1956 he won a seat in Trinidad's Legislative Assembly representing the People's National Movement. This Movement had a clear objective to aim for a programme of self-government for Trinidad and Dominion status for a British Caribbean Federation.

In 1961 he returned to Britain following his appointment as Trinidad High Commissioner in Britain, the first person to hold this position.

In 1962 he was knighted, and he also received the freedom of the town of Nelson, where had played cricket all those years ago.

In 1963 he resigned as Trinidad High Commissioner in London so he could freely speak out on racial issues affecting West Indian immigrants such as the Bristol bus boycott. A bus company in Bristol refused to employ Black workers. A boycott was organised whereby West Indians supported by many white people refused to use the buses. He visited Bristol and spoke out about it. The Trinidadian and British authorities felt that as a senior diplomat he should not be so closely involved in British domestic affairs.

The boycott saw an end to the racial discrimination in the bus company and was seen as a pre-cursor to the 1965 Race Relations Act which made racial discrimination unlawful in public places.

In 1969 he was awarded a peerage in the New Years Honours list in recognition of his hard work for racial equality and his other outstanding achievements. He took on the title of Baron Constantine of Maraval in Trinidad and of Nelson in Lancashire, thus becoming the first Black peer to sit in the House of Lords. However, when he received his peerage he was ill in bed.

In his final years, he served on the Race Relations Board, the Sports Council and the Board of Governors of the BBC. Failing health reduced his effectiveness in some of these roles, and he faced criticism for becoming a part of the British Establishment.

On 1 July 1971 he passed away in London, aged 69, due to a heart attack. His body was returned to Trinidad, where he was given a state funeral. His wife Norma died two months after him.

He was posthumously awarded Trinidad and Tobago's highest honour, the Trinity Cross.

In June 2021, he was inducted into the ICC Cricket Hall of Fame as one of the special inductees to mark the inaugural edition of the ICC World Test Championship final.

First Black mayor of a British Town

Allan Glaisyer Minns – (1858-1930)

Allan Glaisyer Minns was a medical doctor, and the first black man to become a mayor in Britain.

Allan Glaisyer Minns was born in 1858 in the Inagua district of the Bahamas. He was the youngest son of ten children born to John Minns and his wife Ophelia Bunch. His grandfather, also called John Minns, had emigrated from England around 1801 to the Bahamas and became a planter and slave-owner, where he married Rosette, who was a former African slave. He freed her in 1808

Minns was educated at Nassau Grammar School and then moved to London to continue his education at Guy's Hospital. In 1881 he qualified with MRCS, Membership examination of the Royal Colleges of Surgeons and in 1884 LRCP, Licentiate of the Royal College of Physicians. He eventually registered as a doctor with the British Medical Association on 14 February 1884. He was based in Thetford from 1885 where he joined his eldest brother, Pembroke Minns, who was already in medical practice there.

In 1888 he purchased a doctors practice in Thetford. He played an important part in town life being a well-respected physician and community leader. He became Medical Officer at Thetford Workhouse and Honorary Medical Officer of Thetford Cottage Hospital. He published several articles in the Thetford and Watton Times in the early 1900s on themes like 'Fresh Air and Common Sense'. He was also a keen gardener and a founder of Thetford Horticultural Society. He was also an active member of the working Men's Conservative Association.

In 1888 he married Emily Pearson. She died four years later. He met and married Gertrude Ann Morton in 1896. He had children by both wives.

In 1903 he was elected to the Thetford Borough Council. He was the first black member.

In 1904 he was chosen by his fellow councillors to be Mayor making him the first black mayor in Britain. He served two one-year terms as mayor. He was the deputy mayor for the next two years and continued to serve on the Council afterwards. He was also Chief Magistrate of the borough.

In 1923 he left Thetford and moved to Dorking in Surrey,

On 16 September 1930 he died at home aged 71.

First Black mayor in London

John Archer – (1863-1932)

John Archer was a British politician and political activist. In 1913 he was elected Mayor of Battersea, becoming the first black mayor in London. He was a notable Pan-Africanist and the founding president of the African Progress Union.

John Richard Archer was born on 8 June 1863 in Liverpool, to Richard Archer, from Barbados and Mary Theresa Burns, from Ireland. He travelled the world as a seaman, living in the US and Canada, before settling in Battersea with his wife, Bertha, a black Canadian, in the 1890s. He started to study medicine and then ran a small photographic studio.

He became involved in local politics after attending the Pan-African Conference held in London in 1900, where he met leading African members. In 1906 he stood for and was elected as the Progressive, Liberal for the Latchmere ward of Battersea Borough Council. He was appointed to the Baths, Health and Works Committees. He later joined the Board of Guardians, supervising public health and welfare. He became Chair of the Baths Committee maintaining a lifelong interest in the Nine Elms Swimming Club.

There was a lot of infighting within the various left wing factions in the area and he lost the 1909 election. However he was re-elected in 1912.

In 1913 he was appointed to the position of mayor. He was more of a political leader of the council, rather than the ceremonial post. There were negative and racist aspects to the campaign, with allegations that he did not have British nationality. He won by 40 votes to 39 among his fellow councillors, and gave a notable victory speech:

"My election tonight means a new era. You have made history tonight. For the first time in the history of the English nation a man of colour has been elected as mayor of an English borough.

That will go forth to the coloured nations of the world and they will look to Battersea and say Battersea has done many things in the past, but the greatest thing it has done has been to show that it has no racial prejudice and that it recognises a man for the work he has done."

His success was reported in the US journal The Crisis in January 1914.

His views became more left-wing during his years in Battersea and he was re-elected to the council as a Labour representative in 1919. In 1918 he became the first president of the African Progress Union, working for "advanced African ideas in liberal education". In 1919 he was a British delegate to the Pan-African Congress in Paris and two years later, chaired the Pan-African Congress in London.

In 1922 he gave up his council seat to act as Labour Party election agent for Shapurji Saklatvala, who was a Communist Party activist standing for parliament in North Battersea. He convinced the Labour Party to endorse Saklatvala who was duly elected one of the first Indian MPs in Britain. He and Saklatvala continued to work together, winning again in 1924 until the Communist and Labour parties split fully.

In the 1929 general election, he was the agent for the official Labour candidate who beat Saklatvala.

He served as a governor of Battersea Polytechnic, president of the Nine Elms Swimming Club, chair of the Whitley Council Staff Committee and a member of the Wandsworth Board of Guardians.

In 1931 he was elected again for the Nine Elms ward and became deputy leader of Battersea Council.

On 14 July 1932, a few weeks after his 69th birthday he died following a period of ill-health from cardio-renal failure. His funeral was held at the Church of Our Lady of Carmel in Battersea Park Road on 19th July, and he was buried in the council cemetery at Morden.

John Archer had been thought to be the first Black man to be elected as a mayor in Britain, however, in 1904, Mr. Allen Glaisyer Minns, a Black man from the West Indies, was elected mayor of the borough of Thetford, Norfolk. (see above)

Archer House, part of the Battersea Village estate, was named after him when it was constructed in the 1930s. Wandsworth School was renamed in his honour in 1986 but it closed in 1991. There is a John Archer Way in Wandsworth and in Liverpool, a John Archer Hall.

In 2010 he was commemorated with a blue plaque from the Nubian Jak Community Trust.

In April 2013 he was one of six people selected by Royal Mail for the "Great Britons" commemorative postage stamp issue.

In November 2013 a blue plaque was hung at his former home in 55 Brynmar Road, Battersea by English Heritage.

In March 2018 the Ark Academy Network renamed High View Primary school in Battersea as Ark John Archer Academy.

NUBIAN JAK. COMMUNITY TRUST
JOHN RICHARD
ARCHER
1863-1932
MAYOR OF BATTERSEA 1913-1914
(FIRST BLACK LONDON MAYOR)
HAD A
PHOTOGRAPHY SHOP
AND LIVED HERE
1918-1932
WANDSWORTH COUNCIL, EMAS & HERITAGE LOTTERY FUND

First Black mayor of Southwark

Sam Beaver King MBE – (1926-2016)

Sam Beaver King MBE was a Jamaican born campaigner who became the first black mayor of Southwark and a campaigner in support of West Indian immigrants.

Sam Beaver King was born on 20 February 1926 at Priestman's River in Portland, Jamaica. He was one of ten siblings born to his parents, George and Caroline, in a strong Christian household helping on the family's banana farm.

In 1944 like a number of young black men, he responded to an advertisement in the Jamaican newspaper, the Gleaner, calling for volunteers to join the British Royal Air Force (RAF) to fight in the Second World War, for the mother country, England. After carrying out initial training in Kingston, he was posted to an RAF training centre at Filey in Yorkshire and then to RAF Hawkinge, a fighter base near Folkestone, Kent, where he worked as an engineer. At the end of the war, in 1947, he was demobbed and returned to Jamaica.

He found it hard to settle in Jamaica and find work. He saw yet another advertisement in the Gleaner about opportunities helping re-build England and announcing tickets on the ship, the Empire Windrush. He applied and became part of the Windrush generation.

On 22 June 1948, like many others he disembarked at Tilbury Docks from the Windrush. Initially he re-joined the RAF leaving in 1953. His experiences of constant racial discrimination were typical for all black people, facing the "No Blacks, No Dogs, No Irish" signs and constant abuse. He was turned down for work in several areas from carpentry to the Metropolitan Police. He eventually settled in Southwark where he found work as a postman, the start of a 34-year career with the Post Office.

He met and married his wife Mae who was a trainee nurse from Jamaica. They had a son Brian who sadly died in infancy. They had another son called Michael and a daughter called Althea. Unfortunately his wife Mae passed away in 1983. He later married a lady called Myrtle.

He was involved in London's West Indian community and helped in the organisation of the Caribbean-style carnival first organised by Claudia Jones in St Pancras Town Hall in January 1959 which was a precursor of the Notting Hill Carnival. He also helped to found the West Indian Gazette, which was the first British newspaper written specifically for a black people. He was the circulation manager in the mid-1950s.

In 1983 after serving as a local councillor for six months, he was elected mayor of the London Borough of Southwark. He became the first black mayor in the borough and was, at the time, the only black mayor in London.

In 1996 he set up the Windrush Foundation, with Arthur Torrington, to preserve the memories of those who arrived on that voyage and to campaign on behalf of West Indian immigrants. He also advocated for the date of the Windrush's arrival to become a public holiday to mark the contributions of black people to British society.

In 1998 he was awarded an MBE, Member of the Order of the British Empire, as part of the 50th-anniversary celebrations of Windrush Day. He also published his autobiography, Climbing up the Rough Side of the Mountain.

He was a lay preacher, having taken a ministerial course at Goldsmiths College. He was a lifelong advocate of socialism and a fervent supporter of cricket,

On 17 June 2016 he died aged 90 following a bout of illness.

He had been twice married and had two children, three grandchildren and three great-grandchildren.

His funeral took place on Tuesday 19 July 2016 at Southwark Cathedral.

First Black Chief Executive of the Inner London Education Authority

Herman Ouseley, Baron Ouseley Kt – (1945-2024)

Herman Ouseley, Baron Ouseley Kt is a British parliamentarian, who has run public authorities, including local councils and is an adviser and reviewer of public services organisations. He was the first Black Race Equality Adviser in Local government in London Borough of Lambeth in 1978; the first Black Policy Advisor for Ethnic Minorities with the Greater London Council in 1981; the first Black Chief Executive in a local authority in England with the former Inner London Education Authority in 1988 and the first Black Executive Chairman of the former Commission for Racial Equality.

Herman George Ouseley was born in 1945 in British Guiana, now Guyana. He came to England in 1957, when he was 11. He was educated at William Penn School and at Catford College, where he gained a diploma in municipal administration. His mother was a nurse who did several other jobs to keep the family together.

In 1963 he became a local government officer. By determination and his own abilities he achieved increasingly important positions.

From 1981 he served as Principal Race Relations Adviser and head of the Greater London Council's Ethnic Minority Unit. He later became Chief Executive of the London Borough of Lambeth and the former Inner London Education Authority, responsible for over 1000 schools and colleges across London. He was the first black person to hold this position.

In1993 he became the chair and chief executive in the Commission for Racial Equality. He set up the project to tackle racism in football and was the Chairperson of Kick It Out, which was an internationally acclaimed campaign to make football free from discrimination and abuse and to be more inclusive of people of all backgrounds. He did not receive a salary for this work for Kick It Out.

In the 1997 New Years Honours list, he was made a Knight Bachelor for services to community relations and local government.

On 26 June 2001 he was made a life peer as Baron Ouseley, of Peckham Rye in the London Borough of Southwark. He sat in the House of Lords as a crossbencher until his retirement in 2019.

He has had a career as a British parliamentarian, running public authorities, including local councils and as an adviser and reviewer of public services organisations. He has expertise in equality and diversity issues and as the Chairperson of several charitable organisations as well as being a Patron for dozens of organisations. He has been at the forefront of challenging institutional racism in organisations and is an advocate on behalf of individuals from disadvantaged and deprived backgrounds.

He has 13 honorary degrees: from the Universities of Edinburgh, Sheffield Hallam, Bradford, Leicester, Leeds Met, Warwick, Oxford Brookes, Greenwich, London South Bank, London Metropolitan, North East London, Staffordshire, and Brighton.

Outside of politics, he was a director of Brookmight Security and, from 2000, of Focus Consultancy. Between 2000 and 2005 he was the Managing Director of Different Realities Partnership and, since then, has been operating as a self-employed management consultant undertaking reviews of organisations' performance and assignments in pursuit of equality and diversity outcomes.

Sadly on 2 October 2024 Baron Herman Ousley died after a short spell of ill health.

First Black Magistrate

Eric Irons OBE – (1921-2007)

Eric Irons OBE came to Britain from Jamaica in 1944. He was a campaigner for equal rights and in 1962 he became Britain's first black magistrate sitting on the Nottingham bench.

Eric George Irons was born in Spanish Town, Jamaica. His mum was a cook and his father was a policeman. In 1944 like a number of young black West Indian men, he responded to the call for volunteers to join the British Royal Air Force (RAF) to fight in the Second World War for Britain. He was recruited into the RAF in Jamaica in 1944 and in 1945 visited RAF Syerston, near Newark Nottinghamshire but was based at Little Rissington, Bedford. Following this visit, he decided he wanted to live in Nottingham. He extended his service with the RAF for a further five years and married a local girl from Nottingham called Nellie Kelham, They went on to raise 6 children together and had 19 grandchildren.

In 1952 he worked at Chilwell Ordnance Depot in the offices. The depot did not employ many black workers. He began to take up the issue of discrimination with the Nottingham and District Trades Council and through his efforts of negotiation some of the problems were resolved. More black workers were taken on, both in the depot and in other employment.

In 1955 he went on to the Consultative Committee for the welfare of black people, which was set up by a Council of Church/Social Services and the Colonial Social and Sports Club. The remit was to discuss prejudice and local issues. One of the issues was the fact that no black people were taking advantage of educational courses, particularly those held by the WEA.

He challenged and helped lift a city transport embargo on the employment of black workers and also helped the city council to tackle problems highlighted by the 1958 race riots.

In 1958 Nottingham was the scene of racially aggravated violence called race riots, though they were racist mobs attacking the black communities which prompted young Jamaican men in particular to group together and fight back. It began in a St. Ann's pub when some white men had taken exception to a black man having a drink with a white woman. Large-scale violence followed and for weeks after, local teddy-boys walked the streets attacking any black person they could find.

The city asked him to assist in helping to help ease the tension and with his help, the situation became calmer. Slowly the city moved out of the period of fear and racial tensions into a more tolerant time.

However, the racism did not end there. Many of Nottingham's outer suburbs and towns remained poor and were breeding-grounds for groups such as the National Front and British National Party, but Nottingham, in no small part due to his efforts stood out as an example of what could be done. He received death threats, most notably from the Ku Klux Klan, for his efforts.

His lifelong passion for racial equality inspired him to move into public life given the prejudices shown towards black people. He set up the first community group for West Indians, called the Colonial Social and Sports Club, at his own house.

He became prominent as the leader of the Colonial Social and Sports Club and had been serving on the Consultative Committee responsible for the welfare of Black People. He was also a clerk in the City Department of Education.

In 1960 Nottingham the Council appointed him to the specially created post of Organiser for Educational Work Amongst the Coloured Communities. The term coloured was used to refer to Black people. However this was marred due to a campaign designed to abolish the role to create a political divide between how some Black people conducted their activist affairs and how he worked towards social justice.

In 1962 he made history when he was appointed Britain's first black magistrate sitting on the Nottingham bench. He did this for 29 years until he retired in 1991.

In the 1978 New Years Honours list he was awarded an OBE for his championship of social justice.

In 1999 he was awarded an honorary Master of Arts degree by the University of Nottingham for improving race relations in the City.

Irons passed away in 2007.

In October 2019 a plaque was put up in his memory by Nottingham Civic Society at the National Justice Museum in Nottingham.

First Black solicitor to be elected to the Council of the Law Society of England and Wales

Caroline Newman – (1963-)

Caroline Newman is a British solicitor, author, entrepreneur and diversity and equality advocate. In 2002, she was the first black solicitor to be elected to the Council of the Law Society of England and Wales.

Caroline Newman was born on 31 October 1963 at Kingston Public Hospital in Kingston, Jamaica to parents Renel and Girlie Newman. The family including six children, moved to the UK, settling in Newport, Wales.

She attended Newport Duffryn High School gaining 10 GCE O Levels and later attended Newport College of Further Education obtaining a BEC National Diploma in Business Studies and two A levels.

In 1992 she graduated from the University of Westminster with a 2:1 degree, studying part time. She also studied criminology writing a paper on race and injustice outlining the unequal treatment of black people in the criminal justice system and the disparity in incarceration rates.

In 1995 she earned a Masters degree in law and political science at the London School of Economics. Her dissertation was written on the Police and Criminal Evidence Act. Later she enrolled at the College of Law and became a qualified solicitor. She trained at London law firm SJ Berwin. She was the first Black woman to be awarded a training contract at the firm and was initially one of only two black trainees and solicitors.

In 2002 she became the first black solicitor to be elected to the Council of the Law Society of England and Wales. She served on the Council for seven years and chaired several of the Law Society's committees. From 2003 for five years she chaired the Equality and Diversity Committee.

In 2004 she was subjected to abuse when a senior partner at SJ Berwin called her a black sheep. She raised this issue with the management and was able to secure their commitment to introduce diversity policies and training.

In 2006 she founded a business called Lawdacity which was a training and consultancy firm coaching solicitors, barristers, judges, lawyers and legal executives.

In 2014 she was elected as the first chair of the Ethnic Minority Lawyers' Division Committee. She also represented the society on the Institute of Chartered Accountants in England and Wales Investigative Committee, ensuring that issues around diversity were central to investigations.

She also founded the African Women Lawyer's Association (AWLA) which sought to assist and empower women of African descent entering or enhancing their legal career. The ultimate goal was to combat the double discrimination of sexism and racism which black women often face in the legal profession. Some of the AWLA's services include liaison with the Law Societies and Bar Councils, attendance of the Law Society Black and Minority Ethnic and Women's divisions meetings, research for members, advice, workshops and seminars on a range of issues including legislative change, the ability to network with other BAME lawyers and assistance to members who are victims of injustice. She served as a director of the association.

She has been the author of a series of books including Legal Gold for Coaches: How to Sell and Deliver Coaching, Training, and Consulting Services to Lawyers. She was featured in the 2017 anthology Love Unboxed, itemising the struggles of 20 women from different backgrounds and eight countries.

She has delivered equality, diversity and bias training to the legal community, police and armed forces. Under her influence the Solicitors Regulation Authority amended their code of conduct for firms, making it a disciplinary offence to discriminate against an employee.

In 2018 she was awarded the title of Diversity Champion for her advocacy at the UK Diversity Legal Awards in, an event co-sponsored by the Law Society, Solicitors Regulation Authority and General Council of the Bar.

In 2019 she was appointed to the board of the Law Society.

Following the murder of George Floyd on 29 May 2020 and the subsequent protests led by the Black Lives Matter movement, she co-founded a local group promoting Action for Racial Equality and education of the local community. She also co-founded the Diversity, Inclusion, Cohesion and Engagement Committee to assist the parochial church council with research into racial inequality and discrimination in the church and making recommendations for change and inclusivity of all members of the congregation and the local community.

She used her position in the AWLA to speak out against the racism and mistreatment of Meghan Markle in the British press, calling for the racial discrimination to stop and offering her solidarity.

She served as a trustee for the Howard League for Penal Reform for 15 years, pushing the government to adopt humane prison reform. She was part of the Howard League's flagship research programme which ensured the release of girls under the age of 18 from British prisons into more suitable accommodation. She also helped to create the Citizenship and Crime Project in schools, which taught pupils of their rights and responsibilities as citizens.

As a policy manager of the Mental Health Foundation she led the policy development into the needs of mentally disordered offenders, which aimed to divert these offenders into health and social care instead of the criminal justice system.

She married Donald Peter Herbert OBE who is a barrister and founder of the Society of Black Lawyers.

First Black person to become a Permanent Secretary at the Treasury

Dame Sharon Michele White, Lady Chote, DBE – (1967-)

Dame Sharon Michele White, Lady Chote, DBE is a British businesswoman. In 2013, she rose to become the first black person, and the second woman, to become a Permanent Secretary at the Treasury.

Sharon Michele White was born on 21 April 1967 in east London and brought up in Leyton. Her parents had moved to London from Jamaica when her father was 15 and her mother 11. She attended Connaught School for Girls and then Fitzwilliam College, Cambridge, where she gained a BA degree in economics. She later earned an MSc degree in economics from University College London.

In 1989 she joined the Civil Service after working for a church in Birmingham. Initially she worked at the Treasury and later for the British Embassy in Washington, where she met her husband, Robert Chote. He was an economist working for the International Monetary Fund.

The couple married in 1997 and have two children.

During the period of the Ton Blair Labour government she worked at the 10 Downing Street policy unit. She also worked at the World Bank, and as a director general at the Department for International Development from 2003 to 2009 and then at the Ministry of Justice from 2009 to 2011, and also at the Department for Work and Pensions.

While at the Treasury, she supervised a review of the financial management of government and the Treasury's management response to the international financial crisis of between 2007 and 2008. She was Director General for Public Spending at the Treasury from 2012 to 2013.

In 2013 she became Second Permanent Secretary making her the first black person to become a Permanent Secretary at the Treasury, and the second woman after Dame Anne Mueller in the 1980s. Holding this position and the influence that came with it, she was recognised as one of the most powerful Black British people in the UK. The position gave her overall responsibility for managing the UK's public finances, including implementing the ongoing fiscal consolidation.

From March 2015 she became the chief executive of Ofcom.

In 2018 she took up the role of Non-executive Director of Barratt Developments.

In 2020 she stepped down from her role at Ofcom to become the sixth Chair of the John Lewis Partnership.

In the 2020 New Years Honours list she was appointed Dame Commander of the Order of the British Empire (DBE) for her public service.

In the 2021 New Years Honours list she was knighted for her services to the economy and fiscal policy.

In 2022 she was appointed chairman of the UK Statistics Authority.

In 2023 she announced that she planned to step down as Chair of the John Lewis Partnership February 2025 at the end of her five-year term.

In 2025 she was awarded a life peerage to sit in the House of Lords. She was created Baroness White of Tufnell Park in the London Borough of Islington.

First black person to be appointed to the senior judiciary of England and Wales

Dame Linda Dobbs DBE, BSc, LLM, Ph.D – (1951-)

Dame Linda Penelope Dobbs, DBE, B.Sc., LLM, Ph.D. is a retired High Court judge who served from 2004 to 2013 and she was the first black or non-white person to be appointed to the senior judiciary of England and Wales.

Linda Penelope Dobbs was born on 3 January 1951 in Freetown, Sierra Leone. Her father Arthur Ernest Dobbs was an English lawyer who came from Warwickshire and went on to serve as a High Court judge in Sierra Leone. Her mother Loyda Dobbs (née Johnson) was a Creole lady from Sierra Leone.

She attended Moreton Hall School, an independent girls boarding school, near Oswestry in Shropshire, then the University of Edinburgh, where she read music but left after a year. She then attended the University of Surrey, where she studied Russian and law, graduating in 1976. She then studied at the London School of Economics, where she obtained a Master's degree, followed by a doctorate in Soviet criminology and penology.

She was called to the Bar in 1981, practising from 5 King's Bench Walk, the chambers of the then Attorney-General Sir Michael Havers, QC. She had a mixed criminal practice, in later years specialising in fraud and professional disciplinary tribunals, including the General Medical Council and the General Dental Council.

In 1998 she became a Queens Counsel.

She was a member of the General Council of the Bar and chaired its Professional Standards Committee and Race Relations Committee.

In 2003 she became the chairman of the Criminal Bar Association and the same year, she was appointed as a deputy High Court judge despite not having previously held appointment as a recorder.

In 2004 she was appointed as a judge of the High Court and assigned to the Queen's Bench Division without having sat as a deputy High Court judge, becoming the first black or non-white person to be appointed to the senior judiciary of England and Wales. This appointment saw her being recognised as one of the 10 most powerful black women in Britain. At the time there were only 9 black circuit judges out of 623, i.e. 1.4%.

She is a patron of the African Prisons Project and an initiator of the 18 Red Lion Court Award for African advocates. She is also patron of Masicorp, an NGO promoting education in Masiphumelele, South Africa.

On 20 April 2013 she took early retirement from the High Court, aged 62 years. She sits on a number of boards and advisory panels and is a former chair of the Ethics Policy Committee at the London School of Economics, where she sat on the Court of Governors from 2006 to 2015. She holds six honorary doctorates in law, is a Senior Fellow in the Law Department at the School of Oriental and African Studies (SOAS) and is Pro Chancellor at the University of Surrey.

First black Director of Education and Leisure Services in Britain

Gus John – (1945-)

Professor Augustine John is a Grenadian-born award-winning writer, education campaigner, consultant, lecturer and researcher, who moved to the UK in 1964 and has been active in issues of education and schooling in Britain's inner cities. In 1989 he was appointed Director of Education in Hackney, the first black person to hold such a position.

Augustine (Gus) John was born on 11 March 1945 in the village of Concord in Grenada, Eastern Caribbean. His parents were farmers. Aged 12 he won a scholarship to Presentation Boys College, a secondary school in St George's, the capital of Grenada. He joined a seminary in Trinidad at 17, where he spent two years as a theology student.

He moved to England when he was aged 19, transferring to the Theology programme at Oxford University. He became Chair of the Education Subcommittee of the Oxford Committee for Racial Integration (OCRI).

From 1964 to 1967 he was a Dominican friar however he split with the order because of the church's links with apartheid South Africa. In the late 1960s he worked as a gravedigger by day while working by night in an inner-city youth club.

In 1968 he started the first Saturday / Supplementary school in Handsworth, Birmingham, with a group of colleagues. After working on youth and race in Handsworth for the Runnymede Trust, he went to Moss Side, Manchester in 1971 where he continued organising and campaigning around the issues of housing and the specific difficulties for young people to get houses on their own; employment for black school leavers; the way the community was policed; and the quality of schooling outcomes for black school leavers. .

In 1972 he wrote a book called Because They're Black, in collaboration with Derek Humphry, a British-born American journalist and author. It was described as being a social research study of sociological aspects of racial discrimination against Asian and West Indian immigrants in the UK covering intergroup relations, cultural factors, social integration, political aspects, living conditions, employment and the administration of justice The book was awarded the Martin Luther King Memorial Prize for its contribution to racial harmony in Britain. He has been a prolific writer of many notable publications.

He joined the Campaign Against Racial Discrimination (CARD), the civil rights organisation led by David Pitt, who was the second black peer in the House of Lords.

Following the New Cross Fire on 18 January 1981 where 13 young black people lost their lives, he became the northern organiser of the New Cross Massacre Action Committee, and helped organise the Black People's Day of Action, held on 2 March, in response to the massacre.

In July 1981 the inner-city district of Moss Side in Manchester, was the scene of mass protesting starting at the local police station and later moving into the surrounding streets over two days. It was fuelled by racial tension, due to frequent allegations of police officers racially abusing and using excessive force against black youths in the area and mass unemployment brought on by the early 1980s recession. Unemployment was at a post-war high across the nation during 1981, but was much higher than the national average in Moss Side.

After the uprisings in Moss Side, he chaired the Moss Side Defence Committee, and was the adviser to the Liverpool 8 Defence Committee following the Toxteth Uprisings in Liverpool that same year. This also arose in part from long-standing tensions between the local police and the black community. They followed similar disturbances in Brixton, London.

He was the co-ordinator of the Black Parents Movement in Manchester, founded the Education for Liberation book service and helped to organise the International Book Fair of Radical Black and Third World Books in Manchester, London and Bradford.

In 1987 he was a member of the Macdonald Inquiry into Racism and Racial Violence in Manchester Schools and subsequently co-authored Murder in the Playground: the Burnage Report with Ian Macdonald, Reena Bhavnani and Lily Khan. He was a founder trustee of the George Padmore Institute under the chairmanship of John La Rose.

In 1989 he was appointed Director of Education in Hackney becoming the first black person to hold such a position. When the two departments were amalgamated, he became Hackney's first Director of Education and Leisure Services.

After leaving Hackney in 1996, he worked as an education consultant in Europe, the Caribbean and Africa, and became director of his company, Gus John Consultancy Limited. He has been Chair of the Communities Empowerment Network (CEN), an advocacy and campaigning service working for equality and justice in education which was founded in 1999. He was Chair of Parents and Students Empowerment (PaSE), an organisation devoted to empowering students and parents in schooling and education.

He chaired the Round Table for the National Union of Teachers (NUT) in October 2006/March 2007 and produced Born to be Great, the NUT's Charter on Promoting the Achievement of Black Caribbean Boys.

In 2010 he produced The Case for a Learners' Charter for Schools, a charter articulating the educational entitlement of all school students and the rights and responsibilities of everybody engaged in the schooling process, local authorities, school governors, teachers, pupils and parents.

He was a member of Channel 4's Street Weapons Commission and later adviser to London Mayor Boris Johnson on serious youth violence in the capital.

From 2006 he was a member of the African Union's Technical Committee of Experts working on the reunification of Africans as a people. He has advised member states in Africa and the Caribbean (Cameroon, Somaliland, Lagos

State Government, Jamaica) in meeting the Sustainable Development Goals related to education and youth.

Between 2004 and 2012 he worked on Niger Delta affairs and in 2012 collaborated with Kingsley Kuku, the then special adviser to President Goodluck Jonathan, and David Keighe on a development manual entitled Remaking the Niger Delta: Challenges and Opportunities. In 2008 with Samina Zahir, he co-authored Speaking Truth to Power, which resulted from research for Arts Council England on identity, aesthetics and ethnicity in theatre and the arts.

From 2011 he was a consultant to the Methodist Church on implementing Equality and Human Rights legislation, and in 2012 was appointed to chair the Expert Advisory Group on Equality, Diversity and Social Mobility as part of the Legal Education and Training Review (LETR).

He was commissioned by the Solicitors Regulation Authority (SRA) to undertake a comparative review of how it had dealt with disciplinary cases and especially the over-representative number of black and ethnic minority solicitors sanctioned by the SRA, his report was published in 2014. John made a submission to the United Kingdom Parliament's 2017 Youth Violence Commission, which he subsequently published in digest form.

In 2019 he quit an advisory body to the Church of England, expressing his disapproval of the endorsement by Archbishop Justin Welby of the criticism of Labour Party leader Jeremy Corbyn by the chief rabbi Ephraim Mirvis, making allegations of anti-Semitism.

In October 1999 Tony Blair, the then Labour Prime Minister asked him to accept a CBE (Commander of the Order of the British Empire) in the 2000 New Year Honours List, He declined stating that he believed such honours to be anachronistic and an insult to the struggles of African people like himself who spent their life trying to humanise British society and combat racism, which is a core part of the legacy of Empire and which the society and its institutions were perennially failing to confront.

In 2015 his 70th birthday was marked by events honouring his five decades of activism in Britain: on 11 March at Conway Hall, on 14 March at the British Film Institute, in conversation with Gary Younge, and on 19 April at the Phoenix Cinema, in conversation with Margaret Busby.

First Black person to be knighted in Britain

Sir William Conrad Reeves – (1829-1902)

Sir William Conrad Reeves, a Barbados native, received a knighthood from Queen Victoria on January 28, 1889. This made him the first Black person to be knighted in Britain.

William Conrad Reeves was born around 1829/30 in Barbados according to the 1861 census where his recorded age was 31. His father Thomas Phillipps Reeves was a white doctor and member of plantation society in Bridgetown, Barbados. His mother was Peggy Phillis, a former slave, described as a free mulatto or as a free person of colour. They were not married and had two other sons.

He was looked after by his father's sister and was educated at private schools. He gained employment as a journalist on Barbados papers. He was fortunate to be awarded a scholarship to study law in England. He became a student at the Middle Temple in May 1860, being called to the bar on 6 January 1863. He also acted as a correspondent for the Barbados press. In 1864 he returned to Barbados to practise at the local bar.

From May 1867 he acted for a short time as attorney-general of St, Vincent, an island which at that time was under the same governor as Barbados.

In 1868 he married Margaret Rudder and they had a daughter.

In August 1874 he entered the local house of assembly of Barbados as member for St. Joseph, and was appointed Solicitor-General of Barbados in 1875.

In April 1876, following an issue with the governor, Sir John Pope-Hennessy and the crown which he represented, he resigned office and took up the cause of the old constitution of Barbados as against schemes of confederation and crown government.

In 1878 he opposed the proposal introduced by Sir George Strahan for the reform of the elective house of assembly by the introduction of crown nominees. He thus became the champion of the ancient Barbados constitution and was awarded a purse of 1000 guineas.

In 1881 the then governor of Barbados, Sir William Robinson, enlisted his support in creating the executive committee bill. This bill enabled the executive to secure a proper control in matters of finance and administration without interference with the traditions of the house of assembly. The governor acknowledged his support by appointing him attorney-general in February 1882.

In 1883 he was admitted to the Queen's Counsel.

In 1886 he became the first Black Chief Justice of Barbados. The promotion was a rare recognition of worth in a black man. He served in this position until his death. His judgments were clear and well worded. Several of them were collected in a volume by Sir William Herbert Greaves, a successor as chief justice, and Mr. Clark, attorney-general.

In 1889 he was knighted by Queen Victoria, and thus became the first black man to be knighted by a British sovereign. The rank of Knight Bachelor is an ancient honour conferred, presumably to men for public service. The recipient was allowed to use the prefix Sir or the suffix Kt (for Knight). If married, their spouse takes the prefix, Lady.

He died on 5 January 1902, at his home, the Eyrie, St. Michael's, and was given a public funeral with a service in the cathedral at Westbury cemetery.

Sir Conrad Reeves
BAR
AN
PA

First Black Woman to be awarded the MBE

Sybil Phoenix OBE – (1927-)

The Reverend Sybil Theodora Phoenix, OBE is a British community worker of Guyanese birth. In 1973 she was the first black woman to be awarded the MBE in recognition of her outstanding work in the community.

Sybil Phoenix was born Sybil Theodora Marshall on 21 June 1927 in Georgetown British Guiana, (now Guyana) in the West Indies. Her mother died when she was nine. Her father worked in the quarries outside of the capital Georgetown and returned home for only a few days each year. As a result she went, with her brother Percival, to live with her grandfather, who was a Congregational minister, until his death when she was 12.

She then went to live with an aunt and uncle, Mr and Mrs Lynch. Her aunt was her mother's sister and she did not like Sybil very much as she was jealous of Sybil's mother who had lighter skin than her. Due to racism, people who were light skinned got better jobs than people who were darker. Mrs. Lynch took it out on Sybil because her mother was dead. Sybil's aunt and mother had the same mother and father but they were mixed race, which was why one was darker than the other.

When she left school, Sybil became secretary to the minister of the church where her uncle worked as a handyman. She also helped out in the church youth club and did a three-year course of evening classes in social work.

After hearing her sing, two Methodist missionaries offered her free voice training if she sang for the Methodist Church. As a result she joined both the church and the Philharmonic choirs. She also contributed to Clubland, an open youth club responsible for a monthly church service.

She met her future husband, Joe Phoenix, at the youth club, and when she was in her early twenties she moved into a home of her own and set up a business with Joe, making dresses and hats.

Despite initial discouragement from a cousin, she decided to visit England in 1956, at the age of 29 with her fiancé Joe Phoenix. The couple married that June. Soon after arriving, she was asked to lead the youth service at a local Methodist church.

During their early years in England, the couple experienced racism and hostility, both when looking for accommodation and at the local church, where she was already doing youth club work. It was hard for them to find somewhere to live because many places displayed "No Coloureds" or "No Blacks, No Dogs, No Irish" signs which were not illegal back then. At one stage, she lived in a coal cellar and became ill. A church minister asked a church member to help, but the church member told her, "Nobody in my street has taken in coloured people yet and I've got the children to think of."

Their first two children were born in 1960 and 1961, and she gave up her job at a milliner's, to take up a night job as a canteen cook. As she was looking after the children during the day, she got only two or three hours sleep a night, and yet she also found time to do piecework at home.

In 1962 the family moved to 67 Tressillian Road, Brockley. A white friend purchased the house for them using their money and did not disclose that the new owners were black to get around the discrimination they suffered.

She gave up her job in the canteen and began to foster teenage children, as well as having two more of her own, in 1964 and 1965. She also ran the youth club in her local Methodist church and became a community worker, providing support for unwanted children.

In 1971 she founded the Moonshot Club in St John's Hall, Lewisham Way. It became so popular that regularly up to 500 people gathered there every night. She organised events, talked to members and counselled them about their problems, and set up classes to help people get better educational qualifications.

In 1973 she became the first black woman to be awarded the MBE, in recognition of her outstanding work in the community in Lewisham. By then, she had also fostered over 100 children.

Unfortunately the next year she suffered a personal tragedy when she was involved in a car crash while on holiday in Kent. Her ten-year-old daughter Marsha was killed, and she herself was crippled for months. For a time her faith was shaken, but she realised that she was needed at Moonshot and she threw herself back into her work there.

By now the Moonshot Club had sports teams, a young mothers' project, discos and other social events, as well as classes. In 1977, as part of the Royal Jubilee celebrations, Prince Charles paid the club a visit.

On 18 December 1977 the Moonshot Club was gutted in a firebomb attack. According to a national newspaper, the burning down of Moonshot had been discussed at a National Front meeting the previous month. Naturally this led to a good deal of tension in the area, and she had to calm people and find temporary accommodation for the club's activities. She also immediately began to raise money for the rebuilding of the centre, this time in Pagnell Street. This project was the first of its kind to establish a purpose-built centre for the Black community, open to the whole community. She raised £64,000 by herself to commence the project and was instrumental in raising a further £750,000 to see the project to fruition.

In 1979 in partnership with the London Borough of Lewisham she began a supported housing project for single homeless young women aged from 16 to 21. The project was named the Marsha Phoenix Memorial Trust, in memory of her daughter, who died in the car accident in 1974.

In January 1981 thirteen young black people died in a fire which gutted a house in New Cross Road while a party was in progress. The cause of the fire has never been determined. She gave practical assistance to the bereaved families, such as arranging funerals for them and helped them to cope with their grief and anger. The Moonshot Club was the venue for the first meeting after the fire. In 1999 she contacted MP Joan Ruddock to discuss a memorial to those killed in the fire; Ruddock has described Sybil as "one of Deptford's remarkable black community leaders".

In March 1981 there was a happier occasion when Prince Charles returned to Pagnell Street to open the new Centre to replace the Moonshot Club. She stayed as director until November 1981, when she resigned, thinking that it was time to move on.

She has contributed to research about Stop and Search, a police process which was disproportionally used against black people. She has also been involved in welcoming Lewisham people who have become British citizens, after their citizenship ceremony.

She was a Methodist local preacher for many years, working closely with the British Council of Churches to forge links between peoples of all faiths. While based at Clubland Methodist Mission on Walworth Road in South London, she was instrumental in setting up anti-racist training for members of the clergy, known as the Methodist Leadership Racism Awareness Workshop (MELRAW) and as Director she took this work to many countries around the world.

She occasionally acted as a Minister without portfolio for Guyana, and for this was awarded the Medal of Service by Guyana in 1987. She also worked for the Community Liaison Scheme and as Vice-Chair of Lewisham Council for Community Relations.

In 1993 she was awarded an Honorary Fellowship by Goldsmiths, University of London for her services to the local community.

In 1996 she was made an Honorary Freeman of the Borough of Lewisham, and in 1998 was awarded the Freedom of the City of London.

In 2008 she received an OBE for her services to the community.

She remains an inspirational and formidable woman with a steadfast belief in the dignity and rights of human beings, whatever their colour.

First Black woman to be a governor of the BBC and the First Black British Dame.

Dame Jocelyn Barrow DBE – (1929-2020)

Dame Jocelyn Barrow DBE was a British educator, community activist and politician. In 1981 she became the first black woman to be a governor of the BBC and was the founder and Deputy Chair of the Broadcasting Standards Council.

Jocelyn Anita Barrow was born on 15 April 1929 in Port of Spain, Trinidad and Tobago to her Barbadian father Charles Newton Barrow, an engineer, and mother Olive Irene (nee Pierre) from Trinidad and Tobago.

She became active politically in Trinidad and Tobago as a member of the People's National Movement, and at the same time trained to become a teacher at the Port of Spain governmental teacher training college. In 1959, after travelling to Britain she attended the University of London studying English and then postgraduate studies at the Institute of Education.

She taught English at schools in Hackney, which was one of the most deprived areas of east London. She later become a lecturer at Furzedown teacher training college in Tooting, south London. She pioneered the introduction of multi-cultural education. She stressed the needs of the various ethnic groups in the UK. She was a member of the Taylor Committee of School Governors.

She was a founding member of Campaign Against Racial Discrimination (CARD) which was an organisation that ran between 1964 and 1967. Its remit was to advocate for race relations legislation and was responsible for the Race Relations Act of 1968. She also held the positions of general secretary and later vice-chair for CARD.

In 1965 the North London West Indian Association (NLWIA) was set up and she was a leading member. It was a major component of the West Indian Standing Conference, which had been founded in 1958 after the Notting

Hill riots to speak out on behalf of West Indians among other activities. The NWLIA spoke out about prejudice against black children in the state education system, which had been exposed in a leaked report.

In 1968 she was appointed vice-chair of the International Human Rights Year Committee, and from 1968 to 1972 was a member of the Community Relations Commission. She also held the post of vice-president of the National Union of Townswomen's Guilds.

In 1970 she married Henderson Downer, who was a barrister at Lincoln's Inn in London and then a Jamaican appeal court judge, retiring in 2004. For most of their long marriage the couple lived between the UK and Jamaica.

In 1972 she was awarded the OBE for work in the field of education and community relations.

In 1981 she became the first black woman to serve as a governor of the BBC. Prior to her appointment the corporation had been accused of under serving black and minority ethnic audiences and having very little diversity amongst its staff or in senior positions. She left this position in 1988 and was credited with helping to change the face of leadership within broadcasting, helping to pave the way for her successors and working tirelessly to progress race relations in the UK.

In 1984 with Yvonne Collymore, she co-founded Arawidi Publications, a children's publishing house, named after a Caribbean sun-deity. Arawidi published children's books in a variety of language forms including West Indian dialects and Glaswegian.

In 1989 she founded and became the deputy chair of the Broadcasting Standards Council designed to regulate the media. It closed in 1995 and which was the forerunner of Ofcom which was announced in 2001 and launched in 2003.

From 1991 to 1997 she was a governor of the British Film Institute.

In 1992 her work in broadcasting and her contribution to the work of the European Union as the UK member of the Economic and Social Committee was recognised by her being appointed DBE, Dame Commander of the Order of the British Empire, the first black woman to be honoured as a Dame.

In 2005 she was chair of the Mayor's Commission on African and Asian Heritage (MCAAH), set up by the then Mayor of London Ken Livingstone. This produced a report called Delivering Shared Heritage, which set out a code of values for delivering inclusive and healthy heritage management practice for everyone not just the African and Asian communities.

She was instrumental in the establishment of the North Atlantic Slavery Gallery and the Merseyside Maritime Museum in Liverpool. She was a Trustee of the National Museums and Galleries on Merseyside and a Governor of the British Film Institute. She was also the first patron of the Black Cultural Archives having recognised the need for such a monument to educate future generations.

She died aged 90 on 9 April 2020, having been admitted to University College Hospital. Her husband Henderson Downer passed away on 6 January 2023.

She received honorary doctorates from the University of Greenwich in 1993 and from the University of York in 2007.

First Black Woman slave autobiography published in Britain

Mary Prince – (1788-1833)

Mary Prince was a female slave who, while living in London, narrated her life story to Susanna Strickland. This autobiography, titled The History of Mary Prince, was published in 1831, making Mary the first black woman to have her autobiography published, detailing her experiences as a slave.

Mary Prince was born in October 1788 in Brackish Pond, Devonshire Parish, Bermuda. Her father, known only as Prince, was a sawyer enslaved by David Trimmingham, and her mother was a house servant for Charles Myners. Mary had three younger brothers and two sisters, Hannah and Dinah. When Myners died in 1788, Mary, her mother, and her siblings were sold to Captain George Darrell, who gave Mary and her mother to his daughter, making Mary a companion servant to his granddaughter, Betsey Williams.

At the age of 12, Mary was sold for £38 to Captain John Ingham of Spanish Point, Bermuda. Her new owners were cruel, often flogging her and other enslaved people for minor offenses. In Bermuda, salt production was a major industry, and she was forced to work in poor conditions in the salt ponds, often standing in water for up to 17 hours straight.

In 1812, she returned to Bermuda with Robert Darrell and his daughter. She was physically abused and forced to bathe Darrell under threat of further beatings. After defending herself and Darrell's daughter from abuse, she left his service and worked at Cedar Hill, earning money for Darrell by washing clothes.

In 1815, she was sold again to John Adams Wood of Antigua for $300. She worked as a domestic slave but began to suffer from rheumatism, making it difficult for her to work. She joined the Moravian Church in Antigua, where she learned to read and was baptized in 1817.

In December 1826, she married Daniel James, a former slave who had bought his freedom and worked as a carpenter and cooper. However, her floggings increased after her marriage because Adams Wood and his wife disapproved of a free black man living on their property.

In 1828 Adams Wood took her to London as a servant. Despite serving the Woods for over ten years, conflicts arose, and she left their household, finding shelter with the Moravian church in Hatton Garden. She later worked for Thomas Pringle, an abolitionist writer and secretary of the Anti-Slavery Society. Pringle helped arrange for her life story to be transcribed by Susanna Strickland, a writer known as Susanna Moodie. This resulted in the publication of The History of Mary Prince in 1831. This book was the first account of a black enslaved woman's life published in the UK.

The publication of her autobiography contributed to the growing anti-slavery sentiment in Britain. Despite legal challenges and personal attacks from defenders of slavery, the book's direct and authentic tone influenced public opinion and helped galvanize the movement against slavery.

In 1833, the Slavery Abolition Act was passed, taking effect in 1834, which began the process of abolishing slavery in the British colonies. Mary Prince's story and the work of abolitionists like Thomas Clarkson and William Wilberforce played crucial roles in this movement. Her life and autobiography remain significant in the history of abolition, highlighting the personal experiences of enslaved people and their contributions to the fight for freedom.

In recognition of her contributions, a commemorative plaque was unveiled in London in 2007, and the Museum in Docklands opened a permanent exhibition titled London, Sugar & Slavery, crediting Mary as a key figure in the abolition campaign.

The last recorded mention of Mary Prince came in 1833. In 1833, Pringle sued James MacQueen, editor of the Glasgow Courier, for libel, receiving damages of £5. MacQueen defended white West Indian interests and was a vigorous critic of the anti-slavery movement. He claimed Prince was a woman of low morals and a tool of the anti-slavery movement, against her apparently generous and indulgent owners. He attacked the Pringle family character, suggesting they were wrong to accept her into their household.

Later John Wood, to whom she was sold, sued Pringle for libel, holding him responsible as the editor of her book claiming it misrepresented his character. Wood won his case and was awarded £25 in damages. Prince was called to testify in both these trials, but little mention is made of her life after this.

First Black Children's Laureate

Malorie Blackman OBE – (1962-)

Malorie Blackman OBE is a renowned British author who served as the Children's Laureate from 2013 to 2015, the first Black person to hold this position in the UK. She writes primarily for children and young adults.

Malorie Blackman was born on 8 February 1962, in Clapham, London. She grew up in Bromley with her four siblings. Her parents came to Britain from Barbados as part of the Windrush generation. Her father was a bus driver, and her mother worked in a pyjama factory. Her father left the family when she was 13, which helped to make her early years more challenging in addition to dealing with racism and sexism.

In spite of this, she excelled in school and aspired to become an English teacher. However, she was discouraged from this path due to her race. Instead, she pursued a qualification in computer science at Thames Polytechnic, leading to a successful career in computing.

Growing up she loved books but noticed the lack of Black characters in the literature she read and decided to address this gap as a writer. She was hampered by health problems having been diagnosed as having sickle cell anaemia which caused severe pain. The disease predominantly affects black people which meant little was understood or considered by healthcare professionals. As a result her healthy appendix was removed incorrectly when she collapsed in her university bedroom, and it was thought her life expectancy would be to only 30.

Nevertheless, she persevered and after receiving over 80 rejection letters from publishers, she finally published her first book, Not So Stupid!, in 1990. This was a collection of horror and science fiction stories for young adults.

Since then she has authored over 60 books, including the acclaimed Noughts & Crosses series, which tackles themes of love, racism, and violence in a dystopian world. Her work extends to television, including scripts for Byker

Grove and adaptations of her novels Whizziwig and Pig-Heart Boy. She also made history as the first person of colour to write for the BBC TV series, Doctor Who.

Her books have been translated into over 15 languages, and her contributions to literature have earned her numerous awards.

In the 2008 Birthday Honours, she was appointed Officer of the Order of the British Empire (OBE) for services to literature.

In June 2013 she was announced as the new Children's Laureate, succeeding Julia Donaldson, the first black person to hold this position. She helped set up the first UK Young Adult Literature Convention during her time as Children's Laureate and advocated for diverse representation in children's literature and supported campaigns like Let Books Be Books, which opposes gender-specific labelling of children's books.

In her personal life, she enjoys playing the piano, composing, playing computer games, and writing poetry. She resides in Kent with her husband and daughter.

Her memoir, Just Sayin, was published in 2022, and she received the PEN Pinter Prize, becoming the first children's and YA author to win this accolade. The British Library celebrated her career with the exhibition, Malorie Blackman: The Power of Stories, which ran from November 2023 to February 2024, highlighting her journey and the social issues in her work.

She remains an influential figure, using her platform to inspire and bring awareness to important social themes through her storytelling.

First Black presenter of the children's television programme Blue Peter

Diane-Louise Jordan – (1960-)

Diane Johnson, better known as Diane-Louise Jordan, is a well-known British television presenter. She made history as the first black presenter of the children's TV show Blue Peter, where she worked from 25 January 1990, to 26 February 1996.

Diane Johnson was born on 28 June 1960, and grew up in Hatfield, Hertfordshire. Her parents came to Britain from Jamaica as part of the Windrush generation. She studied theatre arts at Rose Bruford College of Speech and Drama in South London. Despite being told she was too short and would be limited in roles due to her race, she secured a nine-month theatre contract before graduating and spent seven years acting across the country.

In 1988 she appeared a chemist shop assistant in a comedy drama film by Mike Leigh called High Hopes.

In 1989 she played the role of Kate Winterton in the soap opera Coronation Street.

Through the 1980s she appeared in a BBC children's TV series called Corners. It was here that she was discovered by Blue Peter producer Lewis Bronze. After several auditions, she became Blue Peter's first black presenter in January 1990. She stayed with Blue Peter for six years.

Unfortunately, tragedy struck the same year she joined Blue Peter when her sister passed away from a virus. She took on the responsibility of raising her niece, Janine. This led to unfair tabloid media scrutiny, when she was falsely accused amongst other things of living off benefits. Eventually, the truth about her situation emerged, and the tabloids lost interest.

She has also presented BBC One's religious programme Songs of Praise and holds several notable positions, including vice-president of Action for Children, council member of the Prince's Trust, patron of the ADHD Foundation, and trustee for BBC Children in Need. She also supported the Bone Cancer Research Trust and served on the Diana, Princess of Wales, Memorial Committee in 1997.

In 2007, she married violinist Giles Broadbent. She presented BBC Radio 2's Sunday Half Hour and Sunday Hour from 2012 to 2017. She is a supporter of CBM, an international charity focused on preventing blindness and helping people with disabilities in poor countries.

In 2023, she received an Honorary Degree as a Doctor of Letters from Loughborough University.

Sadly, her husband Giles Broadbent passed away in September 2023.

First Black well-known Stand-up Comedian

Charlie Williams MBE – (1927-2006)

Charlie Williams MBE was one of the first black footballers in Britain after World War II. He is mainly known as a groundbreaking figure in British entertainment and became the country's first well-known black stand-up comedian.

Charles Adolphus Williams was born on 23 December 1927, in the small mining village of Royston, South Yorkshire. His father was Barbadian who came to Britain in 1914 when he enlisted in the British Army. After World War 1, he settled in Royston and worked selling groceries and then in the coal mines. He married a lady from south Yorkshire called Frances Cook, known as Doris.

Life for Charlie Williams was hard as his father he became ill and had to retire. As a result at the age of 14, Charlie left his school, Ryhill modern school, to take a job in the mines at Monkton Colliery in 1942 to support his family. However, he maintained an interest in football. Sadly his father passed away in 1944, and he moved to Upton, Yorkshire, where he continued to play football.

At the age of 19, he was scouted while playing for Upton Colliery and signed by Doncaster Rovers, where he played as a central defender for over a decade. Despite facing significant racism on and off the field, he let his performance speak for itself and maintained his dignity, becoming a role model for perseverance and grace under pressure.

He faced abuse and death threats but claimed it spurred him on and he let his football do his talking for him. A team mate lauded his ability to turn the other cheek, "He never took the bait and kept his dignity on and off the pitch."

None of these experiences seem to have made him bitter. He recalled that "we'd call each other names during the match but afterwards you would shake hands and be friends. Some fans would even come up and say sorry." The fact is that like all black football players at the time he received little or no support from the football authorities, being expected to just accept racist abuse as being part of the game.

He made 171 appearances for Doncaster as a centre-half from 1949 to 1959, and became a regular first team player in 1955. Yet when the 1956 Encyclopaedia of Association Football was published there was no mention of him or Roy Brown, of Stoke City, despite the fact that they were among the first post-war black players in British football.

He left Doncaster Rovers to play at non-league Skegness Town. He was then offered a well paid, player-coach job in Sydney but when the Australian immigration office realised he was black they blocked his application. A national press campaign resulted in a change of heart from the Australians, but he decided not to bother going as they had rejected him.

He retired from football in 1959 aged 32 he tried his hand as a singer singing in local working men's clubs. However it was his comic chat between the songs that was best received, so he decided to move into comedy full-time He came to prominence from 1971, when he began appearing regularly on the Granada TV show, The Comedians. The show broadcast stand-up routines from relatively unknown but often very experienced club comedians, including Frank Carson, Mike Reid and Bernard Manning. The novel combination of a black man with a Yorkshire accent and his first-hand experience of life in the British working class made him unmistakable. He eventually became Britain's first well-known black television comedian.

His comedy was often at his own expense, and particularly his colour. He used to respond to heckling by saying: "If you don't shut up, I'll come and move in next door to you". Like other popular comedians of his era, his comedy included jokes about "Pakis" and "coons". He reinforced the prejudices and negative race stereotypes prevalent at the time, typified by the rise of the National Front, and TV shows like The Black and White Minstrel Show on the BBC, and the sitcom Love Thy Neighbour, made by Thames

Television for the National ITV network, which he actually appeared in an episode as himself.

Nevertheless, he was a role model for a new generation of British black comedians, such as Lenny Henry and Gary Wilmot, growing up in the 1970s, when almost all other comedians were male and white.

He reached the pinnacle of his comedy career in the early 1970s. In 1972, he spent a six-month season at the London Palladium presenting his own show, It's Charlie Williams, on Granada Television. He was the subject of an episode of This Is Your Life, when he was surprised by Eamonn Andrews at the Batley Variety Club; and he appeared at the Royal Variety Performance.

In 1973, he presented a one-off special Charlie Williams Show on BBC2, and published an autobiography, Ee-I've Had Some Laughs. He was popular enough at this time to be featured as the star of his own one page comic strip in IPC's Shiver and Shake comic at this time. He was also the host of ATV's popular game show The Golden Shot, along with hostess Wendy King, for a six-month period from 1973 to 1974, although he often struggled to hold together a fast moving live show, and it ultimately had a detrimental effect on his career.

In 1976 he toured Rhodesia, and appeared before audiences at packed nightclubs in Salisbury. At that time, the white minority rule government of Rhodesia had unilaterally declared independence from Britain, which had severed all ties with the Rhodesian government.

By the late 1970s and early 1980s, his brand of humour was becoming old-fashioned and the racial slurs and stereotypes unacceptable. As a result his career declined. He caused offence to some, and was praised by others, for defending the Robertson's Golliwog trade mark, and for saying that immigrants to the United Kingdom should conform to the British way of life.

He retired after a final tour in 1995.

In the 1999 Queen's New Year Honours list he was appointed a Member of the Order of the British Empire (MBE) for charitable services to the community in Yorkshire.

In 2000 he was given a lifetime achievement award at the Black Comedy Awards, where it was recognised that he had broken down barriers.

In 2004 he was voted Doncaster Rovers' all-time cult hero by viewers of the BBC's Football Focus programme.

He suffered from Parkinson's disease in his later life, and died on 2 September 2006, aged 78.

He married twice. He was first married to Audrey Crump 1 April 1957. They had two children. He later married a second time, to Janice, who survived him.

He maintained that he had no regrets and he told jokes he thought would suit the audience.

First Black British actor leading a film

Earl Cameron CBE – (1917-2020)

Earl Cameron CBE was a Bermudian actor who lived and worked in the United Kingdom. After appearing on London's West End stage, he became one of the first black stars in the British film industry. With his appearance in the 1951 film, Pool of London, he became the first British-based black actors to take up a starring role in a British film.

Earlston Jewitt Cameron was born on 8 August 1917, in Pembroke, Bermuda, and grew up on Princess Street, Hamilton, the youngest of six children to Edith and Arthur Cameron. His father was a stonemason who died when he was five, after which his mother took on various jobs to support the family. He attended Central school, leaving at 13 to become a plumber's apprentice, then a hotel bellman and waiter.

At the age of 19, he was eager to see the world, leaving Bermuda to work on cruise ships, which eventually brought him to London just as World War II broke out. Stranded in the UK, he faced numerous hardships, including difficulty finding work and accommodation, and a bout of pneumonia. Despite these challenges, he persevered and landed a job as a hotel dishwasher.

His break into acting came unexpectedly. After watching a musical with black cast members, he believed he could do the same. He was soon cast in the musical Chu Chin Chow and later joined the Entertainments National Service Association (ENSA), entertaining British troops. This experience honed his craft and led to further opportunities on stage.

In 1946, he returned briefly to Bermuda but quickly realized his passion lay in acting, prompting him to leave Bermuda. Back in London, he secured roles in various plays, including "Deep are the Roots." He studied acting with Amanda Ira Aldridge, daughter of a renowned African-American Shakespearean actor, and performed in repertory theatre across the UK.

His big break in film came with, Pool of London, in 1951, where he played Johnny, marking him as first black actors in a starring role in a British film. The movie, notable for its portrayal of an interracial relationship, opened doors for him in the industry. He followed this success with roles in The Heart of the Matter, in 1954; Simba in 1955 and Sapphire in 1959, which was voted Outstanding British Film of the Year by BAFTA.

In 1954 he married actress Audrey Godowski and they had five children. The family moved to the Solomon Islands in 1979, where he ran an ice cream shop and served as a Baha'i missionary. They returned to the UK in 1994, shortly before Audrey's passing.

Throughout the 1960s and 1970s, he continued to act in films and on television, often advocating for black British actors. In 1965, he appeared in the James Bond film Thunderball as Sean Connery's chauffeur. He also had a memorable friendship with Sidney Poitier, formed during auditions for the film Cry, the Beloved Country.

In the later years of his career, he took on roles in major films like The Interpreter in 2005 and The Queen in 2006. His contributions to the arts were recognized with several honours, including a Lifetime Achievement Award from the Bermuda Arts Council in 1999.

In the 2009 Queen's New Years Honours list he was awarded a Commander of the Order of the British Empire (CBE) for services to drama.

In 2012 Bermuda's City Hall Theatre was renamed The Earl Cameron Theatre in his honour.

In 2013 he became a Doctor of Letters awarded by Warwick University.

In 2017 on his 100th birthday, he was honoured by the Bermuda Government's Department of Community and Cultural Affairs. On the stage of the theatre now bearing his name, he gave a reading from Othello and was interviewed by veteran journalist Charles Webbe. He also received a tribute by the BFI Southbank.

The bout of pneumonia he suffered in his early years had left him with one functioning lung which incredibly did not slow him down. As the Covid-19 pandemic raged around the world, he died peacefully in his sleep at his home in Kenilworth, Warwickshire on July 3, 2020, aged 102.

He was survived by his second wife Barbara; his five children with wife Audrey, Jane, Simon, Helen, Serena and Philippa; and Quinton Astwood, his eldest son by a relationship with Marjorie Astwood. He also had 8 grandchildren and 2 great-grandchildren.

First Black British actor to win an Oscar

Daniel Kaluuya — (1989-)

Daniel Kaluuya is a British actor known for his outstanding performances both on screen and stage. He has won numerous awards, including an Academy Award, two BAFTA Awards, two Screen Actors Guild Awards, and a Golden Globe Award. In 2021, he made history by becoming the first Black British actor to win an Oscar for his role as Fred Hampton in the film, Judas and the Black Messiah.

Daniel Kaluuya was born on 24 February 1989, in London to Ugandan parents. He grew up in Camden Town with his sister, raised by their mother. His father lived in Malawi, and they reconnected when he was 15. He attended Torriano Primary School and St Aloysius' College, and later took A-levels in History, Drama, and Biology at Camden School for Girls, a mixed semi-comprehensive sixth-form college.

He showed his talent early on, writing his first play at nine and performing in improvisational theatre. He trained at the Anna Scher Theatre School and WAC Arts. In 2006, he landed his first acting role in the BBC drama Shoot the Messenger, and soon after joined the original cast of Skins as Posh Kenneth, also contributing as a writer.

He gained critical acclaim for his performance in Sucker Punch at the Royal Court Theatre, winning the Evening Standard Award and Critics' Circle Theatre Award for Outstanding Newcomer. His career continued to rise with roles in Psychoville, The Fades, Doctor Who, and the iconic Black Mirror episode "Fifteen Million Merits".

In 2009, at the age of 20, he was nominated for a Laurence Olivier Award for his performance in Oxford Street. Daniel's film career includes roles in Johnny English Reborn in 2011, Kick-Ass 2 in 2013, and Sicario in 2015.

His breakthrough came in 2017 with the lead role in Jordan Peele's horror film Get Out, earning him an Oscar nomination. He then appeared in Black

Panther in 2018, Widows in 2018, and starred in Queen & Slim in 2019. In 2018, he received the BAFTA Rising Star Award.

In 2021, his portrayal of Fred Hampton in Judas and the Black Messiah brought him an Academy Award, BAFTA Award, Critics' Choice Award, Golden Globe Award, and Screen Actors Guild Award for Best Supporting Actor. At the age of 32, he became the seventh-youngest winner of the Academy Award for Best Supporting Actor and the first British actor of African heritage to win an Academy Award. He was also included in Time's 2021 list of the 100 most influential people in the world.

In 2022 he starred in the sci-fi horror film Nope alongside Keke Palmer and Steven Yeun, which received positive reviews.

An avid Arsenal fan, he narrated the docu-series All or Nothing: Arsenal, covering the 2021-2022 season.

In 2023, he co-directed the film The Kitchen with Kibwe Tavares, depicting a dystopian future in 2044 London divided by wealth. Daniel Kaluuya's talent and achievements continue to inspire many in the entertainment industry.

In 2024 a statue of him from the film Get Out was raised in Leicester Square, chosen from a poll of 5,000 British film fans as the actor people would most like to see recognised.

First Black filmmaker to win an Academy Award for best picture

Sir Steve McQueen CBE – (1969-)

Sir Steve McQueen CBE is a British film director, film producer, screenwriter, and video artist. He is known for his award-winning film 12 Years a Slave in 2013, an adaptation of Solomon Northup's 1853 slave narrative memoir. This film won him the Academy Award for Best Picture, the BAFTA Award for Best Film, the Golden Globe Award for Best Motion Picture – Drama, and the New York Film Critics Circle Award for Best Director. He became the first black British filmmaker to win the Academy Award for Best Picture.

Steve Rodney McQueen was born on 9 October 1969 in London to a Grenadian mother and a Trinidadian father, his parents both having moved to Britain. He grew up in Ealing, West London and went to Drayton Manor High School. School was not a good experience. He was dyslexic and wore an eye patch due to a lazy eye. He pursued his passion for art and football, playing for the St. George's Colts and studying art at various institutions including Goldsmiths College, University of London.

His early works, such as the 1993 film, Bear, and the 1995 film, Five Easy Pieces, showcased his unique style, often exploring themes of vulnerability and strength. His innovative approach continued with films like Deadpan in 1997, a re-enactment of a Buster Keaton stunt, and Drumroll in 1998, which used multiple cameras to capture the movement of an oil drum through Manhattan.

In 1999 he won the prestigious Turner Prize for his film and video works.

In the Queen's 2002 Birthday honours list he was awarded the Order of the British Empire (OBE) for services to the visual arts.

In 2006 he served as an official war artist in Iraq, creating the poignant artwork Queen and Country to commemorate soldiers who died in the Iraq War.

His breakthrough in feature-length films came with Hunger in 2008, which depicted the 1981 Irish hunger strike and won several awards, including the Caméra d'Or at Cannes. This success was followed by Shame in 2011, a critically acclaimed film about a man's struggle with sex addiction.

In the 2011 Queen's New Year Honours list he was made a Commander of the Order of the British Empire for services to the visual arts.

His next film made in 2013, was 12 Years a Slave based on the 1853 autobiography of Solomon Northup telling the story of a free black man who is kidnapped in 1841 and sold into slavery, working on plantations in the state of Louisiana for twelve years before being released. The film won the Academy Award for Best Picture in March 2014, becoming the first Best Picture winner to have a black director or producer and made him the first black British filmmaker to win the Academy Award for Best Picture.

In 2018 he directed Widows, a heist thriller starring Viola Davis, and in 2020, he created the anthology series Small Axe for the BBC. This focused on London's West Indian community from the late 1960s to the early 1980s. The series received critical acclaim and numerous accolades.

In the 2020 Queen's New Years Honours list he was knighted for services to film.

He lives with his wife, Dutch cultural critic Bianca Stigter, and their two children in Amsterdam and London.

A lifelong fan of Tottenham Hotspur F.C., he continues to impact the worlds of film and art with his powerful storytelling and innovative vision.

First Black British model for Victoria's Secret Angel

Leomie Anderson — (1993-)

Leomie Anderson, a British model, designer, and activist, made her mark in the fashion industry by becoming the sixth Black and first British Black Victoria's Secret Angel in 2019.

Leomie Jasmin Francis Anderson was born on 14 February 1993, in Wandsworth, London, to Jamaican parents. Her journey in the fashion industry began unexpectedly at the age of 14 when she was scouted by Premier Models on her way home from school. Although initially aspiring to be a fashion journalist, she quickly made her mark on the runway, walking for renowned designers like Marc Jacobs at just 17.

She gained recognition after appearing on Channel 4's reality show The Model Agency in 2011 offering insights into the modelling industry. Her influence expanded with the launch of her YouTube channel and blog, Cracked China Cup, providing followers with glimpses into her life as a model and featuring collaborations with renowned brands like Marc Jacobs and appearances in magazines like i-D.

Her career soared as she walked the runway for renowned designers like Marc Jacobs and landed campaigns with major brands such as Giorgio Armani, Burberry, and Fenty Beauty. She made history in 2019 as the sixth Black and first British Black model to become a Victoria's Secret Angel.

Beyond modelling, she is an outspoken advocate for women's rights and racial equality in the fashion industry. She founded the LAPP blog (Leomie Anderson, the Project, the Purpose), later evolving into LAPP Magazine, to advocate for women's mental health, rights, and body positivity.

Additionally, she launched her own clothing brand, LAPP the Brand, focusing on women's athletic wear that merges fashion with functionality.

Her activism extends to speaking engagements at prestigious universities like Oxford and Cambridge, as well as delivering TED Talks addressing racial discrimination and lack of diversity in the industry.

Recognized for her influence, she was featured on Forbes' 30 Under 30 list and launched her podcast, Role Model with Leomie Anderson, in 2021.

In 2023, she took on the role of presenter for the BBC series Glow Up: Britain's Next Make-Up Star, succeeding Maya Jama. Her journey reflects not only her achievements in fashion but also her commitment to driving positive change within the industry and beyond.

First Black model to appear on the front cover of Time, French Vogue, Russian Vogue and American Vogue

Naomi Campbell – (1970-)

Naomi Campbell is an English model, actress, singer, and businesswoman. She began her career at the age of 15 and established herself amongst the most recognisable and in-demand models of the past four decades. She was one of six models of her generation declared supermodels by the fashion industry and international press. She was the first black model to appear on the cover of TIME magazine, French Vogue and Russian Vogue as well as the first British black model to appear on the cover of British Vogue.

Naomi Elaine Campbell was born on 22 May 1970 in Lambeth, South London to Valerie Morris her Jamaican-born mother. Following her mother's wishes, she has never met her father, who abandoned her mother when she was four months pregnant and went unnamed on her birth certificate. She took the surname Campbell from her mother's second marriage. Her half-brother Pierre was born in 1985, Campbell is of Afro-Jamaican descent, as well as of Chinese-Jamaican ancestry through her paternal grandmother, whose surname was Ming.

She spent her early years in Rome, Italy, where her mother worked as a dancer. On their return to London, she lived with relatives while her mother travelled across Europe with the dance troupe Fantastica. From three years old, she attended the Barbara Speake Stage School and at 10 she attended the Italia Conti Academy of Theatre Arts, studying ballet. She also attended Dunraven School in Streatham, London.

In 1978 aged 8 she appeared in the music video for Bob Marley's Is This Love. In 1983 she appeared in the video for Culture Club's I'll Tumble 4 Ya and Mistake number 3, in 1984.

In 1986, while still a student of the Italia Conti Academy of Theatre Arts, she was scouted by Beth Boldt, head of the Synchro Model Agency, while window-shopping in Covent Garden. Her career quickly took off and in April, just before her 16th birthday she appeared on the cover of British Elle.

Over the next few years, her career progressed steadily. She modelled for designers such as Gianni Versace, Azzedine Alaïa, and Isaac Mizrahi and posed for such photographers as Peter Lindbergh, Herb Ritts, and Bruce Weber. By the late 1980s, with Christy Turlington and Linda Evangelista, she formed a trio known as the Trinity, who became the most recognisable and in-demand models of their generation.

When faced with racial discrimination, she was supported by her white friends. She quoted Turlington and Evangelista as telling Dolce & Gabbana, "If you don't use Naomi, you don't get us."

In December 1987 she appeared on the cover of British Vogue, as that publication's first black cover girl since 1966.

In August 1988 she became the first black model to appear on the cover of French Vogue, after designer Yves St. Laurent, threatened to withdraw his advertising from the magazine if it didn't place her on its cover. The following year, she appeared on the cover of American Vogue, which marked the first time a black model graced the front of the September magazine, traditionally the year's biggest and most important issue.

In January 1990 she was named the reigning mega model of them all. Along with Turlington, Evangelista, Crawford and Claudia Schiffer, she formed an elite group of models declared supermodels by the fashion industry. With the addition of newcomer Kate Moss, they were collectively known as the Big Six.

In the mid-1990s, more appearances in videos followed and she branched out into other areas of entertainment. In 1994, she published a novel called Swan, about a supermodel dealing with blackmail. It was ghost written by Caroline Upcher, as she did not have the time to sit down and write a book. It received poor reviews. She also released an album called Baby Woman, named after designer Rifat Ozbek's nickname for her. It was only successful in Japan.

She also had small roles in rom-com Miami Rhapsody and Spike Lee's Girl 6, as well as a recurring role on the second season of American police drama, New York Undercover.

In 1995 along with fellow models Schiffer, Turlington and Elle Macpherson, she invested in a chain of restaurants called the Fashion Cafe, whose directors were arrested three years later for fraud, bankruptcy and money laundering.

In 1998 Time magazine declared the end of the supermodel era. She continued modelling, both on the runway and, more frequently, on print, on many high profile engagements.

Despite her status as the most famous black model of her time, she never earned as many advertising assignments as her white colleagues, and she was not signed by a cosmetics company until 1999. Since 1999, she has released 25 fragrances for women via her perfume house under the Procter & Gamble brand.

Throughout her career she has been outspoken against the racial bias that exists in the fashion industry. Despite being one of the world's top models she was not paid as much as her white peers.

In 2013 she joined fellow black models Iman and Bethann Hardison in an advocacy group called Diversity Coalition. In an open letter to the governing bodies of global fashion weeks, they named high-profile designers who used just one or no models of colour in their fall 2013 shows, calling it a racist act.

In addition to her modelling work she has been involved in a lot of charity work worldwide using her celebrity status to gain wider attention and support. She has received recognition and awards for her support of humanitarian causes.

In 1993 she got engaged to U2 bassist Adam Clayton though they separated a year later. In 1995 she dated Leonardo DiCaprio. From 1998 through 2003, she was in a relationship with Formula One racing head Flavio Briatore becoming engaged before breaking off the relationship. She now considers Briatore her mentor. From 2008 until 2013, she was in a relationship with Russian businessman Vladislav Doronin. She also had relationships with Robert De Niro, Hassan Jameel, Sean "Diddy" Combs, and Usher. In 2019, she dated Skepta an MC and rapper.

In May 2021 she announced the birth of her daughter. In February 2022 she confirmed to Vogue magazine that her daughter was not adopted, posing with her child for a photo shoot. In 2023 she revealed that she also had a son.

First Black teacher employed by the Liverpool Education Authority

Norman Beaton – (1934-1994)

Norman Beaton was a successful British actor from the 1960s to 1990s. In his native Guyana he did some amateur acting while training as a teacher, and developed a parallel career as a Calypso singer. Arriving in Britain in 1960, he became Liverpool's first black teacher, but the experience was not an entirely happy one, and he was soon back making music leading to his acting career.

Norman Lugard Beaton was born on 31 October 1934 in Georgetown, British Guiana (now Guyana). His father William Solomon Beaton was a postmaster who became the country's chief postmaster and won the Imperial Service Medal. His mother Ada Agatha Adeline Mackintosh was a dress designer.

He went to public school and then teacher-training college at Queens College in Georgetown before taking up teaching rising to the post of deputy headmaster at Cane Grove Anglican School in Demerara. At the same time, he followed his love of calypso music by forming the Four Bees vocal group and making 20 singles. The group toured Surinam and French Guyana with the revue Caribbean Cavalcade. He became named the Calypso Champion of Guyana and had a no. 1 hit in Trinidad and Tobago with Come Back Melvina, in 1959.

At the age of 26 in 1960 he sailed for Britain. He studied at London University and obtained a post in the shipping department of a bookshop until his wife and children arrived in London. With his knowledge and experience he went on to become the first black teacher employed by the Liverpool Education Authority. He taught in two Liverpool schools.

However, he still had his interest in music. While in Liverpool, he played guitar for Adrian Henri, Brian Patten and Roger McGough who became the Liverpool Poets. He also made appearances at the famous Cavern Club.

He became increasingly unhappy with his work as a teacher and began writing plays, his first play being the musical Jack of Spades, which was about the doomed relationship between a black man and a white woman and was quite controversial at that time. The play was a hit at the Everyman Theatre, Liverpool. This moderate success gave him enough confidence to give up teaching and concentrate on the theatre.

He moved first to Bristol where he was invited to join the Bristol Old Vic as musical director and composer and then to Sussex where he played the leading role in a musical he had written, Sit Down, Banna, at the Connaught Theatre. This was the beginning of his acting career.

On 24 May 1967 he made his television debut in a play for the BBC called Drums Along the Avon. This was followed by a brief stint as presenter on BBC Bristol's local news programme, Points West. However his progress as an actor was impacted by one of many brushes with the law. This time following an unjust disturbance charge, he received a two-week prison sentence which, put paid to an offer of a 26-week BBC series on education and black youth.

Unfortunately his early career followed a pattern of stage and screen triumphs interrupted by frequent bouts of unemployment, poverty and frustration, further complicated by a chaotic personal life. High points included his stage performances in Jonathan Miller's 1970 production of The Tempest as Ariel and in the energetic and innovative Gilbert and Sullivan adaptation, The Black Mikado in 1975. He worked with Laurence Olivier at the National Theatre, took the lead role in Sergeant Ola and His Followers at the Royal Court in 1979 and played Angelo in Measure for Measure, the first all-black production at the National Theatre in 1981.

He worked with the Black Theatre of Brixton to bring the work of young black playwrights such as Mustapha Matura to wider attention. The venture eventually collapsed, though it laid the foundations for black theatre in the decades that followed.

His early television career followed the standard stereotypically racist and discriminatory path of most black actors. He was frequently seen as a character actor in television dramas and comedies, although often cast in stereotypical black roles, such as that of a London Transport guard in Thirty Minutes Worth with Harry Worth in 1973; a chauffeur in The Protectors in 1974; a drug dealer in Barlow at Large in 1974 and a West Indian in Sykes with Eric Sykes in 1978.

Fortunately in 1975 he got a part in the Horace Ove film Pressure. This film was notable as being Britain's first black feature film. This was followed by his first series role, acting as the father to Lenny Henry's feckless teenager in LWT's all-black sitcom, The Fosters which ran from 1976 to 1977. The show was criticized for its perceived lack of realism, which was a lot to ask of a sitcom, but it did represent a breakthrough of sorts.

He went on to take the lead role in the Anthony Simmons film Black Joy in 1977. This marked a high point in his career. The film was picked as one of Britain's two competition entries at the 1977 Cannes Film Festival, and won highly favourable reviews at home and abroad with many singling out his performance. The icing on the cake came when he was named the Variety Club's Film Actor of 1977, an achievement he described as "the most wonderful moment in my life".

In December 1977 he appeared in the BBC play Black Christmas which led to a part in the BBC series Empire Road which ran from 1977 to 1978. This Birmingham-based series was described as Britain's first black soap opera.

In 1982 he acted alongside Gene Hackman in the film Eureka.

In 1984 he played Lenny Henry's father in the Lenny Henry show.

In 1986 he published his autobiography called Beaton But Unbowed. This described his troubled life. He was married and divorced three times; he went bankrupt with debts of £21,000 in 1982, was jailed for nine months in 1965 for a cheque fraud and received suspended sentences for several other crimes. He once described himself as a "jailbird and hustler" who had "mixed with villains, pimps, prostitutes and con-artists". But, as an actor, he was a leading light of the black community in Britain. At the time of the release of the film Black Joy, he said, "It really upsets me that British films do not incorporate niggers, and television's not much better. It's scandalous."

In 1987 he played the lead role of Willie Boy in the TV comedy Playing Away which was directed by Horace Ové, from a screenplay by Caryl Phillips, about a West Indian cricket team invited to play a rural white team.

In 1989 he acted in the file Mighty Quinn with Denzel Washington.

The highlight of his career came with his title role in Desmond's, by some margin Britain's most successful and popular black sitcom, created by Trix Worrell. Desmond's was different, comfortably transcending the usual black/white racial agenda and concerning itself with more satisfyingly complex issues, notably the very different aspirations and experiences of recent African immigrants and more established Caribbeans. Fundamental to its success was his role as the avuncular but mischievous barber. He received the Royal Television Society Best Comedy Performer Award for his role.

The show proved to be Channel 4's most popular situation comedy and it won international appeal and brought him to the attention of black American star Bill Cosby, who invited him to make a guest appearance in The Cosby Show in 1992.

His untimely death in 1994 inevitably brought Desmond's to a close after six series.

On 13 December 1994 after years of working hard this took a toll on his health. He retired to his home city of Georgetown, Guyana, just as his character in Desmond's was doing the same. He collapsed at the airport from a heart attack and died a few hours later on 13 December 1994 at the age of 60. He was survived by five children from three marriages.

He was married and divorced three times, and had four children with his first wife, two children born in Guyana, two in the UK and one child with his second wife. He spent many years living in Brixton with Jane Cash, whom he referred to as "the wife he never had". Jane died in 2020. He married Jean Davenport in 1988, but they separated later. She died in 2001.

The widespread shock and sadness that greeted the news of his death revealed just how fondly he was regarded, as did the inauguration, in 1995, of the Norman Beaton Award at the Birmingham Film and TV Festival to reward outstanding multicultural work and, in 2003, of the BBC's Norman Beaton Fellowship for new radio acting talent across the UK by encouraging applicants from non-traditional training backgrounds.

He became particularly associated with spirited patriarch roles, most famously as the eponymous barber of Desmond's, but he was a much more versatile actor than his popular image acknowledged. A highly expressive performer who was equally at ease with weighty parts and light comedy, he won great respect on stage and screen but, like many black actors of the time, frequently found consistent television or film roles, particularly ones worthy of his talents, thin on the ground.

First Black living poet to be published in the Penguin Modern Classics series

Linton Kwesi Johnson – (1952-)

Linton Kwesi Johnson, also known as LKJ, is a Jamaica-born, British-based dub poet and activist. In 2002 he became the second living poet, and the only black one, to be published in the Penguin Modern Classics series. His performance poetry involves the recitation of his own verse in Jamaican patois over dub-reggae.

Linton Kwesi Johnson was born on 24 August 1952 in Chapelton, a small town in the rural parish of Clarendon, Jamaica. His middle name, Kwesi, is a Ghanaian name given to boys born on a Sunday. His mother moved to Britain as part of the Windrush generation, He joined her with his father in 1963 to live in Brixton south London. He attended Tulse Hill School in Lambeth. He had been a top pupil in Jamaica, but, like most black children of his generation, in Britain, he was relegated to the bottom stream. He recalls it as being a traumatic period with racist teachers and kids and getting into fights all the time.

While still at school he joined the British Black Panther Movement. He helped to organise a poetry workshop within the movement, while developing his work with a group of poets and drummers called Rasta Love. He enjoyed writing verse and used it as a way expressing the anger and passion of black youth like himself in the struggle against racial oppression

He studied sociology at Goldsmiths College in New Cross, London and graduated in 1973. After this he was employed as the first paid library resources and education officer at the Keskidee Centre in Islington, London. This was Britain's first arts centre for the black community. He got one of his poems called Voices of the living and the dead staged there. It was produced by Jamaica novelist Lindsay Barrett, with music provided by Rasta Love.

He married his wife Barbara, the daughter of his mother's hairdresser. They lived in Brixton.

In the 1970s he wrote for music papers New Musical Express, Melody Maker, and Black Music. He did freelance work for Virgin Records, writing biographies for their reggae artists, sleeve notes and copy for adverts.

His poetry was mainly political, dealing with the experiences of being an African-Caribbean in Britain. He also wrote about other issues, such as British foreign policy and the death of anti-racist marcher Blair Peach.

In 1982 his father died and he wrote, Reggae fi Dada, blaming social conditions. His most celebrated poems, such as Sonny's Lettah, were written during the government of Prime Minister Margaret Thatcher. The poems include graphic accounts of the racist police brutality occurring at the time. He made clever use of Jamaican patois to make the poetry more live and vibrant.

In 1974 his first collection of poetry called, Voices of the Living and the Dead was published in the journal Race Today.

In 1975 his second collection called Dread Beat An' Blood, was published by Bogle-L'Ouverture.

He went on to produce many albums starting with his debut in 1978 Dread Beat an' Blood. His fame surged helped by the rising popularity of reggae music. There was also a punk-reggae anti-establishment coalition with black and white disaffected youths battling against oppression from the authorities. He opened for punk groups, such as Johnny Rotten's PIL, successor to the Sex Pistols and Siouxsie and the Banshees.

His style is more akin to the Jamaican "toasting" tradition which is regarded a precursor of rap, referred to as dub poetry.

In 1977 he won a Cecil Day-Lewis Fellowship, as writer-in-residence for the London Borough of Lambeth.

In 1981 he launched his record label called LKJ Records, working with other reggae artists and dub poets such as Jean "Binta" Breeze.

His poetry gave voice second generation of black Britons, children of Windrush generation. He has been an alternative poet laureate, chronicling the black experience in Britain over three decades, while reflecting on events from South Africa to Eastern Europe.

Back in 1982 his poetry, with its use of Jamaican patois and phonetic spelling, was considered by the authorities to have wreaked havoc in schools and helped to create a generation of rioters and illiterates. By the 1990s he was being celebrated, his poetry translated into other languages. He spawned an international school of dub poetry, while inspiring British poets, from Benjamin Zephaniah and Lemn Sissay to Simon Armitage.

In 1985 he was made an Associate Fellow of Warwick University.

In 1987 he became an Honorary Fellow of Wolverhampton Polytechnic.

In 1990 he received an award at the XIII Premio Internazionale Ultimo Novecento from the city of Pisa for his contribution to poetry and popular music.

In 1998 he was awarded the Premio Piero Ciampi Citta di Livorno Concorso Musicale Nazionale in Italy.

In 2002 he became only the second living poet and the first Black poet to have his work included in the Penguin Modern Classics series, under the title Mi Revalueshanary Fren: Selected Poems.

In 2003 he received an honorary fellowship from his alma mater, Goldsmiths College, University of London.

In 2004 he became an Honorary Visiting Professor of Middlesex University in London.

In 2005 he was awarded the silver Musgrave Medal from the Institute of Jamaica for distinguished eminence in the field of poetry. In 2012, he was awarded the Golden PEN Award by English PEN for "a Lifetime's Distinguished Service to Literature".

He is a Trustee of the George Padmore Institute (GPI), and is a contributor to the GPI's collection of dialogues Changing Britannia: Life Experience With Britain, edited by Roxy Harris and Sarah White (New Beacon Books, 1999).

On 20 April 2017 he was awarded an Honorary Doctorate of Literature (D.Litt.) by Rhodes University in South Africa.

In July 2020 he was awarded the PEN Pinter Prize, established in Harold Pinter's name to defend freedom of expression and celebrate literature, for his commitment to political expression in his work. He was described by the judges as a living legend, poet, reggae icon, academic and campaigner, whose impact on the cultural landscape over the last half century has been colossal and multi-generational.

He is chair of 198 Contemporary Arts and Learning, an art gallery and learning institution in Brixton.

He and his wife Barbara divorced in 1994. They have one daughter Karen, and two sons, Eric and Marcos.

Founder of Britain's first major black newspaper

Claudia Jones – (1915-1964)

Claudia Jones was a Trinidad and Tobago-born journalist and activist. She founded Britain's first major black newspaper, the West Indian Gazette, in 1958, and played a central role in founding the Notting Hill Carnival, the second-largest annual carnival in the world.

Claudia Jones was born Claudia Vera Cumberbatch on 21 February 1915 in Trinidad. When she was eight years old, her family moved to New York City. Her mother died five years later. She was a clever student and won the Theodore Roosevelt Award for Good Citizenship at her junior high school.

In 1932 aged 17, she was struck with tuberculosis, due to poor living conditions. This caused irreparable damage to her lungs leading to lengthy stays in hospitals throughout her life. She graduated from high school, but her family could not afford the expenses to attend her graduation ceremony.

She joined the Young Communist League (YCL) in 1936 after hearing the Communist Party's defence of the Scottsboro Boys, nine African-American boys who were accused of raping two white women in Alabama and who faced execution. She went on to work on the YCL's newspaper, later becoming state education director and chairperson for the YCL.

As a black woman she had limited career choices. Instead of going to college she began working in a laundry, and subsequently found other retail work in Harlem. During this time, she joined a drama group, and began to write a column called Claudia Comments for a Harlem journal.

In 1937 she joined the editorial staff of the Daily Worker, rising by 1938 to become editor of the Weekly Review. After the YCL became American Youth for Democracy during World War II, she became editor of its monthly journal, Spotlight.

After World War II, she became executive secretary of the Women's National Commission, secretary for the Women's Commission of the Communist Party USA (CPUSA), and in 1952 took the same position at the National Peace Council. In 1953, she took over the editorship of Negro Affairs.

She focused on growing the party's support for black and white women, trying to get black women equal respect within the party. She campaigned for job training programs, equal pay for equal work, government controls on food prices, and funding for wartime childcare programs. She insisted on the party developing the training of women comrades, the organisation of women into mass organisations, daytime classes for women, and babysitter funds to enable women to become activists.

As an elected member of the National Committee of the Communist Party USA, she organised and spoke at events. As a result of her membership of CPUSA and various associated activities, in 1948 she was arrested and sentenced to the first of four spells in prison. Incarcerated on Ellis Island, she was threatened with deportation to Trinidad.

Following a hearing by the Immigration and Naturalization Service, she was found in violation of the McCarran Act for being an alien (non-US citizen) who had joined the Communist Party. Several witnesses testified to her role in party activities, and she had identified herself as a party member since 1936 when completing her Alien Registration on 24th December 1940, in conformity with the Alien Registration Act. She was ordered to be deported on 21 December 1950.

In 1951 aged 36 and in prison, she suffered her first heart attack. That same year, she was tried and convicted with 11 others, of un-American activities against the United States government. The charges against her related to an article she had written for the magazine Political Affairs under the title, Women in the Struggle for Peace and Security. The Supreme Court refused to hear their appeal. In 1955 and she began her sentence of a year and a day at the Federal Reformatory for Women at Alderson, West Virginia. She was released on October 23 1955, facing deportation to Trinidad.

She was refused entry to Trinidad and Tobago as it was felt she would cause trouble. She was offered residency in the United Kingdom on humanitarian grounds, after agreeing to cease contesting her deportation. She left America on December 7 1955, arriving in London two weeks later.

The Communist Party of Great Britain (CPGB) sent several Caribbean communists to greet her including her cousin Trevor Carter. However, she was disappointed to find that many British communists were hostile to a black woman. She joined the CPGB and remained a member until her death.

She became involved in the British African-Caribbean community to organise access to basic facilities, as well as the early movement for equal rights. She campaigned against racism in housing, education and employment. She addressed peace rallies and the Trade Union Congress, and visited Japan, Russia, and China, where she met with Mao Zedong.

In the early 1960s with her health failing, she helped organise campaigns against the Commonwealth Immigrants Bill, which was passed in April 1962 making it harder for non-whites to migrate to Britain. She also campaigned for the release of Nelson Mandela and spoke out against racism in the workplace.

In March 1958 above a barber's shop in Brixton, she founded and thereafter edited the West Indian Gazette, its full title subsequently displayed on its masthead as West Indian Gazette and Afro-Asian Caribbean News (WIG). The paper became a key contributor to the rise of consciousness within the Black British community.

She felt that the newspaper served as a catalyst, quickening the awareness, socially and politically, of West Indians, Afro-Asians and their friends. Its editorial stood for a united, independent West Indies, full economic, social and political equality and respect for human dignity for West Indians and Afro-Asians in Britain, and for peace and friendship between all Commonwealth and world peoples.

Always strapped for cash, WIG folded eight months and four editions after her death in December 1964.

In August 1958 four months after the launch of WIG, the Notting Hill race riots occurred, as well as similar disturbances in Nottingham. In view of the racially driven analysis of these events by the existing daily newspapers, she received visits from members of the black British community and various national leaders responding to the concern of their citizens.

Her unconventional response to the events of that summer was the birth of the Notting Hill Carnival. She used the opportunity to uplift the community by celebrating its culture and heritage with the launch of a special showcase for Afro-Caribbean talent. It was suggested that the British black community should have a carnival. She used her connections to gain use of St Pancras Town Hall in January 1959 for the first Mardi-Gras-based carnival. These early celebrations were epitomised by the slogan: "A people's art is the genesis of their freedom."

A footnote on the front cover of the original 1959 souvenir brochure states: "A part of the proceeds [from the sale] of this brochure are to assist the payments of fines of coloured and white youths involved in the Notting Hill events". With the West Indian Gazette she organised five other annual indoor Caribbean Carnival cabarets at London venues such as Seymour Hall, Porchester Hall and the Lyceum Ballroom.

She died in London on Christmas Eve 1964, aged 49, and was found on Christmas Day at her flat. A post-mortem declared that she had suffered a massive heart attack, due to heart disease and tuberculosis.

Her funeral on 9 January 1965 was a large and political ceremony, with her burial plot selected to be that located to the left of the tomb of her hero, Karl Marx, in Highgate Cemetery, North London.

The National Union of Journalists' Black Members' Council holds a prestigious annual Claudia Jones Memorial Lecture every October, during Black History Month, to honour Jones and celebrate her contribution to Black-British journalism.

The Claudia Jones Organisation was founded in London in 1982 by Yvette Thomas and others to support and empower women and families of African-Caribbean heritage.

In August 2008 a blue plaque was unveiled on the corner of Tavistock Road and Portobello Road commemorating Claudia Jones as the "Mother of Caribbean Carnival in Britain".

In October 2008 Britain's Royal Mail commemorated her with a special postage stamp.

On October 14 2020 she was honoured with a Google Doodle.

Many British communists have argued that her participation in the British communist movement has been both obscured and denied by organisations keen to use her image.

A sculpture of her by artist Favour Jonathan, created as part of the 2021 Sky Arts series Landmark, is on display at Black Cultural Archives in Brixton.

First Black British founder of a specialist Caribbean Publishing Company

John La Rose – (1927-2006)

John La Rose was a political and cultural activist, poet, writer, publisher, and in 1966 founded New Beacon Books, the first specialist Caribbean publishing company in Britain. He was originally from Trinidad and Tobago and was involved in the struggle for political independence and cultural and social change in the Caribbean in the 1940s and 1950s and later in Britain, the rest of Europe and the Third World.

John Anthony La Rose was born on 27 December 1927 in Arima, Trinidad and Tobago to his father Ferdinand La Rose, a cocoa trader, and his mother Emily, a teacher. He had four sisters and a brother. He attended the local Roman Catholic school, and at the age of nine won a scholarship to Trinidad's St Mary's College, one of a handful of prestigious secondary schools modelled on the English grammar school. After finishing school he became a teacher at St Mary's before moving on to work for Colonial Life Insurance Company, the first black-owned insurance company in Trinidad and the then biggest insurance company in the Caribbean.

He developed an interest in culture, both the high arts of classical music, painting and poetry, and the popular cultural forms of Trinidad such as carnival and calypso. He was aware of the link between cultural expression and politics of the working classes through their folk language, stories and other art forms.

He helped to found the Workers Freedom Movement and edited its journal, Freedom. He was an executive member of the Youth Council in Trinidad and produced their fortnightly radio programme, Noise of Youth, for Radio Trinidad. In the mid-1950s, he co-authored, with calypsonian Raymond Quevedo, a pioneering study of calypso entitled Kaiso: A Review. This was republished in 1983 as Atilla's Kaiso.

He joined a Marxist study group and became an active member of the Federated Workers Trade Union (FWTU). In 1952 the FWTU, joined by other radicals, formed the West Indian Independence Party and he was appointed its General Secretary contesting a seat in Arima, his home town, in the 1956 elections.

In 1954 he married Irma Andrea Hilaire. They had two sons, Michael and Keith. Irma shared his interest in social justice and politics, being proficient in her own right engaging with world-wide groups and travelling to Romania.

In 1958 he left Trinidad for Venezuela, where Irma taught typewriting and they both taught English. In 1961 he left for Britain to study for a Law degree making his home in London. Irma was left to look after the young family, a difficult task further complicated by the fact that young Keith had bronchitis. Irma, Michael and Keith set sail for England on the SS Antilles in July 1963.

Irma got her first job in London as a bilingual secretary with International paper company Wiggins Teape while devoting her efforts to bring up her two sons and pay the mortgage. Her next job was as an examinations officer at the Institute of Education, University of London in Russell Square, which she held until her retirement. She was also active in the NALGO Trade Union, being on the executive of the Union for many years and acting as welfare officer for foreign students, especially from Africa.

From the mid-1960s he became closely involved in the Black Education Movement, including the fight against Banding, and the wrongful practice of placing West Indian children in schools for the Educationally Sub-normal.

Sadly during this period Irma and John separated.

In 1966 he was a founder member of the Vietnam Solidarity Campaign and a national council member of this important anti-war movement.

In August 1966 together with his new partner Sarah White, he founded New Beacon Books, the first specialist Caribbean publishers, booksellers and international book service. He was editor-in-chief until his death in 2006. He edited the occasional journal New Beacon Review.

In December 1966 he was co-founder with Edward Kamau Brathwaite and Andrew Salkey of the influential Caribbean Artists Movement.

In 1969 he founded the George Padmore Supplementary School, one of the first of its kind, and helped to found the Caribbean Education and Community Workers Association, which published Bernard Coard's, How the West Indian Child Is Made Educationally Sub-normal in the British School System in 1971. He also helped to found the European Action for Racial Equality and Social justice, bringing together anti-racists and anti-fascists from Belgium, Italy, France and Germany in response to concerns about the rise in fascism and xenophobia.

In 1972 he became the chairman of the Institute of Race Relations (IRR). He was also chairman of Towards Racial Justice, which was the vehicle for publishing the journal Race Today.

In 1973 he co-produced and scripted the documentary, The Mangrove Nine, about the resistance to police attacks on the popular Mangrove restaurant with film director Franco Rosso. He also produced a short film on the Black Church in Britain as part of a Full House BBC 2 television programme on the Caribbean arts.

In 1975 he co-founded the Black Parents Movement from the core of the parents involved in the George Padmore Supplementary School after an incident in which a young black schoolboy was beaten up by the police outside his school in the London Borough of Haringey.

The Black Parents Movement later formed an alliance with the Black Youth Movement and the Race Today Collective, which had, with the Race Today journal, by then separated from the IRR. This established a formidable cultural and political movement which was successful in fighting many cases against police oppression and for better state education. The Alliance formed the New Cross Massacre Action Committee in response to the alleged arson attack which resulted in the death of 13 young blacks. This mobilised 20,000 black people and their supporters to march on March 2 1981, the Black People's Day of Action, in protest over the death of the young people and the failure of the police to conduct a proper investigation. He was Chairman of the New Cross Massacre Action Committee.

Later in the 1980s he helped to found the National Association of Supplementary Schools and was its chairman for two years.

In 1982 he was instrumental in the founding of Africa Solidarity aiming to support the struggle against dictatorial governments and tyranny in Africa. He also became Chairman of the Committee for the Release of Political Prisoners in Kenya.

He helped create the International Book Fair of Radical Black and Third World Books which ran from 1982 to 1995. It was held in the UK, initially in London. It brought together people from across the world to participate in debates, forums, readings, musical events, films, plays and other cultural productions, and browse through stalls from a multiplicity of publishers. They celebrated cultural and political achievements, addressed key issues of the times, and mirrored the achievements of black people throughout the world.

In 1991 he helped establish the George Padmore Institute. It was a library, archive and educational research centre housing materials relating to the life experiences of Caribbean, African and Asian communities in Britain. He was the Chairman of the Institute from its inception until his death in 2006.

In addition to publishing, he was an accomplished writer. He published his first collection of poems, Foundations, in 1966 and his second collection, Eyelets of Truth Within Me. In 1992, both were published by New Beacon Books. His poems and essays have been widely anthologised, and his journalism was published regularly in Race Today.

He died of a heart attack on the morning of Tuesday 28 February 2006 in London.

He married Irma Hilaire in 1954 and they had two sons, Michael and Keith. The couple separated and by 1966 he had a new partner Sarah Swinburne White and they had a son Wole. Irma La Rose died in 2019. Sarah Swinburne White died in 2022.

In December 2022 Haringey Council agreed to change the name of Black Boy Lane in Tottenham, London, to La Rose Lane, as a tribute to his huge contribution to Black life in Haringey and across the UK and the role he played in gaining recognition for Black authors and artists, as well as championing inclusive education. This followed two years of consultation by Haringey Council with local residents amid concerns that the name Black Boy Lane had racist connotations.

First British comedy troupe consisting entirely of Black actresses

BiBi Crew – (1991-2005)

BiBi Crew was the first British comedy troupe to consist entirely of Black actresses. They produced work which was focused on the Black British experience.

In 1991 Joanne Campbell, Judith Jacob, Janet Kay, Suzette Llewellyn, Josephine Melville, Beverley Michaels and Suzanne Packer founded BiBi Crew in London. The group was founded in response to a black male troupe called The Posse formed by Brian Bovell, Michael Buffong, Victor Romero Evans, Robbie Gee, Roger Griffiths, Gary McDonald, Eddie Nestor and Sylvester Williams. They wrote and produced their own plays, presenting their shows at the Theatre Royal, Stratford East and touring nationally.

Beverley Michaels saw the troupe perform and thought that there should be a group of women doing the same thing and contacted the other women involved. The group formed after a memorial benefit at the Theatre Royal Stratford East to celebrate the life of actor Calvin Simpson, in which a few of the troupe members participated. Simpson was a talented black actor who was killed in a road accident in 1990.

The troupe's name combines the word for lady in Swahili and Urdu, with the use of the word crew, which was popular with American music groups, and which the group thought gave them some street cred. They were all of Caribbean descent, and devised and produced work with and from an African Caribbean perspective drawing on their personal experiences as black women. They wrote, directed, produced and acted in their productions, which combined music, dance, drama and sketch comedy. They performed regularly at the Theatre Royal Stratford East and contributed to the theatre's mission to reflect the diversity of the local community where it was located. They also toured throughout the United Kingdom and United States.

Sadly, in 2002, Campbell died suddenly as a result of deep-vein thrombosis.

The BiBi Crew reunited in 2005 without Campbell, and Kay, who was pursuing a career in music. They contributed to the emergence of a black comedy circuit in Britain in the 1990s. Along with groups like The Posse, they introduced a new energized performance style into theatre in the early 1990s that was breaking away from old categories and attracting a black audience with sketch-like material, often highly political and rooted in common experience.

First Black British Female standup to sell out a West End theatre.

Angie Le Mar – (1965-)

Angie Le Mar is a multi-talented British comedian, actor, writer, director, presenter, and producer who has achieved many groundbreaking feats in her career. In 2000, she became the first Black female stand-up comedian to sell out a West End theatre and the first Black British performer to appear at Harlem's Apollo Theatre.

Angie le Mar was born on 27 October 1965, in Lewisham, London, to Jamaican parents. She had four older brothers. She attended several schools in Lewisham and later discovered she was dyslexic after finishing her education. Despite challenging school experiences, she found her passion in drama, performing in her first play at age 10 and joining drama clubs and groups such as the Lewisham Drama Club and Second Wave Women's Drama Group.

She attended the Barbara Speake Stage School and the Afro Sax drama club, run by prominent actors Larrington Walker, Ellen Thomas, and Treva Etienne. She co-founded the theatre company Bemarrow Sisters, which operated for seven years.

Her comedy career began in 1985 with open spots and warm-ups at community events. By the 1990s, she was a notable figure in the emerging Black comedy scene, sharing stages with comedians from the BBC series, The Real McCoy. She earned the title, The Queen of Black Comedy.

In 1994, she launched her professional theatre career with Funny Black Women on the Edge, which she wrote, directed, and performed in. The show premiered in London and later appeared at the Edinburgh Fringe Festival. She continued to produce and reprise successful shows, solidifying her reputation in both the UK and the US comedy circuits.

Her reputation took her to the mainstream comedy circuit where she became a regular act at established comedy clubs including Up The Creek, Jongleurs and The Comedy Store, culminating in her performance of her sell-out one woman show, Off The Hook, at the Apollo Theatre, Shaftesbury Avenue, in 2000. She also gained international acclaim when she performed at the Apollo Theatre, Harlem, New York, and the Comedy Act Theatre in Los Angeles. She claimed the distinction of being the first black British comedian to appear at the Harlem Apollo, a noted venue for African-American performers.

She has written and directed numerous plays, such as, The Brothers, in 2006 and, Do You Know Where Your Daughter Is?, in 2007, which was inspired by a real-life phone call she received as a radio presenter. These productions were well-received and toured extensively.

As a way of celebrating 25 years in the entertainment industry, she held An Audience with Angie Le Mar at the Barbican Theatre in 2010. Through her production company, Straight To Audience Productions, she mentors young people and offers workshops in writing, directing, and stand-up comedy.

She has made many television appearances on shows like The Real McCoy, Late Licence, Get Up Stand Up, and Loose Women. She has also been a commentator on Grumpy Old Women and appeared in Holby City. Her radio work includes stints on BBC GLR, Choice FM, and BBC London.

A published author, she wrote her memoir, Full Circle: Turning Your Gift Around, which shared her experiences in show business and aimed to inspire young people and Black women to achieve their dreams. She highlights the challenges and progress in the industry over the years and offers practical advice for aspiring performers.

As a married mother of three, she continues to captivate diverse audiences with her comedy, acting, and speaking engagements. She is a sought-after keynote speaker, addressing various organizations, including UNESCO and major corporations. Through the Angie Le Mar School of Expression, she empowers young people to understand the business side of show business, encouraging them to pursue their passions with confidence.

First Black woman to be employed by the BBC

Una Marson — (1905-1965)

Una Marson was a Jamaican feminist, activist and writer, producing poems, plays and radio programmes. She travelled to London in 1932 and became the first black woman to be employed by the BBC during World War II. In 1942, she became the producer of the programme, Calling the West Indies, turning it into Caribbean Voices, which became an important forum for Caribbean literary work.

Una Maud Victoria Marson was born on 6 February 1905, in St. Elizabeth, Jamaica. She was the youngest of six children. Her father, Reverend Solomon Marson, was a Baptist minister, and her mother, Ada Marson, was a talented organist. She had a middle-class upbringing and attended Hampton High, a girls' boarding school, but her education was cut short due to financial issues following her father's death.

Despite these challenges, she made great strides in her career. After working as a volunteer social worker and then worked for the Salvation Army and YMCA. She became assistant editor of the Jamaican political journal Jamaica Critic in 1926. By 1928, she launched her own magazine, The Cosmopolitan, becoming Jamaica's first female editor and publisher. The magazine featured articles on feminism, local social issues, and workers' rights, encouraging women to enter the workforce and become politically active.

She published her first collection of poems, Tropic Reveries, in 1930, which won the Musgrave Medal from the Institute of Jamaica. Despite the closure of The Cosmopolitan due to financial difficulties, she continued to write and decided to move to London in 1932 to reach a broader audience.

Arriving in London, she faced racial discrimination and became deeply involved in activism. She worked with the League of Coloured Peoples and served as a delegate to the International Alliance of Women. She also worked for the Ethiopian Legation and accompanied Haile Selassie to the League of Nations.

Returning to Jamaica in 1936, she continued her literary and activist work, publishing The Moth and the Stars and staging plays, London Calling and Pocomania at the Ward Theatre, Jamaica. She was active in the Poetry League of Jamaica and founded clubs to support young Black writers and artists. She also established the Jamaica Save the Children Fund to help disadvantaged children.

In 1938, she returned to London, working with the Jamaican Save the Children Fund and the Jamaican Standard. She then began working at the British Broadcasting Corporation (BBC) and was the first black female broadcaster to work there. She started as a script writer in the television studio but later in the War years, she became the producer of, Calling the West Indies, a radio program that enjoyed a lot of popularity among West Indians. It became known as Caribbean Voices. Black World War II soldiers would have their messages read on the radio to their families, The popularity of the programme was underscored by her work as not only did she communicate to West Indians news about what was happening overseas, it became a crucial platform for Caribbean literature.

After the war, she returned to Jamaica and worked with the Gleaner Company as organising secretary and served as general editor of the Pioneer Press. In the 1950s, she moved to Washington, D.C., to continue her writing and education. She married and later divorced Peter Staples, travelling between England, Israel, and Jamaica.

She visited Jamaica twice during 1960, returning for residence in 1961. She went back to serving as executive secretary at the Jamaica Save the Children Fund. She continued travelling to other countries to work on different projects, but her health was intermittently threatened by illness and this made working difficult.

In March 1965, while on assignment in Haifa, Israel, she became ill and decided to return to Jamaica. She was admitted to St. Josephs Hospital, Kingston on the May 5 1965 following a heart attack and she died the next day aged 60.

She was buried on the 10 May at the Half-Way-Tree Parish Cemetery.

She left a legacy of literary excellence and activism, promoting Caribbean culture and championing the rights of women and the marginalized.

First Black British News Reporter

Sir Trevor McDonald OBE – (1939-)

Sir Trevor McDonald OBE is a Trinidadian-born British newsreader and journalist, best known for his career as a news presenter. After working as a print and broadcast journalist in Trinidad he was employed by BBC Radio as a producer, based in London but still broadcasting to the Caribbean. In 1973, he began his long association with Independent Television News as a general reporter and was ITN's first black reporter. He was promoted in 1992 as the sole presenter of News at Ten and became a well-known face on British television screens.

Trevor Lawson McDonald, born George Lawson McDonald, was born on 16 August 1939, in San Fernando, Trinidad and Tobago to his mother, Geraldine, who was of African descent and his father, Lawson, of Indian descent. He was educated at Naparima College, which was a prestigious secondary school in Trinidad. He got his first part-time job at Radio Trinidad and then in International Relations at the University College of the West Indies. After graduating he worked as a journalist for several Trinidadian newspapers including the Trinidadian Guardian and the Daily Mirror. On his first major assignment, he was sent to London in 1962 to report on talks at Marlborough House which culminated in setting a date for Trinidad's Independence.

In 1964 he married Beryl. They had two children Joanne and Tim. They divorced in 1985.

In 1969 he moved to London pursuing a career in broadcasting, joining BBC Radio as a producer and later worked as a newsreader for BBC World Service. In 1973 he joined ITN as a general reporter and was the first black reporter for ITN. He was a talented interviewer using a calm and authoritative delivery.

In 1980 he spent some time with the ITN-produced Channel 4 News returning to ITN in 1989 presenting the early evening news.

In 1986 having divorced Beryl, he married Josephine Goode who he met at ITN, and they had a child called Jack. They divorced in 2020.

In 1989 he became the first black person to be awarded the Royal Television Society's Journalist of the Year award. He has also won several other awards, including two BAFTA Awards.

In the 1992 Queen's New Years Honours list he was awarded the Order of the British Empire (OBE) for his services to broadcasting and charity.

In 1992 he got the position of sole presenter of News at Ten which was ITN's flagship news program and he held this position for seven years. He managed to convey complex stories news stories clear and concise, and he was respected for his impartiality.

In 1999 he was knighted for his services to journalism. He also presented the News at Ten until the program was axed. He moved to present the ITV Evening News. News at Ten was briefly relaunched on 22 January 2001 then axed again and replaced by ITV News at 10.30. Then he presented a current affairs programme called Tonight with Trevor McDonald until 2005.

In 1999 he was awarded the British Academy of Film and Television Art's Richard Dimbleby Award for Outstanding Contribution to Television and in 2011 was given the Academy Fellowship in the TV Baftas.

He is a strong advocate for social justice and has been involved in many philanthropic, charitable and community initiatives.

He has written several books and presented and produced a number of documentaries.

In 2004 he was appointed Chancellor of London South Bank University which held until 2015 to promote the university and raise its profile. He also set up the Trevor McDonald Scholarship Fund providing financial assistance to students from disadvantaged backgrounds.

He is a patron of several charities including the Prince's Trust, the Nelson Mandela Foundation and the National Literacy Trust. He has also worked to raise awareness of social issues such as racism, poverty and homelessness.

He holds honorary degrees from the University of Plymouth and Liverpool John Moores University

He was awarded Newscaster of the year in 1993, 1997 and 1999.

First Black female newsreader on British national television

Moira Stuart CBE – (1949-)

Moira Stuart, CBE is a British presenter and broadcaster. She was the first female newsreader of Caribbean heritage to appear on British national television, having worked on BBC News from 1981.

Moira Clare Ruby Stuart was born at the Royal Free Hospital in London, on 2 September 1949, to Caribbean parents. Her mother Marjorie Gordon was born in Dominica, and her father Harold Stuart was a lawyer from Barbados, though they divorced when she was ten months old. She has two sisters, Sandra and Sharon.

She was educated in London until she was 13, attending Our Lady's Convent RC High School, Stamford Hill. She then moved with her family to Bermuda for a time, returning to London when she was 15 to attend college.

She began working with the BBC in the 1970s as a production assistant in the radio Talks and Documentaries department. She was a continuity announcer and newsreader for both BBC Radio 4 and BBC Radio 2, reading her first Radio 4 news bulletin in 1978. In 1980 she played Darong in series one of game show The Adventure Game. She moved to television news in 1981, when she co-presented News After Noon.

She is acknowledged as being the UK's first female African-Caribbean and black television newsreader. Since 27 August 1981 she has presented on every news bulletin devised on BBC Television apart from the Ten O'Clock News. She has also appeared on The News Quiz and presented the news on the BBC's Breakfast with Frost programme each Sunday and its successor programme Sunday AM with Andrew Marr.

She presented the news for BBC Breakfast. However, BBC Breakfast moved to a new studio with a new look on 2 May 2006 and the entire news content was presented by two main presenters. She retained her slot on BBC's

Sunday AM show and continued to present some weekend television bulletins on BBC One. She also worked on other long-form programmes for other BBC channels, including BBC Four.

In 1988 she was voted Best Newscaster of the Year by the TV and Radio Industries Club Awards.

In 1989 she was voted Best Television Personality by the Women of Achievement Awards.

In 1994 she was named Best Female Television Personality by the Black Journalists' Association.

In 1997 she was named Best Media Personality by The Voice newspaper.

In 2001 she was appointed an Officer of the British Empire (OB) for services to broadcasting.

In 2002 she was named Media Personality of 2002 at the EMMA Awards.

In April 2007 it was announced that she would be leaving Sunday AM, losing a regular TV slot. This prompted an angry public backlash, accusing the BBC of ageism and sexism. The BBC initially declined to comment on why she was no longer being used, but rumours circulated within the BBC and commercial newsrooms that she had been removed because she was considered too old at 57, although Anna Ford had continued anchoring the BBC One O'Clock News until her retirement at 62. This was denied by Director-General of the BBC Mark Thompson when he was questioned by a House of Commons culture, media and sport select committee.

Her 26-year career with BBC Television News was brought to a close on 3 October 2007, when the BBC announced her departure. In total, her experience had spanned 34 years of BBC radio and TV.

A keen music lover, she deputised for Humphrey Lyttelton on his BBC Radio 2 Best of Jazz programme. She has participated in the BBC Jazz Awards as a compère, and features as a narrator on Soweto Kinch's 2006 jazz-rap album A Life in the Day of B19: Tales of the Tower Block.

She has served on various boards and judging panels including Amnesty International, the Royal Television Society, BAFTA, United Nations Association, the Orange Prize, the London Fair Play Consortium, the Human Genetics Commission, the Queen's Anniversary Prize, and the Grierson Trust.

In 2006 she received an honorary doctorate from the University of Edinburgh, which was the university where her grandparents had met. Also in 2006 she had a cameo role playing herself in the Ricky Gervais television comedy Extras, supposedly involved in supplying drugs to Ronnie Corbett.

On 2 June 2007 she hosted the BBC One topical news quiz show Have I Got News for You and was well received by the public.

In 2008, 2009 and 2010, she appeared in a series of advertisements for HMRC promoting tax-return procedures.

In January 2010 she returned to BBC News, reading the news for The Chris Evans Breakfast Show. She presented her last bulletins for the show on 14 December 2018.

In 2012 she was awarded the degree Honorary Doctor of Letters by De Montfort University.

In 2013 received an honorary doctorate from Canterbury Christ Church University

In March 2014 she began hosting the Sunday late-night BBC Radio 2 programme Music Until Midnight. She alternates this Sunday-night slot with Oscar-winning songwriter Don Black. She has also presented music documentary series for Radio 2, including Strong and Sassy - Inspiring Women of Jazz, featuring Carmen McRae, Sarah Vaughan, Adelaide Hall, Anita O'Day and Lena Horne, and Jazz Guitar Greats.

She began as a morning news presenter for Classic FM in February 2019 and, from July 2019 she was a weekend presenter with her own Saturday show.

From 9 August 2020 she has hosted a new Sunday evening series, Moira Stuart Meets..., on Classic FM.

In 2020 she received the Harvey Lee Award for Outstanding Contribution to Broadcasting at Broadcasting Press Guild Awards.

In 2022 she received a Commander of the Order of the British Empire (CBE) for services to media. She also received an honorary degree of Doctor of Letters from Northumbria University, Newcastle.

First Black woman to win a gold medal in the Physics News Award

Margaret Aderin-Pocock MBE – (1968-)

Margaret Aderin-Pocock MBE is a British space scientist and science educator. She is an honorary research associate of University College London's Department of Physics and Astronomy. In 2020 she was awarded the Institute of Physics William Thomson, Lord Kelvin Medal and Prize for her public engagement in physics. She is the first black woman to win a gold medal in the Physics News Award. She has also earned the title of the president-elect of the British Science Association.

Margaret Ebunoluwa Aderin was born on 9 March 1968 to Nigerian parents, Caroline Philips and Justus Adebayo Aderin, in London. She was raised in Camden, London. Her middle name Ebunoluwa comes from the Yoruba words "ebun" meaning "gift" and Oluwa meaning "God", which is also a variant form of the word "Oluwabunmi" or "Olubunmi", meaning "gift of God" in Yoruba. She attended La Sainte Union Convent School in North London. She is dyslexic. As a child, when she told a teacher she wanted to be an astronaut, it was suggested she try nursing, as that was also scientific. She gained four A-Levels in maths, physics, chemistry, and biology.

She studied at Imperial College London, graduating in 1990 with a BSc in physics. She completed her PhD in mechanical engineering in 1994.

From 1996 to 1999 she worked at the Defence Evaluation and Research Agency, a branch of the UK Ministry of Defence. Initially, she worked as a systems scientist on aircraft missile warning systems, and from 1997 to 1999 she was a project manager developing hand-held instruments to detect landmines.

In 1999 she returned to Imperial College on a fellowship from the Science and Technology Facilities Council to work with the group developing a high-resolution spectrograph for the Gemini telescope in Chile. The telescope examines and analyses starlight to improve understanding of distant stars.

She worked on managing the observation instruments for the Aeolus satellite, measuring wind speeds to help the investigate climate change. She is a pioneering figure in communicating science to the public, specifically school children, and also runs her own company, Science Innovation Ltd, which engages children and adults all over the world with the wonders of space science.

She is committed to inspiring new generations of astronauts, engineers, and scientists and has to numerous children, many of them at inner-city schools, telling them how and why she became a scientist, busting myths about careers, class, and gender. She also helps encourage scientific endeavours of young people by being a celebrity judge at the National Science + Engineering Competition where the finals are held annually at The Big Bang Fair to reward young people who have achieved excellence in a science, technology, engineering, or maths project.

She was the scientific consultant for the 2009 mini-series Paradox, and also appeared on Doctor Who Confidential. In February 2011 she presented, Do We Really Need the Moon?, on BBC Two. She also presented In Orbit: How Satellites Rule Our World on BBC Two on 26 March 2012.

As well as presenting The Sky at Night with Chris Lintott, she has presented Stargazing on CBeebies with Chris Jarvis and Out of This World on CBBC with her daughter Lauren. She has also appeared on Would I Lie to You?, Dara O Briain's Go 8 Bit, Richard Osman's House of Games, and QI.

In 2005 she was awarded the Certificate of Excellence by the Champions Club UK

In the 2009 New Years Honours list, she was appointed a Member of the Order of the British Empire (MBE) for services to science education. She also was awarded an honorary doctorate from Staffordshire University for contributions to the field of science education.

In 2011 she won the New Talent award from the WFTV (Women in Film and Television)

In 2013 Yale University Centre for Dyslexia gave her the Out of the box award.

In 2014 an article in the Daily Mail claimed that she, along with Hiranya Peiris, a Sri Lankan-born British astrophysicist, had been selected to discuss results from the Background Imaging of Cosmic Extragalactic Polarization 2 (BICEP-2) experiment on Newsnight because of their gender and ethnicity. The comments were condemned by the mainstream media, the Royal Astronomical Society and their university. The Daily Mail backed down within days acknowledging that the women were chosen because they are highly qualified in their fields. Sadly, this is not an isolated case. Her race and gender are constantly used to question her suitability, rather than acknowledging her undoubted ability.

She is an honorary research associate of University College London's Department of Physics and Astronomy. She also has been made an Honorary Doctor of Science by the University of Bath.

In 2017 she was made an Honorary Doctor of Science by Loughborough University.

In 2018 she was made an Honorary Doctor of Science by the University of Leicester.

In 2020–21 she served as a commissioner on the UK Government's Commission on Race and Ethnic Disparities (CRED). The commission's controversial report concluded that the claim the country is still institutionally racist is not borne out by the evidence, but experts complained that the report misrepresented evidence, and that recommendations from business leaders were ignored. After the report was published, she stated that it was not denying institutional racism existed but said the commission had not discovered evidence of it in the areas it had looked.

In 2020 the Institute of Physics William Thomson awarded her the Lord Kelvin Medal and Prize for her public engagement in physics.

She discussed her life on BBC Radio 4's Desert Island Discs in March 2010 and has been the subject of numerous biographical articles on women in science. She has been ranked in the Powerlist as one of the most influential Black Britons.

Since December 2021, she has been a question-setter for the Channel 4 game show I Literally Just Told You.

She married Martin Pocock in 2002. They have one daughter, Lauren, born in 2010, and live in Guildford, Surrey.

First Black Studies professor in the UK

Kehinde Andrews – (1983-)

Kehinde Andrews is a British academic and author specialising in Black Studies. He is a Professor of Black Studies in the School of Social Sciences at Birmingham City University. He is the director of the Centre for Critical Social Research, founder of the Harambee Organisation of Black Unity and co-chair of the UK Black Studies Association. He is the first black studies professor in the UK and led the establishment of the first black studies programme in Europe at Birmingham City University.

Kehinde Nkosi Andrews was born in January 1983, growing up in Birmingham. His mother is half white English and half Jamaican, and a university graduate born in Britain. His father was born in Jamaica and came to the UK in his early teens, leaving school with limited qualifications. He was a product of a school system that had no interest in the career prospects of black boys.

His parents were committed Black activists, who established numerous organisations and promoted the Black radical intellectual tradition.

He says he suffered an identity crisis in high school. He travelled every day to a good school in a predominantly white area. He saw that black students were pigeonholed destined to not do well. He was one of few black children in the top set, all the others were at the bottom. So to his young self doing well meant following his white friends. Hence he grew up rebelling against everything his parents stood for. He ignored the values and culture he had been brought up with and started emulating the behaviour and interests of his white friends, going to the pub and watch England play, singing patriotic songs, listening to country music.

His parents were focused on improving education and his education in Black studies began when he started picking up books lying around his home. He travelled on a Voluntary Services Overseas youth exchange programme to post apartheid South Africa, where he realised, despite legal changes, Black people were still oppressed. He returned to Britain a completely different person. He completed a Masters degree in Social Research and earned a PhD. in Sociology and Cultural Studies from the University of Birmingham in 2011. His thesis was entitled "Back to Black: Black Radicalism and the Supplementary School Movement."

He was influenced by all the work on nurseries, Saturday schools, bookshops and local organisations that his parents started. He was a founding member of the Harambee Organisation of Black Unity, which ran a hostel, the Marcus Garvey nursery, and the Harriet Tubman bookshop.

He created the Black studies degree course at Birmingham City University which launched in2017. It was designed to create the radical Black education that he grew up with and incorporate it into the university. In the second year of this course, his students take a placement, where they apply their knowledge within an organisation that works in Black communities. Black studies is an interdisciplinary subject that focuses attention on the experiences, perspectives and contributions of people from the African diaspora. It emerged in America in the 1960s and has taken time to reach Britain because despite the diversity of students, the staff and therefore academic interests have remained overwhelmingly exclusive and white. Black British-born staff make up a small fraction of full-time staff, and face barriers to promotion once employed. The fact is that black studies did not emerge sooner because there has not been a critical mass of staff who could teach the subject.

He regularly appears in the media discussing issues of race and racism, colonialism and slavery, and British nationalism. He is a frequent contributor to The Guardian, and has written articles for The Independent, New Statesman, CNN, open Democracy, and often appears as a guest on the BBC and Good Morning Britain.

In 2016 he criticised universities in the United Kingdom for institutional racism, specifically a lack of diversity in students' assigned readings.

In 2017 he spoke at the Oxford Union, arguing that British education perpetuates racism. He also gave a TEDxYouth talk in Birmingham entitled 'How to stay radical within an institution' exploring how Black Studies can exist within the historically racist institution of the university.

In 2018 he tweeted that the sight of the flag of England stirred the same feelings in him as the sight of a Confederate Flag does for African Americans.

In 2019 he took part in a debate on whether or not the West should pay reparations for slavery at Intelligence Squared. He also spoke about his book Back to Black at the John Hope Franklin Centre for Interdisciplinary and International Studies at Duke University and gave a talk at Tate Liverpool on the role of Black radicalism in the United Kingdom and the United States.

In 2019 he appeared on Good Morning Britain, arguing that the RAF bombing of Nazi Germany constituted a war crime and equated the racial views of Winston Churchill to those of Adolf Hitler.

He narrated the film The Psychosis of Whiteness, which explores race and racism through cinematic representations of the slave trade.

In July 2019 he criticised the idea that prominent non-white members of the Conservative Party is automatically a good thing, saying that a "cabinet packed with ministers with brown skin wearing Tory masks represents the opposition of racial progress".

In August 2020 he joined calls to drop Rule, Britannia! and Land of Hope and Glory from the Last Night of the Proms, saying the lyrics contained racist propaganda from a time where Britain was the leading slave-trading nation in the world.

In June 2021 he described Elizabeth II as probably the number one symbol of white supremacy in the entire world.

Sadly in 2022 his wife died of cancer.

He is a dedicated educator looking to advance the knowledge and future for the community and global Black Diaspora.

First Sickle-Cell and Thalassemia nurse specialist

Dame Elizabeth Nneka Anionwu DBE FRCN – (1947-)

Dame Elizabeth Nneka Anionwu DBE FRCN is a British nurse, health care administrator, lecturer, and Emeritus Professor of Nursing at University of West London. In 1979 she became the United Kingdom's first sickle-cell and cell and thalassemia nurse specialist, helping establish the Brent Sickle Cell and Thalassaemia Counselling centre with consultant haematologist Milica Brozovic.

Elizabeth Nneka Anionwu was born Elizabeth Mary Furlong in Birmingham, England, to an Irish mother and a Nigerian father. Her mother, Mary Maureen Furlong, was in her second year studying Classics at Newnham College, Cambridge University. Her father, Lawrence Odiatu Victor Anionwu, was studying law at Cambridge University. This was 1947 so the fallout from their affair was dramatic, but despite pressure to give up her baby for adoption, her mother decided otherwise.

Her upbringing was heavily affected by moving between institutions and family. She spent just over two years living with her mother, a relationship that ended when her stepfather, who did not accept her and drank heavily, started to physically abuse her. She was placed in a catholic children's home where she was cared for by nuns, including several years in the Nazareth House convent in Birmingham.

She left school at 16 with seven O-levels. Her choice of career was influenced by a nun who cared for her eczema. She applied to several London teaching hospitals to train as a nurse, but despite having seven good O-level grades, well above the minimum requirement, she did not receive any replies. She started to work as a school nurse at Paddington General Hospital. She continued her education to become a nurse, health visitor, and tutor.

She travelled to the United States to study counselling for sickle-cell and thalassemia centres as courses were not then available in the UK. In 1979 she worked with Dr Milica Brozovic to create the first UK sickle-cell and thalassemia counselling centre in the London Borough of Brent. This was the first of over 30 centres in the UK to come using the Brent Centre as a model. For six years, she was Britain's first and only sickle cell nurse specialist. The NHS did not consider sickle cell to be a significant public health issue as it mainly affected black people.

Shortly before her 25th birthday she reconnected with her father Lawrence Anionwu, a barrister and former Nigerian Ambassador to Italy and the Vatican. She visited Nigeria frequently and later changed her surname to Anionwu. She has credited her father as the first person to provide her with career advice. Sadly he died in 1980 aged 59.

In 1981 she gave birth to her daughter, Akuza. However the relationship with Akuza's father broke down and fortunately she received support from her family and friends.

In 1990 she was a lecturer at the Institute of Child Health, University College London, later promoted to senior lecturer, with the help of Professor Marcus Pembrey, she taught a course at University College London for National Health Service (NHS) staff members working with communities affected or at risk of sickle-cell disease, cystic fibrosis, Tay–Sachs disease and thalassaemia.

She was appointed Dean of the School of Adult Nursing Studies and a Professor of Nursing at the University of West London. In 1998 she created the Mary Seacole Centre for Nursing Practice at the University of West London.

In 2005 she wrote, A Short History of Mary Seacole. In 2003 she became a Trustee and subsequently Vice-Chairperson of the Mary Seacole Memorial Statue Appeal. Following the unveiling of the statue at St Thomas' Hospital in June 2016 she was appointed a Life Patron of the Mary Seacole Trust.

She is also a Patron of other charities; the Sickle Cell Society, the Nigerian Nurses Charitable Association UK. She was the Vice President of Unite/Community Practitioners and Health Visitors Association and the Honorary Advisor to England's Chief Nursing Officer's Black & Minority Ethnic Strategic Advisory Group

She has published many journals and informative pamphlets for family members of sickle-cell patients, nurses who care for sickle-cell patients, and information for the general population.

In the 2001 Queen's Birthday Honours list, she was appointed Commander of the Order of the British Empire (CBE) for her services to nursing.

In 2004 she was awarded the Fellowship of the Royal College of Nursing (FRCN) for developing the sickle-cell and thalassemia counselling centre.

In 2007 she retired. Following her retirement, she was appointed Emeritus Professor for Nursing at the University of West London.

In 2010 she was inducted into the Nursing Times Nursing Hall of Fame for the dedication to the Development of Nurse-led Services. She also received the 2015 Lifetime Achievement Award on Divas of Colour.

In 2016 she published her memoirs called Mixed Blessing from a Cambridge Union.

In the 2017 Queen's New Years Honours list, she was appointed Dame Commander of the Order of the British Empire (DBE) for services to nursing and the Mary Seacole Statue Appeal. She was awarded a Fellowship of the Queen's Nursing Institute in October 2017.

In 2019 in recognition of her major contribution to nursing, research and campaigning, the University of St Andrews conferred on her the degree of Doctor of Science, honoris causa. Also, in 2019 she was awarded an honorary doctorate from Birmingham City University, in recognition of her major contribution to the nursing profession.

In October 2019 at the Pride of Britain Awards, she received the Lifetime Achievement Award, in recognition of her passion for nursing and dedication to reducing health inequalities. The presentation was made by Janet Jackson.

On 31 May 2020 she was the subject of an episode of Desert Island Discs on BBC Radio 4. She was on the list of the BBC's 100 Women (BBC) announced later that year on 23 November.

In May 2023 she carried the Sovereign's Orb in the Royal procession at the Coronation of King Charles III and Camilla.

First Black person to have a number-one hit in the UK Singles Chart

Winifred Atwell – (1910-1983)

Winifred Atwell was a Trinidadian pianist who enjoyed great popularity in Britain and Australia from the 1950s with a series of boogie-woogie and ragtime hits, selling over 20 million records. She was the first black person to have a number-one hit in the UK Singles Chart and is still the only female instrumentalist to do so.

Una Winifred Atwell was born in Tunapuna in Trinidad and Tobago. Her actual birth date is either 27 February 1910 or 27 April 1914. She played piano from the age of four. Her family owned a pharmacy and she trained as a pharmacist and joined the family business.

She continued playing the piano performing locally and for American servicemen at the Air Force base. She learned to play the popular boogie-woogie style.

She left Trinidad in the early 1940s travelling to the United States to study piano. A newspaper clipping revealed that she played in a concert at The Town Hall in New York on 10th May 1945, as part of a presentation by the Altruss Opera Company starring Paul A. Smith, a well-known tenor.

She left for England and from 1946 studied at the London Royal Academy of Music eventually becoming the first female pianist to be awarded the highest grade for musicianship. She played honky-tonk piano at London clubs and theatres to support herself.

On 21 October 1946 she appeared on BBC TV in the Stars In Your Eyes show and this was quickly followed by several radio appearances on the Light Programme. In January 1947 she was heading the bill of Come to the Show at the Empire Theatre, Belfast, where she was billed as, radio's most versatile pianist. Many radio appearances followed including the Variety Bandbox show. She appeared on the variety stages too, sometimes with another pianist called Donald Thorne.

In 1946 she met Lew Levisohn and they married a year later. Levisohn was a variety artiste who gave up his stage career to become her manager. They had no children. Encouraged by Levisohn, she turned her attention to playing ragtime music.

She attracted attention with an unscheduled appearance at the Casino Theatre, where she was substituting for an ill star. She caught the attention of impressario Bernard Delfont, who put her on a long-term contract in 1948. She was championed by popular disc jockey Jack Jackson, who introduced her to Decca promotions manager Hugh Mendl.

She released a number of discs for Decca in 1951 that were well received. Jezebel sold well, however, Cross Hands Boogie was hugely popular. Black and White become a radio standard.

Lew Levisohn staged her performances by having her first play a concert grand piano, then a beaten-up old upright piano. This was purchased from a Battersea junk shop for 50 shillings and became famous as her other piano. It travelled with her all over the world. Richard Stilgoe revealed that he was the owner of the famous "other piano".

When she first came to Britain, she initially earned only a few pounds a week. By the mid-1950s, this had shot up to over $10,000. By 1952 her popularity had spread internationally. Her hands were insured with Lloyd's of London for £40,000, the policy stipulating that she was never to wash dishes. In 1951, she signed a record contract with Decca, and her sales were soon 30,000 discs a week. She was by far the biggest selling pianist of her time. Her 1954 hit Let's Have Another Party was the first piano instrumental to reach number one in the UK Singles Chart.

In 1952 she appeared in the first Royal Variety Performance for the new queen, Elizabeth II. She closed her act with Britannia Rag, which she composed specially for the occasion. It reached Number Five in the pop charts.

She is the only holder of two gold and two silver discs for piano music in Britain and was the first black artist in the UK to sell a million records. Millions of copies of her sheet music were sold, and she went on to record her best-known hits.

Her peak came in the second half of the 1950s. She also made several TV performances. Her career earned her a fortune and would have extended further to the US but for issues of race. Her breakthrough appearance should have been on The Ed Sullivan Show in 1956, but on arrival in America she was confronted with problems of selling the show in the south with a British-sounding black woman. The appearance was never recorded.

In 1955 she arrived in Australia as an international celebrity. Her tour broke box-office records bringing in £600,000 in box-office receipts. She was paid AUS$5,000 a week (the equivalent of around $50,000 today), making her the highest paid star from a Commonwealth country to visit Australia up to that time.

Her popularity in Australia led to her settling in Sydney in the 1970s. She became an Australian citizen two years before her death

She was also a skilled interpreter of classical music and never made a secret of the fact that her heart lay with classical music. Despite her success with ragtime music, she never lost sight of her original ambition to become a concert pianist.

In 1969 she was awarded Trinidad and Tobago's national award, the Gold Hummingbird Medal, for her achievements in music.

She bought an apartment on the beach front in Flight Deck, an apartment complex in Collaroy in Sydney, as a base for her worldwide performance commitments. However, she was nevertheless keenly aware of prejudice and injustice and was outspoken about racism in Australia. She always donated her services in a charity concert on Sundays, the proceeds going to orphanages and needy children. She spoke out against the third world conditions endured by Australian Aborigines, which made headlines during an outback tour of the country in 1962.

Dismissing racism as a factor in her own life, she said she felt she was spoiled by the public. She also created headlines in the 1960s with her dieting, slimming from sixteen to twelve stone on what appeared to be a protein diet.

Though a dynamic stage personality, she was, in person, a shy, retiring and soft-spoken woman of modesty. Eloquent and intellectual, she was well read and keenly interested in and informed about issues and current events. Voracious in her reading habits and a devotee of crosswords, she had a e love of mangoes, a dislike of new shoes, and a keen interest in televised cricket, supporting England. She was also a devout Catholic and modestly played the organ for her parish church.

Though she attempted to keep up with music trends, rock and roll hastened the end of her career. By the 1960s tastes in popular music had changed rapidly and her rapid style of piano playing, with its famous tinny bar-room sound, went out of fashion.

Sadly in 1977 her husband Lew Levisohn passed away.

She often returned to her native Trinidad, and bought a house in Saint Augustine. In the early 1980s, her sense of loss following her husband's death made her consider returning to Trinidad to live, but she found the weather too hot.

She suffered a stroke in 1980 and officially retired in 1981. Her only non-private performances were as an organist in her parish church.

In 1983 following an electrical fire that destroyed her home, she suffered a heart attack and died while staying with friends. She is buried beside husband Lew Levisohn in South Gundurimba Private Cemetery in northern New South Wales.

She left her estate to the Australian Guide Dogs for the Blind and a small amount to her goddaughter. However, a cousin of Lew Levisohn contested her will and is reported to have been granted $30,000 from her estate.

There is some uncertainty over her date and year of birth. Many sources suggest 27 February 1914, but there is a strong suggestion that her birthday was 27 April. Most sources give her year of birth as 1914, but her gravestone states that she died at the age of 73, suggesting that she was born in 1910.

She was one of the most successful and beloved entertainers of her time, as well as the first Caribbean artist to become a household name in an era when Black performers in Britain had more chance of success if they were American.

Elton John and several other musicians called Atwell one of their musical heroes.

In November 2020 a Nubian Jak Community Trust black plaque honouring Atwell was unveiled at the former site of a hair salon she owned in Chaucer Road, Brixton, south London.

First Black female book publisher

Margaret Yvonne Busby, CBE, Hon. FRSL – (1944-)

Margaret Yvonne Busby, CBE, Hon. FRSL, also known as Nana Akua Ackon, is a Ghanaian-born publisher, editor, writer and broadcaster, resident in the UK. She became Britain's youngest and first black female book publisher when in 1967 she co-founded the London-based publishing house Allison and Busby with Clive Allison.

Margaret Yvonne Busby was born in 1944, in Accra, Ghana, to parents Dr George Busby and Mrs Sarah Busby (née Christian), who both had family links to the Caribbean. She comes from a family of doctors and lawyers. Her father, the son of a tailor, won a scholarship to study medicine, first in Trinidad then Edinburgh and Dublin. He practised in London before serving in the Ghanaian countryside; a blue plaque now commemorates his pre-NHS commitment to the poor people of Walthamstow.

Her parents sent her and two siblings to England to be educated when she was five. She first attended a school in the Lake District followed by Charters Towers School, an international girls' boarding-school in Bexhill-on-Sea, Sussex, with her sister. After passing her O-levels aged 14, she left school at 15, went back to Ghana and took her A-levels at 16, then spent a year at a college in Cambridge.

From the age of 17 she studied English at Bedford College, where she edited her college literary magazine as well as publishing her own poetry. She graduated at 20 with a BA Honours degree.

She was married to British jazz musician and educator Lionel Grigson.

She met Clive Allison, her future business partner, while at university and they decided to start a publishing company. After graduating, she worked briefly at the Cresset Press, while setting up Allison and Busby (A & B) with Allison. Their first books were published in 1967, making her the then youngest publisher as well as the first black African woman book publisher in the UK.

She was Allison & Busby's Editorial Director for 20 years, publishing many notable authors including Sam Greenlee (author of The Spook Who Sat by the Door, the first novel published by A & B, in 1969). Allison & Busby was bought out by WH Allen in 1987. There was no job for her, but Allison was kept on. She became editorial director of Earthscan which is an English-language publisher of books and journals on climate change, sustainable development and environmental technology for academic, professional and general readers, before pursuing a freelance career as an editor, writer, and critic.

As a journalist, she has written for The Guardian (mainly book reviews or obituaries of artists and activists), The Observer, The Independent, The Sunday Times, the New Statesman and elsewhere, for both the general press and specialist journals.

In the 1980s she was a founding member of the multi-racial organization Greater Access to Publishing (GAP), which ran campaigns promoting increased Black representation in British publishing, holding a conference in November 1987 to highlight publishing as an option for Black women.

In 1992 she published an anthology, Daughters of Africa: An International Anthology of Words and Writings by Women of African Descent from the Ancient Egyptian to the Present. She used her own bookshelves and experience of looking for things which were not taught at school or university. It included contributions from over 200 women across many genres.

It pioneered African writing, by not only writing about their families, communities and countries, but also writing themselves into the African literary history and African historiography. It helped establish women writers and reclaim the woman's role as the creator and carrier of many African societies' narratives, as the traditional storytelling session was a women's domain.

In the 2005 New Years Honours list she was awarded the Officer of the Order of the British Empire (OBE), for services to Literature and to Publishing.

She edited a follow-up in 2019 entitled New Daughters of Africa: An International Anthology of Writing by Women of African Descent, featuring over 200 writers from across the African Diaspora.

In connection with the 2019 anthology, the Margaret Busby New Daughters of Africa Award was created by the publisher, in partnership with SOAS, University of London, to benefit an African woman student. The award would cover tuition fees and accommodation at International Students House, London.

She has contributed to a number of books including co-authoring, co-editing, writing introductions and forwards

She was a prominent participant in the major 2019 exhibition Get Up, Stand Up Now: Generations of Black Creative Pioneers at Somerset House, celebrating the impact of 50 years of Black creativity in Britain and beyond. It contained the work of about 100 artists and she wrote an introductory essay for the catalogue, as well as participating in events.

She worked regularly for radio and television from the late 1960s, including presenting and providing content.

She has also written for the stage including Sankofa in 1999, Yaa Asantewaa – Warrior Queen in 2001 and An African Cargo in 2007. She has also been a song lyricist.

In 2014, following the death of Maya Angelou, she scripted a major tribute entitled Maya Angelou: A Celebration, which took place on 5th October at the Royal Festival Hall during the Southbank Centre's London Literature Festival..

She has worked continuously for diversity within the publishing industry and was the patron of Independent Black Publishers (IBP), a trade association chaired by Verna Wilkins. The aim of IBP, as she was quoted as saying, was to "provide a forum for progressive black publishers to share initiatives, maximise mutual strengths and identify common difficulties, with a view to having a more effective impact on the book trade and the wider publishing industry",

She was appointed chair of the 2020 Booker Prize judges.

She has judged several other literary competitions, including the Caine Prize for African Writing, the Orange Prize, the Independent Foreign Fiction Prize, the Wasafiri New Writing Prize, the OCM Bocas Prize for Caribbean Literature, the Commonwealth Book Prize Africa39, and the Wole Soyinka Prize for Literature in Africa, being the chair of judges in 2018.

In 2021 she was a judge in the Trade category of the British Book Awards, and in 2022 judged the PEN Pinter Prize.

In the 2021 Birthday Honours list she was appointed Commander of the Order of the British Empire (CBE) for services to publishing.

She has served on the boards or in advisory positions for other cultural organisations, including the Drum Arts Centre, The Africa Centre, London, English PEN, the Royal Literary Fund, the African & Caribbean Music Circuit, the Hackney Empire theatre, the Organization of Women Writers of Africa, the Etisalat Prize for Literature, and Wasafiri magazine.

She is currently a trustee of jazz education organization Tomorrow's Warriors, and of Nubian Jak Community Trust, and Prize Ambassador of the SI Leeds Literary Prize.

She is a patron of Friends of the Huntley Archives at London Metropolitan Archives, a charitable foundation building on the archival legacy of Jessica Huntley and Eric Huntley, who co-founded publishing house Bogle-L'Ouverture Publications.

Over the years she has received a number of accolades and awards for her work,

First Black Headteacher in Britain

Yvonne Conolly CBE — (1939-2021)

Yvonne Conolly CBE was a Jamaican born teacher who arrived in Britain in 1963 as part of the Windrush generation. In 1969 she became the first black female headteacher in the UK.

Cecile Yvonne Conolly was born in Jamaica in 1939. She trained for three years as a primary school teacher. She arrived in the UK from Jamaica on 11 August 1963, as part of the Windrush generation, with just £36 in her pocket. She had travelled with a teacher friend called Elizabeth Heybeard on one of a number of ships, which brought thousands of workers from the Caribbean. This was in response to the British government's request for people to come to Britain to help rebuild the country after WWII.

Britain was a culture shock for her after Jamaica with its greyness, lack of space and smoke coming from chimneys. She settled in Canfield Gardens in West Hampstead, north London, taking jobs as a babysitter, cleaner and typist, as well as securing work as a supply teacher.

As a supply teacher, she was aware of the level of racial tensions in a number of schools where she taught. This became even more apparent when she secured her first full-time appointment as a teacher at the George Eliot School in Swiss Cottage, north London. This came after writing numerous letters to the London County Council to get a job.

For five years she excelled and eventually became deputy-head of the primary school. She had originally planned to return to Jamaica after three years. In January 1969, and much to her own and her colleagues surprise, she was offered a promotion to become headteacher at Ring Cross Primary School on Eden Grove in Holloway, Islington. At just 29 years of age, she was the country's first black female headteacher.

She received racist abuse and had to have a bodyguard to accompany her to work. Her appointment received a lot of British media attention. She was subjected to repeated attacks in some national newspapers, as well as receiving hate mail at home. In an interview, she remembers, "When I was appointed as headteacher, somebody threatened to burn the school down. I had newspaper articles which had announced my appointment, sent to me, crossing out my photograph with nasty comments. Happily, the parents were only interested in whether their children would get a good education and that certainly was my focus."

She did not let the negative reaction to her headship stop her from delivering an effective education service. For example, to show her pupils that people are all the same but different, she invited her dentist, who was black, to give a talk in school. The children sat open mouthed as they couldn't believe that a dentist was black. She felt that showing representatives from different ethnic groups to show achievement could help children to realise that they could also achieve. She was a prime example.

She went on to set up the Caribbean Teachers Association which was designed to give confidence and practical advice to black teachers who wanted to become school heads. There were few black teachers in the system, and those that were there were not being promoted.

She spent nine years as headteacher of Ring Cross Primary School and, in 1978 she left to take up a position as a member of the multi-ethnic inspectorate created by the Inner London Education Authority (ILEA). As an inspector she investigated methods of dealing with racism, in particular examining schools in Camden and Islington. She was an Ofsted inspector from 1977 to 1986. She was also very vocal in the home secretary's advisory council on race relations.

She felt that we would never get rid of racism as wherever human beings go there will be some discrimination, prejudices and lack of empathy. She also felt that the nature of racism had changed from the days of the No Blacks, No dogs, No Irish signs to being more subtle

She formally retired in 2001, after 40 years of service in education, but remained chair of the Caribbean Teachers' Association. She has since been treated for the incurable blood cancer myeloma.

In 2019 the Yvonne Conolly Garden in Wray Crescent Park in Islington was dedicated to her.

In the 2020 Queen's Birthday Honours list she was made a Commander of the Order of the British Empire (CBE) for services to education.

She was also honoured for her services to education with the Honorary Fellow of Education award from the Naz Legacy Foundation. On announcing the award, HRH Prince of Wales, Prince Charles, now King Charles said she had character and determination which helped her break barriers for black educators.

Sadly on Wednesday 27 January 2021 she died of myeloma at the Whittington Hospital, Islington, at the age of 81 years. She is survived by her daughter and grandson.

First Black Headteacher in Wales

Betty Campbell MBE – (1934-2017)

Betty Campbell MBE was a Welsh community activist, who trained as a teacher and became the teacher of Mount Stuart Primary School in Butetown, Cardiff. This made her the first black head teacher in Wales.

Betty Campbell was born Rachel Elizabeth Johnson on 6 November 1934 in Butetown, Cardiff. The area was popularly known as Tiger Bay, and was built up around Cardiff docklands. It had a large immigrant community and was one of the UK's first multi-cultural communities. Her mother, Honora, known as Nora, was Welsh Barbadian. Her father, Simon Vickers Johnson, had come to the UK from Jamaica when he was 15. He was killed in World War II when his ship the Ocean Vanguard was torpedoed by a U-boat in 1942. Her mother struggled financially after his death and occasionally worked as an illegal street bookmaker.

She excelled at school, being top of her class. She won a scholarship to the Lady Margaret High School for Girls in Cardiff and wanted to be a teacher. She was discouraged by one of her teachers who told her she would never make it as a working-class black girl as the problems would be insurmountable. This made her cry, but also made her more determined to achieve her goals.

However, she became pregnant at the age of 17, while she was doing her A-levels. She left school when she married Rupert Campbell, a fitter's mate, in 1953. By 1960 she had three children. Fortunately by then, Cardiff Teacher Training College had started to enrol female students. She applied and was one of only six female students to be admitted.

Her first teaching post was in Llanrumney. She soon returned to Butetown, getting a job at Mount Stuart Primary School, where she taught for 28 years, becoming the headteacher and thus becoming the first black headteacher in Wales.

As a black teacher she experienced hostility from parents. Some had never seen a black teacher before and felt that if a teacher was black then they would not be quite as good as a white teacher.

She was inspired by a trip to America where she learned about anti-slavery activists such as Harriet Tubman and the civil rights movement. Hence in the 1970s when she became Wales' first black head teacher at Mount Stuart, she began teaching children about slavery, black history and the system of apartheid which was in operation at the time in South Africa.

Speaking later in the Senedd, the Welsh Parliament, she explained that she was determined to help enhance the black spirit and black culture as much as she could. She was responsible for helping to create Black History Month and taught a series of workshops on the role of Butetown's citizens and their countries of origin in the Second World War.

From 1991 to 1995 she was a Butetown councillor on Cardiff City Council.

From 1999 to 2004 she was an independent councillor for Butetown on Cardiff City Council.

The profile of Mount Stuart School was raised under her leadership and her teaching became a template for multicultural education across the United Kingdom.

She became a member of the Home Office's race advisory committee and a member of the Commission for Racial Equality.

She became a part of the Paul Hamlyn Foundation Commission on Education, which published a number of research papers on education. In 1993 it published the book "Learning to Succeed" where practice examples from Mount Stuart Primary School were cited.

In 1994 Prince Charles attended the Mount Stuart Primary School's annual St David's Day eisteddfod.

In 1998 she was invited to meet Nelson Mandela on his only visit to Wales, because she was a member of the Commission for Racial Equality,

She was a board member of BBC Wales in the 1980s and was made an honorary fellow of Cardiff Metropolitan University.

In the 2003 Queen's Birthday Honours list, she was awarded a Member of the Order of the British Empire (MBE) for services to education and community life. She was also made an honorary fellow of Cardiff Metropolitan University

In 2015 she received a lifetime achievement award from Unison Cymru's Black Members' group, for her contribution to black history and Welsh education.

She died at the age of 82 on 13 October 2017, having been ill for several months.

She had four children, one of whom had special needs. She had 14 grandchildren and 17 great-grandchildren.

At her funeral, hundreds of people lined the streets of Cardiff to pay their respects. The First Minister of Wales, Carwyn Jones described her as a true pioneer and an inspiration to other black and ethnic minority people.

In 2021 a statue of her was erected in the plaza of Central Square, Cardiff.

First Black Headteacher in London

Beryl Gilroy – (1924-2001)

Beryl Gilroy was a Guyanese teacher, novelist, and poet who arrived in Britain in the 1950s as part of the Windrush generation. She joined Beckford school in West Hampstead eventually becoming the head teacher and the first Black headteacher in London

Beryl Agatha Gilroy was born Beryl Agatha Answick on 30 August 1924, in Skeldon, Berbice, Guiana. She grew up in a large, extended family, influenced by her maternal grandmother, Sally Louisa James, who was a herbalist and managed the family small-holding,

From the age of two she was raised by her grandmother following a period of illness. Through her childhood years she was mainly homeschooled, attending school infrequently. Her grandfather taught her to read while her grandmother schooled her in the art of herbs, local medicine and aspects of life. She did not enter full-time schooling until she was 12.

She was inspired by her grandmother's teaching and stories using the same methodology when it came to schooling her own children. They were homeschooled with the same focus on freedom that her grandmother had given her.

From 1943 to 1945, she attended teacher training college in Georgetown, gaining a first-class diploma. She subsequently taught and lectured on a UNICEF nutrition programme. After several years teaching, in 1951, at the age of 27, she was selected to attend university in the United Kingdom leaving Guiana.

Between 1951 and 1953 she attended the University of London, gaining a Diploma in Child Development. She assumed that as a qualified and respected teacher from Guiana, she would not have a problem getting a teaching job in London. However, racism was very strongly prevalent.

Prospective employers refused to hire her because she was a black woman and would not accept that she could possibly be a teacher.

To gain a living she worked as a maid, dishwasher and at a mail order store in east London, as a clerk. In her memoirs, she recounted one of her first experiences of racism. She was mates with a work colleague called Sue. Her mate Sue moved to Swiss Cottage in north London and told Gilroy not to visit. "I don't want 'em to see me 'obbnobbin with nigs," Sue told her. Years later, now living in a halfway house, Sue appeared at the school where Gilroy was head teacher, looking to place her twin girls in the nursery. "Poor Sue!" wrote Gilroy. "Time had savaged her."

Her first job in education came when she was employed by the Inner London Education Authority at a Catholic school in a poor area, teaching a class of seven-year-olds who were scared of her and hid under the table when she arrived. Most of the white pupils she taught throughout her career copied remarks made by their bigoted parents. Things such as Black people living in trees, or roasting and eating people. Using patience, strength, wit and incredibly imaginative teaching, she turned the most troublesome of classes into engaged learners. She became reportedly the first black woman appointed as a teacher in London.

She taught for a couple of years. She married scientist Patrick Gilroy, who was an active anti-colonist. She left teaching, spending the next 12 years at home bringing up and educating her children Darla and Paul whilst furthering her own higher education. She also read and reviewed works for a publisher.

In 1968 she returned to teaching and eventually became the deputy head and then the first Black headteacher in London at Beckford School, now known as West Hampstead Primary School, in West Hampstead. This was a difficult time for her as many of her co-workers resented her and were prejudiced against her. She also received a low wage compared to other teachers at her school, despite being the head teacher. However, she continued teaching regardless of these issues.

Her experiences as a teacher led to her writing her novel Black Teacher in 1976 to show the experience of a black female teacher. It was part autobiography, part fiction. Many reviewers of the book were other teachers, who disputed her experiences as outlined in the book. They tried to discredit it, by claiming it was easier than she had described to get a job as a teacher, and that the racism in the book was not likely to be as bad as she perceived it to be.

She stated that the purpose behind Black Teacher and much of her other writing was to set the record straight from a woman's perspective. There had been Ted Braithwaite's To Sir With Love in 1959 and Don Hinds' Journey to an Illusion in 1966 but the woman's experiences had never been stated given the double issues of sexism and racism.

Black Teacher book was republished by Faber in July 2021, meeting with more positive reviews based on real evidence indicating that the experiences portrayed were real.

She worked as a multi-cultural researcher at the Institute of Education, University of London, and developed a pioneering practice in psychotherapy, working mainly with Black women and children.

In the early 1980s, she was a co-founder of the Camden Black Sisters group, a support organisation supporting women in Camden, London.

In 1987 she gained a PhD in counselling psychology from an American university whilst working at the Institute of Education.

She had been writing creatively from her childhood. In the 1960s, she began writing Praise of Love and Children which was later published by Peepal Tree Press. Between 1970 and 1975, she wrote several books for her children's series Nippers, which contained possibly the first reflection of the Black British presence in UK writing for children.

Although many of her peers writing Caribbean Literature were being published, hers were initially rejected. They were seen as being too colonial, and unknowing, and psychological and strange. Some of her writings were not published for more than 30 years after she had written them.

In 1986 her first novel Frangipani House, set in an old person's home in Guyana, was published, winning a GLC Creative Writing Prize.

In 1989 her novel, Boy Sandwich was published, followed by Stedman and Joanna: A Love in Bondage in 1991, and a collection of poems, Echoes and Voices. The next novels were Sunlight and Sweet Water, Gather the Faces, In Praise of Love and Children and Inkle and Yarico, all published in 1994. Her last novel, The Green Grass Tango was published posthumously in 2001, after her death.

In 1998 a collection of her non-fiction writing, entitled Leaves in the Wind, came out from Mango Publishing. It included her lectures, notes, essays, dissertations and personal reviews. Her early work examined the impact of life in Britain on West Indian families and her later work explored issues of African and Caribbean Diaspora and slavery.

Her writings used inspiration from stories her grandmother would tell her about British Guiana; her own life experiences, such as her work before becoming a teacher, and the racism she experienced as a teacher and head teacher.

After many years of being over looked during her life, she finally began receiving recognition and honours for her work late in her career as a writer. She wrote The Nippers series throughout the 1960s-1970s. They were several short stories made for children and won her over sixteen awards.

In 1990 she was honoured by the Greater London Council for all of her services in education.

In 1995 she received an Honorary Doctorate from the University of North London.

In 1996 she was honoured by the Association of Caribbean Women Writers and Scholars.

In 2000 she was made an Honorary Fellow by the Institute of Education.

In 2004 an orange skirt suit she wore was included in an exhibition titled Black British Style at the Victoria and Albert Museum in honour of her.

She died of a heart attack at the age of 76 on 4 April 2001.

First Black British person to win the Booker Prize

Bernardine Evaristo, OBE FRSL FRSA – (1959-)

Bernardine Evaristo, OBE FRSL FRSA is a British author and academic. Her novel Girl, Woman, Other, won the Booker Prize in 2019, making her the first black woman and the first black British person to win the Booker. She is also Professor of Creative Writing at Brunel University London and President of the Royal Society of Literature, the second woman and first person of colour to hold the role since it was founded in 1820.

Bernardine Anne Mobolaji Evaristo was born on the 28 May 1959, the fourth of eight children, in Woolwich, south east London, to an English mother, of English, Irish and German heritage, and a Nigerian father, of Nigerian and Brazilian heritage. Her father was a welder and local Labour councillor, the first black councillor in the Borough of Greenwich; her mother was a schoolteacher.

She was educated at Eltham Hill Girls' Grammar School, the Rose Bruford College of Speech & Drama, and Goldsmiths, University of London, where she earned her PhD in Creative Writing in 2013. She spent her teenage years at Greenwich Young People's Theatre, which was where she first became involved in the arts.

In the 1980s she co-founded Theatre of Black Women, Britain's first black women's theatre company with Paulette Randall and Patricia Hilaire.

In the 1990s she organised Britain's first black British writing conference, held at the Museum of London, and also Britain's first black British theatre conference, held at the Royal Festival Hall.

In 1995 she co-founded and directed Spread the Word, London's writer development agency with Ruth Borthwick. She organised Britain's first major black theatre conference, Future Histories, for the Black Theatre Forum, at the Royal Festival Hall. In 1997 she organised Britain's first major conference on black British writing, Tracing Paper, at the Museum of London.

She has taught creative writing since 1994. She has also been awarded many writing fellowships and residencies. She taught the University of East Anglia-Guardian "How to Tell a Story" course for four seasons in London up to 2015. Since 1997 she has accepted over 130 international invitations as a writer. These have involved writer-residencies and visiting fellowships, British Council tours, book tours, teaching creative writing courses and workshops as well as keynotes, talks and panels at many conferences and literary festivals.

In 2006 she got together an Arts Council-funded report delivered by Spread the Word writer development agency into why black and Asian poets were not getting published in the UK. It revealed that less than 1 per cent of all published poetry is by poets of colour.

After the report was published, she set up The Complete Works poetry mentoring scheme, with Nathalie Teitler and Spread the Word. In this national development programme, 30 poets were mentored, each over a one- or two-year period. Many went on to publish books, win awards and receive serious recognition for their poetry.

From 2011 she has taught at Brunel University, London, becoming Professor of Creative Writing.

In 2012, being a longstanding advocate for the inclusion of writers and artists of colour, she founded the Brunel International African Poetry Prize.

She has authored two non-fiction books, eight books of fiction and verse fiction exploring aspects of the African Diaspora. She has experimented with form and narrative perspective, occasionally merging the past with the present, fiction with poetry, the factual with the speculative, and reality with alternate realities. One of her novels, Blonde Roots, is a satire inverting the history of the transatlantic slave trade, replacing it with a universe where Africans enslave Europeans. The book won the Orange Youth Panel Award and Big Red Read Award, and was nominated for the International Dublin Literary Award and the Orange Prize and the Arthur C. Clarke Award.

She has won awards for her other books, some of which have been adapted into plays.

She chaired the 32nd and 33rd British Council Berlin Literature Seminar in 2017 and 2018

In 2017 she served on the Council of the Royal Society of Literature.

Her novel Girl, Woman, Other, concerns about 12 primarily black British women whose ages range from 19 to 93. They are a mix of cultural backgrounds, sexual orientations, classes and geographies, and the novel charts their hopes, struggles and intersecting lives. In July 2019 the novel made the Booker Prize shortlist, alongside books by Margaret Atwood, Lucy Ellmann, Chigozie Obioma, Salman Rushdie and Elif Shafak. On 14 October it won the prize jointly with Atwood's The Testaments. This made her the first black woman and first black British author to win the prize.

In 2019 she was appointed Woolwich Laureate by the Greenwich and Docklands International Festival, reconnecting to and writing about the home town she left when she was 18.

She delivered the New Statesman/Goldsmiths Prize lecture on 30 September 2020.

In October 2020 she gave the opening keynote address at the Frankfurt Book Fair's Publishing Insights conference, where she called on publishers to hire more people representing a wider range of communities rather than sticking to clichés and stereotypes.

In 2020 she was recognised as one of the United Kingdom's most influential people of African or African Caribbean heritage for her writing by being included in the 2021 edition of the annual Powerlist.

In 2020 she won the British Book Awards: Fiction Book of the Year and Author of the Year, as well as the Indie Book Award for Fiction as well as many other awards.

She became the first woman of colour and the first black British writer to reach number one in the UK paperback fiction charts. She held the top spot for five weeks and spent 44 weeks in the Top 10.

In 2022 her novel, Girl, Woman, Other was included on the "Big Jubilee Read" list of 70 books by Commonwealth authors chosen to celebrate the Platinum Jubilee of Elizabeth II.

She has written short fiction, drama, poetry, essays, literary criticism, and projects for stage and radio. Two of her books have been adapted into BBC Radio 4 dramas, The Emperor's Babe in 2001 and Hello Mum in 2010. She has made many British podcast interviews.

She has also written many articles, essays, fictions and book reviews for publications and magazines including: The Times, Vanity Fair, The Guardian, The Observer, Vogue, The Independent, Harper's Bazaar UK, The Times Literary Supplement, Conde Naste Traveller, Wasafiri, and the New Statesman.

She is a lifetime Honorary Fellow of St Anne's College, University of Oxford and International Honorary Fellow of the American Academy of Arts & Sciences.

In 2021 she became the President of Rose Bruford College of Theatre and Performance and she was Vice-Chair of the Royal Society of Literature (RSL). In 2020 she became a lifetime vice president, before becoming president in 2022, which made her the first Black writer and only the second woman to hold the position in the Society's 200-year history.

In the Queen's 2009 Birthday Honours list she was appointed a Member of the Order of the British Empire (MBE) for services to literature

In the Queen's 2020 Birthday Honours list she was appointed an Officer of the Order of the British Empire (OBE) again for services to literature.

Two major arts television documentaries have been made of her, The South Bank Show, with Melvyn Bragg by Sky Arts in Autumn 2020 and Imagine, with Alan Yentob, Bernardine Evaristo: Never Give Up, on BBC One in September 2021. She has given many other interviews.

She is married to writer David Shannon, whom she met in 2006, and whose debut novel was launched in March 2021.

First Black British Woman to win the Book of the Year award

Candice Carty-Williams – (1989-)

Candice Carty-Williams is a British writer who has written for several publications. At the British Book Awards in June 2020 she became the first black woman to win the Book of the Year award for her novel Queenie.

Candice Carty-Williams was born on 21 July 1989 in St Thomas' Hospital, Westminster to her Jamaican-Indian mother and Jamaican father. She was raised in south London and with her mother they started out in Clapham, and spent a few years in Norbury, south London, before moving in with her grandparents in Streatham. When she was 15 her mother had a second daughter, prompting a move to Lewisham with her stepfather.

She struggled at secondary school where she was loud and she was placed in the lower academic sets. An exclusion from school for a week turned out to be a blessing in disguise as her stepfather sent her to Lewisham library every day and reading became her refuge, though, growing up she never felt she could write.

Racism and discrimination was a constant factor in her life, ranging from boys at school telling her they'd love to go out with her but their parents would never allow them to date a black girl, to women she had never met before thinking it was ok to feel up and touch her hair.

After leaving school, she studied for a degree in communication and media studies at the University of Sussex, having been told she was not clever enough to study English. Her university friends introduced her into the possibilities of a career in publishing. However, as she had no family or friends working in publishing, her path into the industry was to do internships. Her first one at the age of 23 was with Melville House. She then did a two-week internship at 4th Estate and then got a job as a temporary editorial assistant at Vintage. She did this for six weeks and then 4th estate asked her to come back and be a marketing assistant.

It became apparent to her that there was an underrepresentation of black and minority ethnic authors and writers in publishing. To combat this she created the Guardian and 4th Estate BAME Short Story Prize, which aimed to offer assistance towards publishing or literary agent representation. The prize was small but gave a hugely valuable step in supporting writers from minority backgrounds, and helping them gain the visibility that their work deserved. There was a budget of £48, the cost of setting up a website to field submissions. She did all the sifting, through about 300 stories, and it was a great success. She was amazed at the impact that the prize had. She felt that it was sad that it had to exist but pleased that it did.

In September 2016 she joined Vintage Books, a trade paperback publishing imprint of Penguin Random House, where she was senior marketing executive and was also a mentor on the Penguin Books Write Now scheme, eventually leaving in May 2019.

As a fervent reader, she struggled to relate to most of the fiction she read. Unable to find one she one she really connected with, she chose to write her own. The result was Queenie. A novel with a compelling yet flawed protagonist navigating the challenges of being a young black woman in today's world, the plot drawing on her own experience and the experiences of Black women around her; the family, the workplace politics, the relationships and struggles with mental health.

Set in Brixton, it outlines a number of the challenges faced by twenty-somethings trying to make their way in the city, from the extortionate and broken world of private renting, to gentrification, casual and not-so-casual racism, and the complexities of multiculturalism. It a very relatable London that rarely finds literary pages. She felt it was important to show that black women are like everyone else but also different, because they see things through a different lens and perspective.

She used humour and pathos to examine social and racial politics such as the housing crisis faced by millennials. With regard to the racial element she was aware that people would always accuse there was an overreaction and it was wrong to get upset about these things. However the #MeToo and Black Lives Matter movements showed that there was a need to express where things are demonstrably wrong. This Windrush debacle also affected her as her grandparents were part of the Windrush generation who came to Britain to work and now they were faced with being told go back home we don't want you here anymore.

After submitting a first draft of Queenie to literary agent Jo Unwin, it became the subject of a four-way bidding war between publishers. She eventually chose to sign with Orion, who reportedly paid a six figure sum. The book was published in 2019, being marketed as a black Bridget Jones. She thought this initially but felt that it was more political as a personal yet universal story. It was not autobiographical but using themes from her and her friends' lives. The book received positive critical attention, described by reviewers as both a smart and breezy comic debut and astutely political, an essential commentary on everyday racism.

On its release Queenie entered the Sunday Times Bestseller hardback chart at number two, and by the end of 2019 it had won Blackwell's Debut Book of the Year award. It was also shortlisted for Book of the Year by Waterstones, Foyles and Goodreads as well as being runner-up for the Costa First Novel Award. It won the Book Awards' Book of the Year Award in 2020.

She has written for publications including The Guardian, i-D, Vogue, The Sunday Times, Refinery29, BEAT Magazine, and Black Ballad. She contributed an essay to the anthology New Daughters of Africa, in 2019, edited by Margaret Busby. In January 2020 she was appointed the new weekly books columnist of The Guardian. She gave this up after lockdown in 2021 to concentrate on her second novel, People Person.

She is a contributor to Dear NHS, edited by Adam Kay, a 2020 anthology of personal stories from famous people about how they have been helped by the National Health Service.

She wrote a short story for Prada's holiday 2020 campaign, photographed by Steven Meisel.

In October 2021 she published a young adult novella, titled Empress & Aniya, which follows two teenage girls from different backgrounds, who accidentally cast a body swap spell on their 16th birthday.

In May 2021 she was commissioned by the BBC to write Champion, a London-based musical television drama. It aired for one series from July to August 2023, focusing on the musical rivalry between two up-and-coming musicians, siblings Bosco and Vita Champion, and the ramifications and fallout of that rivalry which could drive their family apart in their quest for musical stardom.

In 2022 she published her second novel, People Person about a group of 5 half-siblings, the same dad with 4 mothers. They meet in response to a crisis as adults and start shaping themselves into a family. It's a warm novel, funny and full of emotional intelligence. The tone is light-hearted and comic. Similar to Queenie she uses humour and pathos to examine social and racial politics.

In 2024 an eight-episode television drama series based on Queenie was aired by Channel 4.

Despite lacking confidence in her abilities and creativity as a youngster she has come a long way and her success is remarkable and laudable and clearly well deserved.

First Black women's theatre company

Theatre of Black Women — (1982-1988)

Theatre of Black Women was Britain's first black women's theatre company. It was founded by Bernardine Evaristo, Patricia Hilaire and Paulette Randall in 1982. The three ladies had met while taking the Community Theatre Arts course from 1979 to 1982 at Rose Bruford College of Speech and Drama. It was a progressive course which was designed to produce individuals who would be capable of creating their own theatre in order to become a force for change in society.

Theatre of Black Women was a small scale touring company. The company defined themselves as Black Feminist and their work often engaged in debates about the historical exclusion of black women from the women's movement.

Theatre of Black Women's aim was to produce plays by and about black British women at a time when parts for black women were almost non-existent in theatre. This was at all levels and spheres within theatre. Black women faced the double issues of racism and sexism.

They wanted to explore black women's experience using theatre as a powerful means of communication. They considered issues such as Black women in education, health housing, and feminism in history and in the Arts. They looked at black women's lives and struggles hoping to be able to provide an opportunity for Black women's voices to be heard positively through theatre. They wanted to use theatre to promote positive and encouraging images of Black women as individuals, examining and re-defining relationships with men, living independent lives, giving and receiving support from other Black women, discovering their own Black identity, and celebrating their Black womanhood.

In 1982 as a part of their Young writers Season, the Royal Court Theatre staged their first three short one-woman plays. The plays were Evaristo's

Tiger, Teeth Clenched Not To Bite, Hilaire's Hey Brown Girl and Randall's Chameleon. The pieces were also taken to the 1982 international women's theatre festival at the Melkweg in Amsterdam, Holland.

Other plays to be staged included Silhouette by Evaristo and Hilaire; Pyeyucca, by Evaristo with additional material by Hilaire; Chiaroscuro by Jackie Kay, and Miss Quashie and the Tiger's Tail, a children's play by mother-and-daughter team Gabriela and Jean Pearse. The company mainly toured the UK making occasional appearances in Europe. They worked with other women such as Joan Ann Maynard, who directed Chiaroscuro, and Gail Ann Dorsey, who composed the music for Chiaroscuro.

As well as producing theatre, the company ran drama workshops for young black women both nationally in the UK and in Europe.

The efforts of the Theatre of Black Women were well received. However the company was forced to disband in 1988 when Arts Council funding was stopped. The three ladies remained in theatre: Bernadine Evaristo OBE is an author and academic, Paulette Randall MBE is a theatre director and Patricia St. Hilaire is a playwright, director, poet and academic.

First Black British F1 Grand Prix World Champion

Sir Lewis Hamilton, MBE Hon FREng Kt – (1985-)

Sir Lewis Hamilton, MBE Hon FREng Kt, is a prominent British racing driver. He joined the McLaren Young Driver Programme in 1998, which led to his Formula One debut with McLaren from 2007 to 2012, making him the first black driver in the series. In his first season, he set several records and finished runner-up to Kimi Räikkönen by one point. The next year, he became the youngest and first black Formula One World Champion. He has since won a joint-record seven World Drivers' Championship titles, tied with Michael Schumacher.

Lewis Carl Davidson Hamilton was born on 7 January 1985, in Stevenage, Hertfordshire. His father is Anthony Hamilton, who is black and of Grenadian descent, and his mother is Carmen Larbalestier, who is white and British. His parents separated when he was two, and he lived with his mother until he was twelve before moving in with his father. Raised as a Catholic, he attended The John Henry Newman School, where he took up karate at age five to defend himself from bullying. He enjoyed playing football and cricket.

His racing career began at five when his father bought him a radio-controlled car. By six, he had a go-kart, and his father worked multiple jobs to support his racing ambitions. He faced significant racist abuse as the only black child in racing but continued to excel, winning the British Kart Championship at ten. A chance meeting with McLaren boss Ron Dennis led to his inclusion in the McLaren driver development programme, which paved the way for his future in Formula One.

From 1998 to 2000, he won numerous European and world karting championships and became the youngest-ever driver ranked number one in the sport at fifteen. He progressed to car racing in 2003, winning the British Formula Renault championship and later the Formula Three Euroseries and GP2 titles.

In 2007 he joined the McLaren F1 team and had an impressive first season, finishing second in the world drivers' championship, the first and only black man to compete at F1. In 2008, he won his first drivers' championship. He continued to perform well with McLaren.

In the 2008 Queen's Birthday Honours list, he was awarded a Member of the Order of the British Empire (MBE), after he won his first championship.

In 2012, he moved to Mercedes-Benz. Despite initial struggles, he dominated the 2014 and 2015 seasons, winning his second and third drivers' championships. He has since added more titles, matching Schumacher's record of seven championships in 2020.

He lost the 2021 championship to Max Verstappen in a controversial last race of the season. He led but due to dubious race director decisions, Verstappen was enabled to overtake him winning the race. Verstappen went on to dominate the sport in 2022 and 2023.

At the beginning of 2024, he announced his decision to leave Mercedes to drive for Ferrari in 2025, which was a childhood dream.

In 2024 he won the British Grand Prix, this was his first win since 2021.

His 2025 career has been difficult with a win in the sprint race in China being a highlight.

Throughout his career, he has faced and spoken out against racism, advocating for diversity in motorsport. Following the murder of George Floyd in 2020, he was very vocal in supporting the Black Lives Matter movement and demands for racial equality. He launched the Hamilton Commission to promote STEM education among black youth and created Mission 44 to support underrepresented young people. He has also launched the Ignite foundation with Mercedes to increase diversity in motorsport.

His activism extends to environmental issues, animal rights, and social causes. He adopted a vegan lifestyle in 2017 and has pushed for sustainability within his team. He has supported numerous charities, worked with

UNICEF and Save the Children, and established the Lewis Hamilton Foundation.

In the 2021 Queen's Birthday honours list he was knighted for services to motorsports, after equalling Michael Schumacher's record of seven championship wins. His records stand – most wins – 105, pole positions – 104, podiums - 202.

He is interested in music and fashion, collaborating with Tommy Hilfiger on clothing. He has a vegan restaurant chain called Neat Burger. He part owns an NFL team, the Denver Broncos, and competes in the all-electric off-road racing series Extreme E with his X44 team.

He resides in Monaco but also owns properties in New York and Colorado. He continues to inspire with his dedication to racing, advocacy for equality, and commitment to various humanitarian and environmental causes.

First Black British London Tram driver and First Black British Olympian

Louis Bruce - (1875-1958)

Louis Bruce gained a tram licence in 1900 after taking a job as a tram driver for London United Tramways making him one of the first and possibly only Black tram drivers in London. In 1908 he was one of 14 members of the Hammersmith AWC to feature at the Olympic Games in London making him the first and earliest known Black person to have represented Great Britain at the Olympic Games.

Louis Bruce McAvoy Mortimore Doney aka Louis Bruce was born on 17 December 1875, in Edinburgh, Scotland. He was raised in Plympton, Devon living with his grandmother and two aunts after his father's death and his mother's remarriage. He moved to Hammersmith, London, in the early 1900s and became one of the first, if not the only, Black tram drivers in London when he obtained his tram license in 1900. He worked for London United Tramways (LUT) at Fulwell Depot and was highly regarded in his profession.

In addition to his career as a tram driver, he was an entertainer, performing as a dancer, ragtime singer, and comedian at social events. His diverse talents extended to sports as he was an active member of the Hammersmith Amateur Wrestling Club (AWC) and participated in heavyweight wrestling matches. Despite facing racial prejudice, he gained recognition in the sporting world.

In 1908, he became the first known Black person to represent Great Britain at the Olympic Games in London. Competing in wrestling, he won his first match but was defeated in the second round. His participation was a significant milestone. He continued to be involved in sports, excelling in race walking and heavyweight boxing, where he won a championship title in 1913.

His professional achievements included rising to the rank of tram inspector by 1911. That year, he married Ethel Elizabeth Dunn, and they had a son named Dennis in 1917. He worked with LUT until at least 1921 and later became a shopkeeper in Sutton, Surrey.

Louis Bruce passed away on March 31, 1958, at the age of 82.

He was initially misidentified in records as "Lawrence Bruce" until recent research by Olympic historians corrected this and confirmed his status as a pioneering Black British Olympian, predating the previously recognized Harry Edward.

First Black British Olympian on the track

Harry Edwards – (1898-1973)

Harry Edward was a British runner known for his achievements in the 100 and 200 meters races at the 1920 Summer Olympics in Antwerp. He won bronze medals in both events, making him the first Black person to earn Olympic track medals for Great Britain. Although once believed to be Britain's first Black Olympian, Edward was preceded by Louis Bruce, a Black heavyweight wrestler who competed in the 1908 London Olympics.

Harry Francis Vincent Edward was born on 15 April 1898, in Berlin. His mother was Prussian, and his father, originally from Dominica, worked as a circus entertainer and later as a maître d' in Berlin. Harry grew up in Germany, excelling academically and athletically, and became fluent in English, German, and French.

At 16 he showed his potential by winning the 200m and placing second in the 100m at a competition held in the stadium built for the 1916 Olympics. However, the outbreak of World War I led to his internment in a prisoner-of-war camp in Ruhleben, near Berlin, due to his status as a British subject. Despite initially participating in sports and making friends, conditions in the camp deteriorated towards the war's end.

After the war he was released from the concentration camp in late 1918. He arry moved to London, where he became a teacher of German and French. He also pursued amateur athletics, quickly making a name for himself. His performance at the 1920 Amateur Athletics Association meeting earned him a spot on the British Olympic team.

At the 1920 Antwerp Olympics, he reached the finals in both the 100m and 200m, winning bronze medals in each event. He continued to compete successfully in British athletics meetings, notably making history in 1922 by winning the 100, 200, and 400-yard finals within an hour at the main

AAA meeting, a feat never surpassed. His achievements earned personal congratulations from King George V.

In his personal life he married twice, first to Antoinette Kohler Regner in 1922, and then to Gladys Hirst in 1938, with whom he had a son. In 1923, he moved to the United States, where his athletic performance was less successful. He worked various jobs in New York and Philadelphia and was involved in significant cultural and social projects, including the Federal Theatre Project and the Office of Price Administration during World War II.

After the war, he joined the UN Relief and Rehabilitation Administration, working in Greece and later for the New York Employment Office. He continued to volunteer, including initiating a foster-children program in Vietnam and assisting with dignitary visits in New York.

He passed away in 1973 after a heart attack while visiting his sister in Germany.

His memoir, "When I Passed the Statue of Liberty I Became Black: The Autobiography of an Ex-European," details his life's journey and is available at the Amistad Center in New Orleans. He was remembered as a kind-hearted, intelligent advocate for human rights, having witnessed and influenced many major events of the 20th century.

First Black British female Olympian

Anita Neil OLY – (1950-)

Anita Neil OLY is a retired British international sprinter. At just 18, she represented Great Britain at the 1968 Olympics in Mexico, sprinting in the 100m and the 4x100m relay, and making history as the first Black British woman Olympian. She later competed at the 1972 Munich games.

Doris Anita Neil was born on 5 April 1950, in Wellingborough, Northamptonshire. She was the daughter of an African American staff sergeant who met her mother, Florence, during World War II. Her father, often travelling between the USA and Britain, eventually left the family when she was six. Growing up, Anita and her siblings were the only mixed-race students at their school, facing racism from peers and teachers. Despite these challenges, her extraordinary speed was apparent early on.

At 13, her PE teacher, Roger Beadsworth, recognized her potential and began coaching her twice a week. By 14, she won the long jump at the All England school championships. At 15, she joined the London Olympiads Ladies club, where meeting her idol, Mary Rand, provided a burst of inspiration. Rand's encouragement and advice were invaluable.

An unexpected opportunity came when Rand's injury led to Anita being drafted to represent Great Britain in Lille, France. It was her first trip abroad, a daunting experience. At 16, she visited Cuba, her first encounter with a predominantly Black nation, where she received a warm welcome and was often mistaken for Cuban.

Training was tough due to poor facilities in Wellingborough, relying on basic school amenities. Financial struggles meant she had to balance full-time work as a seamstress with her training, leaving little time for a social life. Her dedication paid off when she set a national record of 10.6 seconds in the 100 yards at a Portsmouth competition and helped her relay team break a world record, earning them a visit to Buckingham Palace and a memorable meeting with footballer George Best.

Confirmation of her place in the 1968 Olympics brought both excitement and profound experiences. Competing in the 100m and 4x100m relay, she advanced to the second round in the 100m and the relay final, witnessing firsthand the Black Power salute by John Carlos and Tommie Smith.

In 1969, she won bronze medals in the 100m, 200m, and 4x100m relay at the European Athletics Championships in Athens. She secured a silver medal in the 4x100m relay at the 1970 British Commonwealth Games in Edinburgh.

At the 1972 Munich Olympics, she once again reached the second round in the 100m and the relay final, competing amidst the tragic backdrop of the Black September terrorist attack.

Throughout her career, she juggled her athletic pursuits with a full-time job, leading a double life of intense competition and daily financial struggles to support her family. Retiring at 23 due to lack of support, she faced the heartbreak of watching former teammates compete without her. This early retirement led her to a more reclusive life, hiding away her achievements.

A significant slight occurred when the Olympic torch passed through Wellingborough for the 2012 London Games, and she was overlooked. However, the British Olympic Association has since recognized her as Great Britain's first Black female Olympian. Her local community's recognition and support have been heart-warming. She continues to reside in Wellingborough, engaging in local events and enjoying the belated acknowledgment of her pioneering role in British athletics.

First Black British woman to win an Olympic gold medal

Tessa Sanderson CBE – (1956-)

Tessa Sanderson CBE is a former British javelin thrower, known for her remarkable achievements in athletics. She competed in every Summer Olympics from 1976 to 1996 and won a gold medal in the javelin throw at the 1984 Olympics. Notably, she was the second track and field athlete to compete in six Olympics and the first Black British woman to win an Olympic gold medal.

Theresa Ione Sanderson was born on 14 March 1956, in St Elizabeth, Jamaica. When she was five, her parents moved to England as part of the Windrush generation, leaving Theresa and her siblings with their grandparents. At six, she and her siblings joined their parents in Wolverhampton, where her father worked as a sheet-metal worker and her mother held various jobs, including as a hairdresser. Theresa attended Ward's Bridge High School, where she faced racism and challenging conditions. Despite these obstacles, her talent in sports was recognized by her PE teacher, Barbara Richards, who encouraged her to train seriously.

At 13, she joined her first athletics club, Wolverhampton & Bilston, and began excelling in javelin throwing. By 1971, she was competing nationally and internationally, breaking records along the way. However, financial difficulties posed a significant challenge, as she had no funding or sponsorship and had to work full-time while training.

In 1977 her fortunes changed when she met Michael Samuelson, a film producer and charity president, who helped secure sponsorship for her. This support was crucial for her preparation for the 1984 Olympics, where she won the gold medal with a record throw making her the first Black British woman to win an Olympic gold medal.

In the 1985 New Years Honours list she was appointed a Member of the Order of the British Empire (MBE) for services to sports.

In 1986 her autobiography, Tessa: My Life in Athletics, was published.

Her career was marked by a fierce rivalry with fellow javelin thrower Fatima Whitbread, which, while spurring her on, also highlighted issues of favouritism and racial bias within British athletics. Despite these challenges, she continued to succeed, winning multiple medals in various competitions and setting records.

After initially retiring in 1988 due to injury, she made a comeback and continued competing until 1997.

In the 2004 New Years Honours list, she became a Commander of the Order of the British Empire (CBE) for services to sport.

In 2006 she founded an academy in Newham which helped to find and train athletes to represent Britain in the 2012 Summer Olympics.

In 2009 she set up The Tessa Sanderson Foundation and Academy to encourage young people and people with disabilities to take up sport with mentoring and support.

On 3 May 2010 she married former judo Olympian Densign White at St Paul's Cathedral in London. Her bridesmaids were fellow Olympic teammates Sharron Davies, Kelly Holmes and Christine Ohuruogu. The couple fostered and then adopted twins Cassius and Ruby Mae.

She transitioned into roles that supported and encouraged young athletes, particularly through the Tessa Sanderson Foundation and Academy, which she established to help young people and those with disabilities pursue sports.

She has spoken about the discrimination she has experienced as a black woman. She felt that sexism was the reason women athletes were not adequately paid. She experienced racist language and behaviour from her school days, including being spat on. She has spoken about receiving a racist letter saying that she was not truly British after her 1984 Olympic gold medal. She felt that Black athletes now have more of a voice and she had to fight her own battles. She remains disappointed at the continuing lack of Black, Asian and minority representation in sports governing bodies.

First British man to win 100 metres gold at the Olympic Games, World Championships, European Championships and Commonwealth Games.

Linford Christie OBE – (1960-)

Linford Christie OBE, a Jamaican-born former British sprinter, is a legendary figure in athletics. He's the only British man to have won gold in the 100 meters at the Olympic Games, World Championships, European Championships, and Commonwealth Games. He was also the first European to break the 10-second barrier in the 100 meters and held the British record in this event until 2023.

Linford Cicero Christie was born on 2 April 1960, in Saint Andrew, Jamaica. He joined his parents in London at the age of seven. He attended Henry Compton Secondary School in Fulham, where he excelled in sports and competed in the first London Youth Games in 1977. He did not take athletics seriously until he was 18, but his career took off in 1979 under coach Ron Roddan.

His early career was challenging, but he achieved his first major win in the 100 meters at the 1986 European Championships. He gained international attention at the 1988 Seoul Olympics, where he won silver in the 100 meters after Ben Johnson was disqualified for doping.

In 1992 at the Barcelona Olympic Games, he became the third British athlete to win the Olympic 100 metres, after Harold Abrahams and Allan Wells. Carl Lewis, his great rival missed the race, and he ran 9.96 seconds in the final, and at the age of 32 years 121 days became the oldest Olympic 100 metres champion by four years and 38 days.

In 1993 he became the first man in history to hold the Olympic, World, European and Commonwealth titles in the 100 metres when he won at the Stuttgart World Championships in his fastest ever time of 9.87 seconds. That year he was also voted BBC Sports Personality of the Year by the British public. The following year, in 1994, he defended his Commonwealth title in Victoria in his second fastest ever 100 metres time of 9.91 seconds.

His career faced controversies, including a disciplinary hearing for a positive drug test at the 1988 Olympics and a doping scandal in 1999 involving nandrolone. Despite being banned from athletics, he maintained his innocence and continued to advocate against steroid use.

He retired from international competition in 1997 but remained influential in the sport.

In the 1990 Queens Birthday honours list he was appointed a Member of the Order of the British Empire (MBE)

In the 1998 Queens Birthday honours list he was appointed an OBE

In 2009 he was inducted into the London Youth Games Hall of Fame.

In 2010 he was inducted into the England Athletics Hall of Fame.

With 24 medals, he is one of Britain's most decorated athletes. He has eight children and continues to be a significant figure in athletics.

First British athlete to win two gold medals at the same world championships

Sir Mohamed Farah CBE OLY – (1983-)

Sir Mohamed Farah CBE OLY, widely known as Mo Farah, is a celebrated British long-distance runner with an impressive track record. He has won ten global championship gold medals, including four Olympic and six World titles, making him the most successful male track distance runner and British track athlete in modern Olympic history. Notably, he was the first British athlete to win two gold medals at a single World Championships.

Mohamed Muktar Jama Farah, originally named Hussein Abdi Kahin (Somali: Xuseen Cabdi Kaahin), was born on 23 March 1983, in Somaliland, which was then part of Somalia. His early life was marked by hardship. At the age of four, his father died in a civil war, and he was separated from his mother, spending several years in Mogadishu. At nine, he was trafficked to Britain via Djibouti, given the name Mohammed Farah, and forced to work as a domestic servant.

Despite these challenges, he eventually gained British citizenship in July 2000. Initially not allowed to attend school, he began his education at Feltham Community College, where his athletic talent was discovered by his physical education teacher, Alan Watkinson. This led to his joining the Borough of Hounslow Athletics Club and marking the start of his running career.

His early achievements included representing Hounslow in the London Youth Games and winning multiple English school titles. Philanthropist Eddie Kulukundis helped him complete his naturalization as a British citizen, facilitating his participation in international competitions. Training at St Mary's University, Twickenham, he became a full-time athlete and won the European Junior 5,000m title in 2001.

His career took off in 2006 with a silver medal in the 5,000m at the European Championships and a win at the European Cross Country Championships.

He married Tania Nell in 2010 and has four children: stepdaughter Rihanna, twin daughters Aisha and Amani, and son Hussein. He was also named track-and-field athlete of the year by the British Olympic Association.

His career highlights include winning the 5,000m and 10,000m double at the 2010 European Championships, becoming the first British man to run the 5,000m in under 13 minutes.

In 2011 he became the first British man to win the 5,000m at the World Championships, a few days after winning a silver medal in the 10,000m. He smashed the European 10,000m Record with a time of 26:46.57 and improved the British 5,000m Record to 12:53.11.

The next year was the London 2012 Olympics. In his first race, he capped off what became known as Super Saturday for the Great Britain team, by winning the 10,000m gold medal in a time of 27:30.42. This was Great Britain's first ever Olympic gold medal in the 10,000m. A week later he completed the long distance double by winning the 5,000m in a time of 13:41.66, becoming the first British athlete to win two gold medals at the same world championships.

His 2012 became even better for his family when his wife Tania gave birth to twin daughters to whom he dedicated each of his Olympic Gold Medals.

In the 2013 New Years Honours list he was appointed Commander of the Order of the British Empire (CBE) for his services to athletics.

At the Moscow World Championships in 2013, he won another long distance double in the 5,0000m and 10,000m. He repeated this feat at the 2014 European Championships in Zurich making him the most successful individual in the history of the European Athletics Championships, with five titles. He exceeded this by again winning the long distance double at the 2015 World Championships in Beijing, before ending the 2015 season by winning the Great North Run.

He became recognised as one of the greatest distance runner of all time at the 2016 Rio Olympic Games, by winning both the 5,000m and 10,000m. He became the second athlete to complete the long distance double-double. The 10,000m had been somewhat difficult as he had been accidentally tripped during the race, falling to the floor and then having to catch up with the leaders before finally winning in an engrossing finish. This time he dedicated his two Gold medals to his daughter Rhianna and son Hussein to complete the set!

In the 2017 Queen's Birthday Honours list he was knighted for his services to Athletics. The same year he was voted the BBC Sports Personality of the Year

In 2017 he transitioned to road racing setting records in the marathon. He announced his retirement from marathon racing in 2023, finishing his last London Marathon in ninth place. He holds numerous records, including European records for the 10,000m, half marathon, and marathon, as well as British records for the 5,000m and 3,000m.

He is also known for his philanthropic efforts, including the Mo Farah Foundation, and has faced and spoken out against racial discrimination. His autobiography, Mo Farah, Twin Ambitions, was published in 2013, and a 2022 BBC documentary, The Real Mo Farah, detailed his true childhood story, earning critical acclaim.

GREAT BRITAIN
TDK
FARAH

First Black singer to feature on BBC Radio

Evelyn Dove – (1902-1987)

Evelyn Dove was a groundbreaking British singer and actress, often compared to Josephine Baker early in her career. Of Sierra Leone Creole and English heritage, she made history in 1939 as the first black singer to feature on BBC Radio.

Evelyn Mary Dove was born on 11 January 1902 in London. She was the daughter of Francis Dove, a prominent Sierra Leonean barrister, and Augusta Winchester, an Englishwoman. Her family was accomplished. Her older brother Frank was a decorated war hero, and her younger sister Mabel became a noted journalist and politician.

She studied singing, piano, and elocution at the Royal Academy of Music, graduating in 1919. Despite her classical training, racial barriers in Britain pushed her towards cabaret and jazz revues. She performed with the Southern Syncopated Orchestra, an all-black band that promoted black music in the UK. She managed to survive a tragic shipwreck in 1921 where members of the orchestra and around 27 other passengers drowned when their ship sailing from Glasgow to Dublin collided.

Her career flourished internationally in the 1920s and '30s. She toured Europe with the revue, Chocolate Kiddies and performed in major cities such as Berlin, Moscow, and Paris. In 1936, she headlined at a Harlem nightclub in New York. Her popularity extended to Italy, France, and India, where she was hailed as a leading entertainer.

She reached the pinnacle of her career in Britain between 1939 and 1949. She did a lot of notable work broadcasting with the BBC as the first Black singer to feature on BBC radio. She became a prominent figure on BBC Radio, where she was as beloved as Vera Lynn during World War II.

One very successful programme was the series Serenade in Sepia from 1945 to 1947, for which she made more than 50 broadcasts with Trinidadian folk-singer Edric Connor. This attracted so many listeners that the BBC decided to make a television version.

In 1947 along with Connor and other artists she performed in Variety in Sepia. This was a TV special dedicated to Black talent, which was filmed live on 7 October 1947 at the RadiOlympia Theatre, Alexandra Palace, London, and aired on BBC TV.

Despite her success, she faced challenges later in life. After travelling and working abroad, she returned to Britain in the 1950s, but struggled to find work and battled health issues. She appeared in a few television roles and stage productions, but her fame waned.

She spent her final years in a nursing home and passed away from pneumonia on March 7 1987, at the age of 85.

Her legacy was largely forgotten until recent years. She was featured in a 1993 BBC Radio series, and her life story is detailed in the biography "Evelyn Dove: Britain's Black Cabaret Queen" by Stephen Bourne, published in 2016.

In 2019, Google honoured her with a Doodle on her 117th birthday, celebrating her contributions to music and entertainment.

First Black Daily Radio Show / First National Black Newspaper

Alex Pascall OBE – (1936-)

Alex Pascall OBE is a British broadcaster, journalist, musician, composer, oral historian, and educator. He played a significant role in developing the Notting Hill Carnival and was a key figure behind the creation of Britain's first national Black newspaper, The Voice. Alex was one of the first regular Black radio voices in the UK, presenting the pioneering programme Black Londoners on BBC Radio London for 14 years, making it the first daily Black radio show in British history from 1978.

Alex Pascall was born in November 1936 on the island of Grenada. He was the eldest of ten children. His family valued education and creativity, leading him to excel in school and perform on stage, which ignited his passion for the arts. After moving to London at 22, he worked in various jobs before establishing a career in music and broadcasting.

In 1964, he married Joyce, a fellow Grenadian nurse, and together they raised two children while founding a multicultural choir and a company promoting Caribbean culture. Despite facing racism, he continued to make strides in the arts and media. One notable incident involved a life-saving act by a white taxi driver who rescued him from an attack by a gang.

He gained national prominence as a broadcaster through his work with the groundbreaking BBC Radio London programme Black Londoners, which was first aired on 22 November 1974. He fronted it for 14 years. The show initially ran once a month, then moved to once a week and then from 1978, it was broadcast daily, becoming Britain's first daily Black radio magazine programme.

The programmes hour-long format was half phone-in and half news content each day. It became an important vehicle for the discussion of issues affecting the black community, in particular the New Cross Fire in 1981. It gave a mouthpiece for many black musicians, artists and politicians who either lived in or passed through the capital. Prominent guests on the programme from the worlds of politics, sport, literature and the arts included Muhammad Ali, Alex Haley, Bob Marley, Marvin Gaye, C. L. R. James, Maurice Bishop, Michael Jackson, Arthur Ashe, Althea McNish, Mustapha Matura, Jeremy Corbyn MP, Leon Britton MP, Angela Davis, Miriam Makeba and the Mighty Sparrow.

The development of the programme began in 1973 when people working in race and community relations recognised there was a lack of black representation in the British media. They approached BBC local radio and succeeded in obtaining a slot for black programming. The responsibility for its development was placed in the hands of Barry Clayton as producer and Alex Pascall as a presenter. They devised a magazine-style format programme for broadcast in November 1974.

Black Londoners was aired by BBC Radio London for 14 years, going on to become the first black daily radio programme broadcast in Britain from 1978 till 1988, when the station changed its name and the general format. Black women were also featured as an integral part of the programme, which did not happen often enough on the British Radio airwaves.

It was broadcast by BBC Radio London but he shaped its tone and content, even writing the signature tune. As a musician and songwriter he had a classic radio voice and an easy, intimate style that drew listeners in. Although the BBC had launched the programme in 1974 in response to community lobbying, its attitude towards it was not always helpful. There were people at the ground level who were supportive, but it was also clear that there were very negative people at the senior levels of the BBC who were not exactly keen.

In 1981, he helped launch The Voice newspaper, though he eventually parted ways with the project. He then focused on his radio show and later became involved with the Notting Hill Carnival, working to preserve its cultural significance amid negative media coverage.

He continued entertaining and teaching. He toured the country, giving talks and performances on Caribbean music and culture. In the mid-90s, he was asked to film one of his musical workshop sessions for children. He ensured that the children chosen were a representative mix. The show went on to become the programme Teletubbies, and he became known to millions of children worldwide for his appearances on the show, singing songs to groups of youngsters, he was also a programme consultant.

When his radio programme ended in 1988, he felt let down and forgotten by the BBC, despite spending 14 years presenting a pioneering series. He felt he could have gone on to achieve more but was disregarded by the BBC. Despite this he has produced and presented a number of radio programmes highlighting Black talent.

Throughout his career, he has been dedicated to promoting Caribbean music and history. He has spoken out on issues affecting the Black community and held various influential positions, including chair of the Black Members' Council of the National Union of Journalists. He has also worked as a playwright and cultural strategist, with his play, Common Threads, exploring the history of the sugar and coal industries.

Alex and his wife Joyce have a daughter, Deirdre, an arts educator and musician, and a son, Ayandele, a film editor.

In the 1996 Queen's Birthday Honours list he was made an Officer of the Order of the British Empire (OBE) for services to community relations.

First Black person to be an on-camera reporter and interviewer on British Television

Barbara Blake-Hannah – (1941-)

Barbara Blake-Hannah is a Jamaican author, journalist, filmmaker, politician, and cultural consultant renowned for promoting Rastafari culture and history. She made history in 1968 as the first Black on-camera reporter and interviewer on British television for Thames Television's evening news program, Today. Unfortunately, she was dismissed after viewers complained about seeing a Black woman on screen. Returning to Jamaica, she served as an independent senator from 1984 to 1987.

Barbara Makeda Blake-Hannah was born on 5 June 1941, in Jamaica. She was raised in an affluent Kingston neighbourhood by her father, Evon Blake, a prominent magazine editor. She attended the prestigious Hampton boarding school, where she and her sister were among the few Black students. After her father's finances declined, she left school to attend secretarial school, gaining valuable work experience in journalism, copywriting, and television.

In 1965, she moved to Britain for a role in the film, A High Wind in Jamaica. Despite her qualifications, she faced significant racism, struggling to find decent accommodation and starting her career from the bottom. She eventually worked for various publications, including The Caribbean Times and The Sunday Times, while dealing with pervasive racism.

In 1968 she became a reporter for Thames Television's Today programme. She was the first black person to be an on-camera reporter and interviewer on British television. She interviewed notable figures like Prime Minister Harold Wilson and actor Michael Caine. She was shielded from a lot of the racism and prejudice when conducting interviews in public, mainly because most people were flattered by the presence of a camera. People wanted their 15 minutes of fame to be on television and it did not matter who was ask the questions. Unfortunately, being a journalist did not protect her from racism within her own profession.

Her appointment made every daily newspaper, apart from the Daily Express, which had a rule that no Black people were allowed on the front page. One day in 1968, she was sent to report at the Houses of Parliament. She was sat on a bus passing by South Africa House in Trafalgar Square and white people were using the N-word and shouting, "Go back home…." up at her face. The irony was this was the year of the bill proposing amendments to the 1965 Race Relations Act 1965, making it illegal to refuse housing, employment or public services on the grounds of race. In March, It was also the year when Enoch Powell made his infamous Rivers of Blood speech in objection to the bill.

After nine months as a television reporter, she was dismissed without formal explanation, although her producer said the company was under pressure from a negative response from viewers for them having a black woman on television and said that the station had had calls from viewers, telling them to "get the Nigger off the screen". This was at a time when black acts like Shirley Bassey regularly appeared on television so blacks were allowed in an entertainment capacity, but not as serious news people, delivering serious stories.

The timing of her dismissal from Today was significant as Thames Television could have acted on the Race Relations Act but they didn't. Instead of following the letter and spirit of the law, they allowed the racists to win. Her dismissal highlighted the racial prejudice in British media.

She managed to get another job in TV, at Associated Television in Birmingham. However, she still suffered from racism finding it more pronounced than in London. It was difficult to get any accommodation and she was forced to commute every day from London, until she found a room at the YWCA. This was the 1960's so making 2 daily journeys between London and Birmingham would have been unbearable.

She also had to deal with the racism of her colleagues. She had to listen without reacting when the production staff asked, 'What 'wog' story are we doing today?'" She was deliberately kept away from the studio on a day when Enoch Powell was being interviewed. Following this, she worked as researcher on the BBC's documentary series Man Alive.

A few years later, she was asked to do public relations for the Jamaican film The Harder They Come. She decided to leave the UK and return to Jamaica permanently where she embraced Rastafari and black consciousness. Her career flourished as she became a successful filmmaker and author, writing about her experiences and promoting Rastafari culture.

She got into Jamaican politics and 1984 she became the first Rastafarian to serve in the Jamaican parliament as an independent senator. Her son, Makonnen David Blake Hannah, made history in 1998 as the youngest technology consultant appointed by the Jamaican government.

She has remained engaged with British issues, campaigning against deportations and criticizing the ongoing racism in British media. She has highlighted how little has changed since her dismissal, pointing to the treatment of Meghan Markle as an example.

In 2020, the Press Gazette launched the, Barbara Blake-Hannah Prize, to recognize emerging journalists from minority backgrounds, with the award including a trip to Jamaica to meet her. She has received numerous lifetime achievement awards and an Order of Distinction from the Jamaican government. The journalism award holds special significance for her, as it ensures her legacy will inspire future generations of diverse journalists.

Today
STUDIO 4
ON AIR
THAMES

First Black presenter of a British TV cooking show

Ainsley Harriott MBE – (1957-)

Ainsley Harriott is one of Britain's most recognized TV personalities and chefs. His journey to fame began after extensive training and experience in professional kitchens. In the early 1990s, he became the resident chef on BBC TV's Good Morning with Anne and Nick, which led to his role on Ready, Steady, Cook, making him the first Black presenter of a British TV cooking show.

Ainsley Denzil Dubriel Harriott was born on 28 February 1957, in Paddington, London. He is the son of Chester Leroy Harriott, a pianist and singer, and Peppy Harriott, both of Jamaican heritage. He attended Wandsworth Comprehensive School and trained at Westminster Kingsway College, where he apprenticed at Verrey's restaurant in London's West End.

Alongside his culinary career, he followed his father's musical footsteps, forming the Calypso Twins with school friend Paul Boross. The duo released a hit album in the early 1990s and performed widely, including in the United States.

His cooking career flourished as he became head chef at the Long Room of Lord's Cricket Ground and worked in several prestigious London restaurants, such as The Dorchester and The Hilton. He also presented More Nosh, Less Dosh, on BBC Radio 5 Live and appeared on TV as an extra with comedians Hale and Pace.

In 1992 he joined Good Morning with Anne and Nick as the resident TV chef, eventually becoming the main presenter of Can't Cook, Won't Cook, establishing him as the first Black presenter of a British TV cooking show. He also appeared in the sci-fi comedy series Red Dwarf and hosted the U.S. show, The Ainsley Harriott Show, which ran for over 100 episodes from 2000.

He has marketed his own range of food products, including couscous, risotto, soups, and cereal bars. In 2008, he participated in the genealogy show, Who Do You Think You Are?, where he discovered his great-grandfather's distinguished military career and his family's complex history with slavery.

He has authored numerous best-selling cookbooks, starting with, In The Kitchen in 1996, and has sold over two million cookery books worldwide. His TV appearances include, Something for the Weekend, GMTV with Lorraine, and cooking shows such as, Ainsley's Barbecue Bible, and, Ainsley's Gourmet Express.

In the 2020 New Years Honours list he was appointed Member of the Order of the British Empire (MBE) for services to broadcasting and the culinary arts.

He also helped rescue his sister from drowning at the 2022 Chelsea Flower Show and won the Christmas special of The Masked Singer in 2023, as Partridge in a Pear Tree.

He married former costume designer Clare Fellows, with whom he has two children. Though separated in 2012, they remain on good terms. He is a supporter of Arsenal F.C. and has reflected on the shocking racism he faced in his career, being rejected from jobs despite his qualifications due to his race.

With over 18 years as a popular TV chef, he is celebrated for his charisma, professionalism, and contribution to making cooking both entertaining and accessible.

First Black musician to win the BBC Young Musician award

Sheku Kanneh-Mason MBE – (1999-)

Sheku Kanneh-Mason MBE is a British cellist who gained fame after winning the 2016 BBC Young Musician award, becoming the first Black musician to achieve this since the competition began in 1978.

Sheku Kanneh-Mason was born on 4 April 1999, in Nottingham. He is the third of seven children. His father, Stuart Mason, is a luxury hotel business manager of Antiguan descent, and his mother, Dr. Kadiatu Kanneh, originally from Sierra Leone, was a lecturer at the University of Birmingham. He attended Trinity School in Nottingham, where he studied Music, Maths, and Physics for his A-levels.

He began playing the cello at the age of six after briefly playing the violin. His interest was sparked by seeing his sister perform in Stringwise, a course for young string players. By the age of nine, he had passed the Grade 8 cello exam with the highest marks in the UK and won the Marguerite Swan Memorial Prize. He received an ABRSM junior scholarship to join the Junior Academy of the Royal Academy of Music.

In 2015 he competed on Britain's Got Talent with his siblings, reaching the semi-finals.

He achieved further recognition in 2016 by winning the BBC Young Musician of the Year, the first Black musician to do so. He also won the Royal Philharmonic Society Young Instrumentalist Duet Prize. His local authority, Nottingham, honoured him by naming a bus after him.

He is a member of the Chineke! Orchestra, which was founded by Chi-chi Nwanoku to promote diversity among classical musicians. Inspired by the lack of diversity in classical music. He found Chineke! particularly motivating.

In June 2016 he signed with Enticott Music Management and later with Decca Classics. His debut recording featured Shostakovich's Cello Concerto No.1, which he performed to win the BBC Young Musician contest. He was also the subject of the BBC Four documentary, Young, Gifted and Classical: The Making of a Maestro."

He has performed at prestigious events such as the British Academy Film Awards (BAFTA) and the BBC Proms. His debut album, Inspiration, released in January 2018, included his arrangement of Bob Marley's No Woman, No Cry. The album achieved significant success, becoming the highest-charting debut by a British cellist and the best-selling British debut of the year.

He performed at the wedding of Prince Harry and Meghan Markle in May 2018 and again at the Royal Variety Performance later that year. He won multiple awards, including Male Artist of the Year and Critics' Choice Award at the Classic BRIT Awards in June 2018.

In 2020 he released his second album, Elgar, featuring the London Symphony Orchestra conducted by Sir Simon Rattle.

In March 2020 he won the public vote for Best Classical Artist at the Global Awards.

In the 2020 New Years Honours list he was appointed a Member of the Order of the British Empire (MBE) for his services to music.

In November 2021 he released an album called Muse with his sister Isata playing piano.

He comes from a prodigious musical family. His six siblings all share exceptional musical talents. Isata plays the piano, Braimah plays the violin and Konya and Aminata both play violin and piano. Jeneba and the youngest, Mariatu both play cello and piano. In November 2020 an album featuring all seven siblings called Carnival was released. It was recorded at London's Abbey Road Studios featuring melodies by Saint-Saëns,

Tchaikovsky and Eric Whitacre, alongside the voice of actress Olivia Colman reading poems by Michael Morpurgo.

The family planned to tour Australia in 2020 and 2021, but this was delayed due to the COVID-19 pandemic. The whole family toured six Australian cities over 16 days in July/August 2022, including a performance with the Melbourne Symphony Orchestra of Shostakovich's Cello Concerto No. 2 and a wide variety of compositions by Frank Bridge, George Gershwin, Felix Mendelssohn, Maria Theresia von Paradis, Eric Whitacre, Franz Schubert, Samuel Coleridge-Taylor, Franz Liszt, Jerry Bock, and Bob Marley's Redemption Song.

In 2022 with Decca Classics, he released an album called Song which displayed his innately lyrical playing in a wide and varied range of arrangements and collaboration

On 26 May 2022 he was appointed as the Royal Academy of Music's first Menuhin Visiting Professor of Performance Mentoring.

He was diagnosed with Type 1 diabetes at the age of 12. In September 2018 the Juvenile Diabetes Research Foundation (JDRF) announced that it had appointed him as a global ambassador. He is also an ambassador for the charities Music Masters and Future Talent.

First professional orchestra in Europe to be made up of majority Black, Asian and ethnically diverse musicians

Chineke! Orchestra — (2015-)

Chineke! Orchestra is a pioneering British orchestra, the first in Europe to be composed primarily of Black, Asian, and ethnically diverse musicians. The name "Chineke" comes from the Igbo language, meaning "God." Founded by musician Chi-chi Nwanoku in 2015, the orchestra held its debut concert at Queen Elizabeth Hall in London. The orchestra for its first two concerts comprised exclusively black, Asian and minority ethnic musicians, but it has since included white musicians.

The Chineke! Foundation was also established by Chi-chi Nwanoku CBE in 2015. Its mission is to create outstanding career opportunities for Black and ethnically diverse classical musicians in the UK and Europe. The foundation's motto, "Championing change and celebrating diversity in classical music," reflects its goal to increase the representation of these musicians in British and European orchestras. The foundation supports musicians through the Chineke! Orchestra, the Chineke! Junior Orchestra, and various educational and community engagement initiatives.

Chi-chi Nwanoku CBE, the founder, artistic, and executive director of the Chineke! Foundation, was born in June 1956 in Fulham to a Nigerian father and an Irish mother. She discovered her passion for music at a young age, starting with the piano and later excelling in the double bass. Her early career as a 100-meter sprinter ended due to a knee injury, which led her to focus on music. She studied at the Royal Academy of Music and became a prominent double bass player, founding member of the Orchestra of the Age of Enlightenment, and professor at the Royal Academy of Music.

She has been recognized for her contributions to music and diversity with numerous awards. The idea for Chineke! was inspired by a conversation with Ed Vaizey, the UK Minister of Culture, and a concert by the Kinshasa

Symphony, which highlighted the lack of diversity in classical music audiences and performers.

In the 2001 Queen's Birthday honours list she was appointed a Member of the Order of the British Empire (MBE) for her services to music.

The Chineke! Foundation quickly garnered support from cultural organizations like the BBC and Arts Council England, raising significant funds and attracting diverse talent. The orchestra's debut featured works by Black British composers and marked the first concert for conductor Wayne Marshall. Since then, Chineke! has performed at prestigious venues, including The Proms, and made its first commercial recording in 2017.

In the 2017 Queen's Platinum Jubilee Birthday honours list she was appointed a Commander of the Order of the British Empire (CBE) for her services to music and diversity

The Chineke! Junior Orchestra provides a platform for young Black and ethnically diverse musicians aged 11-22, offering mentorship and bridging the gap between youth programs and higher education. This initiative aims to increase the number of diverse candidates studying music at the tertiary level, with many junior members achieving notable successes in national competitions and gaining admission to elite music schools.

Chi-chi Nwanoku, Founder of Chineke! Foundation and Orchestra

First Black woman to be appointed to a professorial chair in History in Britain

Olivette Otele FRHistS FLSW – (1970-)

Olivette Otele FRHistS FLSW is a historian and Professor of the History of Slavery at Bristol University where she is also Vice-President of the Royal Historical Society and Chair of Bristol's Race Equality Commission. She specializes in the connections between history, memory, and geopolitics, particularly regarding French and British colonial pasts. Notably, she holds the distinction of being the first Black woman appointed to a professorial chair in History in Britain.

Olivette Otele was born in Cameroon in 1970 with a Cameroonian heritage. She grew up in Paris, France, and studied at Sorbonne University, focusing on European colonial and post-colonial history. She is multilingual, fluent in French, English, some German, and three Cameroonian languages.

After completing her education, she became an associate professor at Université Paris XIII before joining Bath Spa University, where she eventually became a Professor of History in 2018, becoming the first Black woman to hold such a position in the UK. She has been vocal about the challenges she faced in academia due to her caring responsibilities and being a woman of colour, highlighting broader issues of discrimination within the university system.

Her expertise extends beyond academia. She is a Fellow of the Royal Historical Society and serves on several boards, including Historians Against Slavery and The British Society for the Eighteenth-Century Studies. Her research focuses on post-slavery societies, Afro-European identities, and the Atlantic slave trade.

She has led significant research projects, including one exploring the legacy of the slave trade in Bristol, funded by UK Research and Innovation. Her work has been recognized through various honours and awards, including the establishment of the Olivette Otele Prize by the Institute of Historical Research to recognize outstanding research by Black PhD students.

In 2020 she began a two-year research project at Bristol University to examine Bristol's connection to the transatlantic slave trade, aiming to reshape the way Britain acknowledges and teaches this history. She was also appointed as the independent Chair of Bristol's Commission on Race Equality in June 2020, demonstrating her commitment to promoting racial justice and inclusivity.

Beyond her academic achievements, she is an advocate for social justice, driven by her belief in the importance of understanding history to combat racism and discrimination. She has authored multiple books, contributed to numerous publications, and engaged in media activities to raise awareness of these issues.

In recognition of her contributions, she received an honorary doctorate from Concordia University in Canada in 2022 and was appointed as a Distinguished Research Professor at SOAS University of London in April 2022.

First Black Professor in Scotland

Sir Godfrey Palmer KT OBE CD – (1940-)

Sir Godfrey Palmer KT OBE CD is a Professor Emeritus in the School of Life Sciences at Heriot-Watt University in Edinburgh, Scotland, and a human rights activist. In 1989, he became the first black professor in Scotland, becoming a professor emeritus after he retired in 2005. Emeritus is an honorary title granted to someone who retires from a position of distinction. He was knighted in the 2014 New Year Honours.

Godfrey Henry Oliver Palmer was born on 9 April 1940 in St Elizabeth, Jamaica. His father left home when he was seven years old. His mother travelled to England to work as a dressmaker in England in 1948, as a part of the Windrush generation. He grew up in Kingston, Jamaica, in the care of his eight aunts.

He joined his mother to live in North London in March 1955, shortly before his 15th birthday. Too young to work, he was told he had to go to school. His only schooling in Jamaica had been Sunday school. He was assessed as being educationally subnormal at his first school, and he was sent to Shelborne Road Secondary Modern. Fortunately, his cricketing skill gained him a place on the London Schools' cricket team, and a place at Highbury Grammar School. He left school in 1958 with six O-levels and two A-levels, in botany and zoology, finding a job as a junior lab technician at Queen Elizabeth College, London University. He gained further qualifications studying one day a week at a local polytechnic. So much for being regarded as educationally subnormal!

In 1961 he went to the University of Leicester earning a 2:2 degree in botany in 1964. He sought post-graduate work and applied to study for an MSc at the University of Nottingham, funded by the Ministry of Agriculture. He also met Maggie at Leicester, who would go on to become his wife.

In 1965 he began a doctorate to study for a PhD in grain science and technology jointly with Heriot-Watt College and the University of Edinburgh. He completed his PhD thesis entitled Ultra-structure of cereal grains in relation to germination in 1967. He then began work at the Brewing Research Foundation in Surrey in 1968 on the science and technology of barley. He moved back to Heriot-Watt University in 1977. He received a Doctorate of Science in 1985, and was offered a personal Chair at Heriot-Watt in 1989. His mother joked, 'What are they giving you a Chair for? Tell them to give you money.' He made history as Scotland's first black professor, a title he earned through his expertise in grain science and technology. His pioneering work in understanding the processes of barley and other cereals led to significant advancements in brewing and distilling industries. Notably, he was instrumental in establishing the International Centre for Brewing and Distilling at Heriot-Watt University, showcasing his ability to bridge academia with industry.

Beyond his academic pursuits, he is a tireless advocate for human rights, particularly focusing on issues of racial equality and social justice. His involvement in various charity works and community initiatives reflects his dedication to improving the lives of others, especially those from marginalized backgrounds.

In April 2021 he was appointed as the Chancellor of Heriot-Watt University, for an initial term of five years. The role was central to promoting Heriot-Watt's prominence and profile in research in the university's campuses in Scotland, Malaysia and Dubai.

In the 2003 Queen's Birthday Honours list, he was appointed Officer of the Order of the British Empire (OBE) In recognition of his work and achievements in the field of grain science

In 2007, the Bicentenary of the passage of the Slave Trade Act 1807 by Parliament, which abolished the slave trade, he was named among the 100 Great Black Britons, as well as on the 2020 updated list.

In 2008 he became the fourth person, and the first European, to be honoured with the American Society of Brewing Chemists Award of Distinction, considered the Nobel Prize of brewing, for distinction in scientific research and good citizenship. He received the award in Boston, Massachusetts.

He has been awarded Honorary Doctorates by Abertay University in 2009, the Open University in 2010, the University of the West Indies in 2015, and Heriot-Watt University in 2015.

In the 2014 New Years Honours list, he was knighted for services to human rights, science, and charity.

As a prominent figure in Edinburgh, his influence extends beyond academia. He has played pivotal roles in commemorating historical events, advocating for the reinterpretation of monuments, and challenging systemic injustices, such as his involvement in the protests following the murder of George Floyd.

On 14 November 2022 he received the Edinburgh Award from the Edinburgh City Council. This award was established in 2007 and honours an outstanding individual who has made a positive impact on the city and gained national and international recognition for Edinburgh. He was presented with an engraved Loving Cup from the Lord Provost and had his handprints set in stone at the City Chambers, in recognition of his ground-breaking contributions to academia, and his indefatigable defence of human rights in Edinburgh and beyond,

In December 2022, with the Lord President of the Court of Session, Lord Carloway, he unveiled a plaque commemorating the 1778 Knight v Wedderburn case, which ruled that slavery was incompatible with Scots law.

In March 2024 King Charles III appointed him a knight of the Most Ancient and Most Noble Order of the Thistle (KT), the highest order of chivalry in Scotland

He has lived in the town of Penicuik in Midlothian since 1977. He is married to educational psychologist Margaret Palmer. They met while studying in Leicester in the 1960s.

First Black fighter to win a British boxing title

Dick Turpin – (1920-1990)

Dick Turpin was an English middleweight boxer. He was British and Commonwealth middleweight champion, and in 1948 became the first black fighter to win a British boxing title and the first black athlete to win a British title in any sport. He was elder brother and trainer of the more famous Randolph Turpin, who became world middleweight champion after beating Sugar Ray Robinson in 1951.

Dick Turpin was born on 26 November 1920 in Leamington Spa, Warwickshire. His father Lionel Turpin was black, born in British Guyana and his mother Beatrice Elizabeth Whitehouse was a local white lady. Lionel had stowed away to get to Britain to join the army during World War I. Life was hard for the family as this was a time when there was not much ethnic diversity in Britain. Sadly, Lionel died in 1929. He had fought at the Battle of the Somme and never fully recovering from the injuries he sustained in a gas attack. Beatrice was thus left to raise the children alone.

Probably due to their challenging circumstance of needing to protect themselves from racist attacks, Dick and his two younger brothers, Jack and Randolph, all took up boxing during childhood. Dick and Randolph were both middleweights, while Jack fought at featherweight.

Dick fought his first professional bout in March 1939 against Jimmy Griffiths, in Coventry. He lost on points over ten rounds. He later won a rematch.

Like his father, he would also serve in the forces, refusing an exemption in order to fight on the African, Italian and German fronts during World War II. He returned unharmed and resumed his career in the ring.

He went on to build up a domestic record of 86 fights with 68 wins, 12 losses, 5 draws and one no-contest, before his first title fight. This was for the

Commonwealth middleweight title, in May 1948, and was against Richard Bos Murphy of New Zealand. Turpin won the fight, at Coventry, by a knockout in the first round to become Commonwealth champion.

He suffered continuously from racial discrimination. Incredibly as a black man he was not allowed to challenge for any British boxing title by law. This was introduced in 1911, amid anxieties over the fitness of the white race, and concerns over how a coloured fighter defeating a white opponent would affect the colonies.

Naturally, there were many non-white and highly-skilled boxers around the world. One was American fighter Jack Johnson, who became the world heavyweight champion in 1908 and subsequently successfully defended his title several times. However, Johnson was unpopular with many white Americans, not least those in power. He received almost equal contempt in Britain. Johnson further annoyed them by being very much his own man and refusing to bow to the expectations placed on him by the white ruling classes. His success made him a global star. In 1911, he was set to fight Britain's 'Bombardier' Billy Wells in London.

There was a considerable backlash to the prospect of a white man facing a black opponent on British soil, especially given the likelihood of the black man winning. Winston Churchill, the then British Home Secretary was lobbied by many people including the Archbishop of Canterbury and Lord Lonsdale, to step in and stop the fight from happening. On 26 September, Churchill bowed to this pressure and declared the bout to be illegal. Johnson eventually fought in Europe in France and Spain, but never in Britain.

Churchill's decision did not just put a stop to this fight between Johnson and Wells fight, it set a precedent that would be used time and again to stop any black or non-white boxer from competing for the British title. It was not until 1948, almost 37 years later that it was repealed, eventually falling to mounting public and press opposition, though some within the sport still did not agree with white men fighting people of other races, especially if it was likely that the white men would lose.

The repeal of the 1911 law opened the door for Dick Turpin, whose career was peaking at just the right time. His British title fight against Hawkins came only one month after he had knocked out Richard Bos Murphy of New Zealand to become Empire champion.

On 28 June 1948, he out-fought Hawkins over 15 rounds in front of 40,000 people at Villa Park stadium in Birmingham. The fight took place in pouring rain, with both boxers slipping on the drenched canvas. Almost a decade after his debut he would become Empire and British champion, beating Vince Hawkins on points.

The significance of him simply competing for a British title was made evident by the BBC's decision to cover the fight on radio. The Birmingham Gazette described the event as the Midlands' biggest boxing attraction for many years, and his achievement was even mentioned in the African-American press.

During late 1948 and early 1949, he fought European boxers, drawing and then losing on points against Tiberio Mitri, of Italy, then being knocked out in seven rounds in a non-title fight against the then world middleweight champion, Marcel Cerdan, of France. He then won by a disqualification against another Frenchman, Robert Charron.

In June 1949 he defended his British and Commonwealth titles against Albert Finch, winning on points after fifteen rounds. In September 1949 he defended his Commonwealth title against Australian, Dave Sands. The fight was at Harringay Arena, and he was knocked out in the first round, leaving him with only the British title.

He then won his next four fights, losing the fifth, on points to American, Baby Day, before defending his British title against Albert Finch, whom he had beaten in his previous defence. The fight was held in April 1950, in Nottingham and Finch won on points after fifteen rounds.

Following the loss of both his titles, he had only two more fights, against the Belgian, Cyrille Delannoit, in Brussels, losing on a technical knockout in the sixth, and finally against his old rival Albert Finch, losing on a technical knockout in the eighth. This last fight was in July 1950.

He retired and became a trainer for his brother Randolph, who went on to beat Sugar Ray Robinson to take the world middleweight title in 1951.

He died aged 69 in 1990.

In 2021 a blue plaque paying homage to him as the first black boxer to win a British title has been unveiled on Parkes Street in Warwick, the town where he was born and lived much of his life.

First British boxer to win Olympic gold at super-heavyweight division

Audley Harrison MBE – (1971-)

Audley Harrison MBE is a British former professional boxer who competed from 2001 to 2013. As an amateur, he represented Great Britain at the 2000 Olympics, winning a gold medal in the super-heavyweight division. He was the first British boxer to achieve this. He turned professional in 2001 after signing with BBC Sport, having 17 fights broadcasted before the BBC ceased airing boxing.

Audley Hugh Harrison was born on 26 October 1971, in Harlesden, London, to Jamaican parents. He had a troubled youth involved in street gangs and petty crime, resulting in a three-year prison sentence for robbery and assault. During his imprisonment, he decided to change his life.

After his release, he focused on amateur boxing and education, graduating from Brunel University with degrees in sports science and leisure management. He trained at Repton Amateur Boxing Club, becoming British super-heavyweight champion in 1997 and 1998, and won gold at the 1998 Commonwealth Games.

In 2000 he won gold at the Sydney Olympics, defeating Mukhtarkhan Dildabekov of Kazakhstan in the super-heavyweight division, the first Black British fighter to do this.

In the 2001 Queen's New Years Honours list he was appointed a Member of the Order of the British Empire (MBE) for his services to sport, in recognition of his Olympic Gold medal.

Following his Olympic success, he turned professional. He wrote his autobiography titled, Releasing the Dream, and founded A Force Promotions to manage his career, securing a £1 million broadcast deal with the BBC.

He debuted professionally at Wembley Arena, quickly establishing a winning streak. He fought in the United States, continued his success, and won the World Boxing Foundation World belt in 2004. After suffering a hand injury, he had a brief hiatus from boxing.

He faced significant challenges, including a split decision loss to Danny Williams and a knockout defeat by Michael Sprott. Despite setbacks, he made a comeback, winning the Prizefighter tournament in 2009 and the European Boxing Union belt in 2010. However, his attempt at a world title against David Haye ended in a third-round defeat.

He participated in the BBC show "Strictly Come Dancing" in 2011 and later announced a boxing return. He continued to fight sporadically, winning the Prizefighter tournament again in 2013 but faced defeats, including a notable loss to Deontay Wilder.

After several retirements and comebacks, he finally retired from professional boxing in March 2014. He lives in Los Angeles with his wife Raychel, daughter Ariella, and son Hudson.

In 2015, he revealed that he was suffering from traumatic brain injuries, which affected his vision and mood.

First British boxer to reach the final of the World Amateur Boxing Championships

David Haye – (1980-)

David Haye, a former professional boxer from Britain, made a significant mark in the boxing world between 2002 and 2018. He achieved multiple world championships in two weight classes and notably became the first Black British boxer to reach the final of the World Amateur Boxing Championships, earning a silver medal in 2001.

David Deron Haye was born on 13 October 1980, in Bermondsey, London, to Jamaican father Deron Haye and English mother Jane Haye. He displayed an early passion for boxing. His journey began at the age of six when he expressed his ambition to become the heavyweight champion of the world. Remarkably, at just 10 years old, he won his first fight by knockout in a mere 12 seconds, setting the stage for his future in the sport.

As a teenager, his talent became evident as he faced opponents much older than himself. His dedication led him to compete in the 1999 World Amateur Boxing Championships, where he caught the eye of fashion photographer Bruce Webber, leading to a lucrative modelling opportunity with Abercrombie & Fitch.

At the age of eighteen, he competed in the light-heavyweight division at the 1999 World Amateur Boxing Championships in Houston, Texas. He knocked out the-ABA light-heavyweight champion Courtney Fry but missed out on the 2000 Sydney Olympics after a controversial defeat in the qualifier in which he was eliminated by experienced American Michael Simms early in the contest.

At the 2001 World Championships in Belfast, he fought at heavyweight defeating Sebastian Köber to reach the final, where he was stopped by Cuban Odlanier Solís in the third round to earn a silver medal. Thus becoming the first British boxer to reach the final of the World Amateur Boxing Championships

Turning professional at the age of 22 in December 2002, he swiftly rose through the ranks, securing numerous victories and titles in both the cruiserweight and heavyweight divisions. His achievements include unifying cruiserweight world titles and becoming a world heavyweight champion.

In addition to his boxing career, he established his own promotional company, Hayemaker Promotions, in 2008, further solidifying his influence in the sport. Throughout his career, he faced various challenges and setbacks, including injuries and controversial matches, but remained a formidable force in the ring.

After announcing his retirement in June 2018, he briefly returned to the ring in 2021 for an exhibition bout against friend and businessman Joe Fournier, which he won.

Despite his retirement, his legacy in boxing continues to inspire aspiring athletes, showcasing the determination and resilience required to succeed in the sport.

He married make-up artist Natasha in 2008, with whom he has a son named Cassius (named after Cassius Clay), though they divorced after eight.

First Black man to play rugby for England

James Peters — (1879-1954)

James Peters was an English rugby union player and, later, a rugby league footballer. He is notable as the first black man to play rugby union for England in 1906, and the only black England player until 1988.

James Peters was born on 7 August 1879 at 38 Queen Street in Salford, Lancashire, England to his Jamaican father George Peters and his mother Hannah Gough from Wem, Shropshire. He was the eldest of four children. His father George was a travelling showman in the circus. This was quite common for black people in Victorian Britain as they were seen as minorities and oddities. George was mauled to death in a training cage by lions. His mother, Hannah was unable to look after him so he was moved to join another circus troupe as a bareback horse rider. He broke his arm when he was 11 and was abandoned by the circus in Dorset.

Destitute and possibly begging just to stay alive; his plight touched the heart of a Miss Daniel, who was the daughter of the doctor/surgeon to Lord and Lady Portman who brought him to their attention. The details are a bit sketchy but he ended up at James Fegan's Christian Orphanage for Boys in Southwark, London. Life in the orphanage was strict, and the boys were well educated, paying special attention to religion and sport. He was a natural athlete, and became the captain of the rugby and cricket teams. Aged 13 he was moved to Fegan's other orphanage Little Wanderers' Home in Greenwich.

At the annual sports day in 1894, held at Stamford Bridge stadium, he won all seven events, but generously gave away one of his prizes to his nearest competitor. He was moved back to Southwark, where he trained as a printer. Later he re-trained as a carpenter. At the age of 19 he left Fegan's to get a job as a carpenter in Bristol. He was finally re-united with his mother, two brothers and sister, after ten years away. He also met his mother's new husband, William Hart. .

His trade brought him to Bristol, where he played as a fly-half for Dings Crusaders, Knowle and Bristol Rugby Club, and represented the Somerset County team between 1900 and 1903. His presence at Bristol was opposed by some on racist grounds. A committee member at Bristol resigned in protest at his selection for the team, whilst a local newspaper described him as a "palid blackamoor" and complained that he was "keeping a white man out of the side".

He moved on to Plymouth in 1902 where he worked as a carpenter in Devonport Dockyard. He also represented Plymouth RUFC and the Devon county side until 1909. By 1904 he was Devon's star player, earning the nickname Darkie Peters. He was overlooked for selection to the England team for a further two years, despite the national side having six other Devon players in the team. He shone in the Devon side which won the County Championship in 1906, resulting in the press calling for his selection for the national team.

On 17 March 1906, he won his first cap for England against Scotland, England's first black player. However, the Yorkshire Post pointed out, "His selection is by no means popular on racial grounds". In the match, he set up two tries for England: The Sportsman commented that the "dusky Plymouth man did many good things, especially in passing." He was to play a further game, against France, in which he scored a try.

Later in 1906 his Devon county team were chosen to play against a touring South African side. On match day, they noticed he was black, and the Springboks refused to play with him in the team. After a lot of debate, and possible political intervention, the game went ahead with him, in front of an 18,000 crowd. South Africa won.

For the following international game, South Africa v England game, he was dropped, and not even selected for the trials. He'd gone from being England's top half-back, to not being in the top six due to racial discrimination. He was also dropped from England's next game.

Once the South Africans had left, he was soon back in favour with the England side, and played against Ireland in 1907, followed by two further international games against Scotland and Wales. The latter was in dense fog, ironically the last time he would be seen in an England shirt. He had played five times for England, a great achievement, but it could have been so much more.

Unfortunately in 1909 he suffered a terrible machining accident, losing three fingers. His Plymouth teammates arranged a benefit game for him. However as this meant him receiving money, the Rugby Union authorities saw this as professionalism, and duly banned him, when he had remarkably got back into the Plymouth team, despite his accident.

Plymouth and several other clubs in the south-west of England tried to form a Western League, which would later become Rugby league and play competitive fixtures. He was suspended for accepting payment from Devon Rugby Club, which was illegal according to the codes of rugby union. Many players, including Peters, and also RFC Plymouth were suspended by the RFU. Plymouth's ground closed, signalling the end of Plymouth RFC. The rules of professionalism often owed more to politics than finance.

Somewhat disillusioned by rugby union, aged 34, he was accepted into rugby league. Returning to his native north-western England, he played for Barrow in 1913, and then transferred to St. Helens in 1914 until his retirement from rugby. Sadly racial discrimination was a constant irritation.

With the outbreak of World War I, he was recalled to work in Devonport Dockyard. He worked there until 1921, but also had a shop selling beer and worked as a builder's carpenter. He lived in Plymouth for the rest of his life. He was a fit man, walking everywhere, never catching the bus. Teetotal and religious, with a keen sense of humour, he was never seen without his pipe or dog.

He was married to Rosina Finch for 47 years and they had 2 children, Rowena and Jack

He died on 26 March 1954, aged 74, and is buried in Plymouth.

He was the first black man to represent England at rugby in 1906, and he remained the only black England player for another 82 years until Chris Oti represented England in 1988.

First Black captain for Great Britain in any sport

Clive Sullivan MBE – (1943-)

Clive Sullivan MBE was a Welsh rugby league footballer. A Great Britain and Wales international winger, he played for both Hull F.C. and Hull Kingston Rovers in his career, and also for Oldham and Doncaster. Captaining Great Britain in 1972, he was the first black captain for Great Britain in rugby league or any sport. He was part of the Great Britain team which won the 1972 Rugby League World Cup.

Clive Anthony Sullivan was born on 9 April 1943 in the Splott, an inner-city suburb of Cardiff. His mother's family was of Antiguan descent and his father was Jamaican. They were the only black family in the area.

He began playing rugby at school, but from the age of 14, he suffered injuries which required surgery on his knees, feet and shoulders. Doctors felt it would be unlikely that he would ever be able to walk normally again let alone play rugby. Fortunately he recovered.

In 1961 after leaving school, he worked briefly as a motor mechanic and then joined the army. He was posted to Catterick in the North Riding of Yorkshire for his basic training and went on to be trained as a radio operator. Once qualified, he volunteered to become a paratrooper and after gaining his wings, he joined 216 Parachute Signals Squadron at Farnborough, Hampshire.

While he was at Catterick, he was picked for an inter-corps rugby match because he was Welsh. He chose to play the match as admitting he had a major injury would have led to him being invalided out of the army. He planned to play badly to avoid being picked again. However, instinct took over and after scoring a long distance try with no ill effects, he decided to make the most of the army training to further progress his hopes of playing rugby.

He was spotted playing in a game at the army barracks and given a trial at Bradford Northern. This trial was not successful and he was not signed by Bradford. However, after the game he was offered a trial at Hull. In this trial he scored three tries and was signed as a professional the following day. He wanted to serve in the Army and play professional rugby.

His first three seasons were restricted by his army duties. He also had three knee operations and a nearly fatal car crash in October 1963, although he returned to play again just three months after the accident.

He saw active service with his unit in Nicosia, Cyprus in January 1964. He was subsequently attached to the United Nations Peacekeeping Force and awarded the United Nations Medal for his service. He left the army after this spell in Cyprus and being free of his army commitments he returned to Hull in time to play the last game of the season.

In his début for Hull, he had an outstanding game, gaining the support of the Hull club and city. He became known for his exceptional speed and upper body which was deceptively strong. His main issues were his knees which needed constant attention and further operations. He played a total of 352 games for Hull, scoring 250 tries. In his 213 games for Hull Kingston Rovers he scored 118 tries.

In 1967 his international career for Great Britain began. The following year he played three World Cup matches, grabbing a hat-trick against New Zealand. In 1970 he toured Australasia, though he only played in one test due to injury. However, he won a further three test caps against New Zealand in 1971.

In 1972 he was handed the captaincy of Great Britain, making him the first Black captain for Great Britain in rugby or any sport. He played two tests against France. The World Cup took place that same year, and he captained Great Britain to become world champions. He scored a try in each of Great Britain's four games and scored a try to level 10–10 against Australia in the World Cup Final, after a length of the field run.

In 1973 his Great Britain career came to an end with three tests against Australia. He was captain-coach of Hull F.C. from 1973 to 1974.

In the 1974 New Years Honours list, he was awarded a Member of the Order of the British Empire (MBE) for services to rugby league.

In the 1975 Rugby League World Cup, he led Wales in all four matches, scoring a try in the victory over England in the second game for the Welsh team. Wales finished third in the five-team World Cup.

He shocked everybody in Hull by switching to rival team Hull Kingston Rovers.

On 13 December 1977 he played left wing and scored a try in Hull Kingston Rovers' 26–11 victory over St. Helens in the 1977 BBC2 Floodlit Trophy Final at Craven Park, Hull.

On 18 December 1979 he played left wing in the 3–13 defeat by Hull F.C. in the BBC2 Floodlit Trophy Final at the Boulevard, Hull

On 3 May 1980, in the 1979-1980 Challenge Cup Final, he played left wing in the Hull Kingston Rovers' 10-5 victory over Hull F.C at Wembley Stadium, London.

In 1982 he was unexpectedly called back into the Hull F.C. team, at the age of 39, playing right wing, He played for Hull F.C. until his retirement in 1985.

Six months after retiring, he died of cancer on 8 October 1985, aged 42.

He was survived by his wife Rosalyn who he married in 1966 and a son Anthony and a daughter Lisa.

The city of Hull held him in such high esteem that a section of the city's main approach road, the A63 between the Humber Bridge and the city centre, was renamed Clive Sullivan Way in his honour.

Since 2001 the Clive Sullivan Memorial Trophy has been awarded to the winner of the Rugby League local derby match between Hull and Hull Kingston Rovers in recognition of his service to both local clubs.

In December 2020 he was named as one of three Welsh rugby league players to be honoured with a new statue in Cardiff Bay, the other two being Billy Boston and Gus Risman.

In April 2021 he was honoured in a Google Doodle to celebrate what would have been his 78th birthday.

He still holds two records for Hull, which include the most tries in a career (250) and most tries in a match (7, against Doncaster on 15 April 1968), and is one of fewer than twenty-five Welshmen to have scored more than 1,000 points in their rugby league career.

He represented Great Britain 17 times and appeared at three World Cups, 1968 and 1972 with Great Britain, and in 1975 for Wales.

First Black British Chair of a major sport in England

Tom Ilube CBE – (1963-)

Tom Ilube CBE is a successful British entrepreneur and educational philanthropist. In his early life he developed a keen interest in rugby, though his professional career took him to work in the technology sector. However he retained his interest in rugby and became involved in the community game for a number of years. On 1 August 2021 he became chair of the Rugby Football Union making him the first black chair of a major sport in England.

Thomas Segun Ilube was born in July 1963, near Richmond, Surrey. His father came from Nigeria and his mother from Richmond. His father had joined the West African part of the British army and came to Britain in 1956 to be trained initially in Harrogate in north Yorkshire, then as an electrical engineer. He moved to London where he met his wife and Tom was born. His father was one of the first black engineers working for the BBC.

Tom Ilube CBE has led an inspiring life journey, starting from his roots in Surrey, England, to becoming a trailblazing figure in both technology and philanthropy. Born in July 1963, to a Nigerian father and a mother from Richmond, his upbringing was marked by cultural diversity and academic pursuit.

The family lived in Sunbury where he went to school. However, in 1969 the family relocated to Uganda when his father was asked to help establish Ugandan Television. It was a chaotic time in Uganda due to the rule of Idi Amin and after three years the family escaped back to Britain. Tom then attended Teddington Boys School which he enjoyed. He loved science and rugby which he played both in school and for his local club, the London Welsh in Richmond.

The family then returned to Nigeria which was a big culture shock though he enjoyed his time, making lots of friends and learning a lot. He went to Edo

College in Benin City, in the south-west of Nigeria. This was the best school in the region and was modelled on British schools.

In 1980 he went to the University of Benin in Nigeria to study physics. He was introduced to computers, though he never actually saw one.

In 1984 he graduated from university and returned to Britain. He decided he wanted a career in IT

His IT journey was marked by determination and resilience. He famously applied to every company listed in the Computer User's Yearbook, starting with those beginning with the letter A, until he landed a job at British Airways. This marked the beginning of a successful career that saw him work for prestigious institutions like the London Stock Exchange and Goldman Sachs.

In 1996 he embarked on his entrepreneurial journey, founding Lost Wax, a company that evolved from creating websites to developing advanced multi-agent systems. His entrepreneurial spirit led him to co-found Egg, an internet bank that achieved remarkable success in a short span.

Throughout his career, his commitment to leveraging technology for societal good remained unwavering. He co-founded Garlik, a cybersecurity company, and spearheaded initiatives like Noddle, which aimed to empower individuals with free access to credit reports.

Beyond his entrepreneurial ventures, his impact extended to education and philanthropy. He played a pivotal role in establishing institutions like the Hammersmith Academy and the African Science Academy, advocating for innovation and inclusion in education.

His achievements have been widely recognized, earning him numerous accolades, including being named the most influential black person in the UK by Powerlist.

In 2017 he received the Beacon Award for innovation in philanthropy. The New African magazine listed him as one of Africa's most influential people.

He was a non-executive director of the BBC, from April 2017, stepping down in June 2021 to take up the role of chair of the Rugby Football Union.

In the 2018 Birthday Honours list he was appointed a Commander of the Order of the British Empire for services to Technology and Philanthropy

In 2018, he was appointed Commander of the Order of the British Empire (CBE) for his contributions to technology and philanthropy.

In 2018 he was awarded an honorary doctorate by City University, London. He was also elected an advisory fellow of St Anne's College, Oxford, and subsequently elected an honorary fellow in 2021.

In 2020 he was elected an honorary fellow of Jesus College, Oxford. He was awarded honorary doctorates by the University of Benin in 2021, the University of Portsmouth in 2022 and Coventry University in 2022.

In August 2021 he was appointed the new chairman of the Rugby Football Union, the most senior position in English rugby, hoping that he could inspire others to make a difference at all levels of the game. This made him the first black chair of a major sport. He said he had a big and exciting vision for rugby union over the next decade, exemplifying his commitment to breaking barriers and fostering inclusivity in sports leadership.

Reflecting on his journey, he emphasized the importance of progress and inclusion, noting that despite challenges, each generation pushes boundaries forward.

First Black person to play football at international level

Andrew Watson – (1856-1921)

Andrew Watson was a Scottish footballer and is widely recognized as the world's first black individual to play football at the international level. He played three matches for Scotland between 1881 and 1882. It had been thought that Arthur Wharton was the first black player, as he was the first black professional footballer to play in the Football League, but Watson was playing football over a decade before him. Watson was paid professionally in 1887 while playing for Bootle, this was two years before Wharton was a professional with Rotherham Town, however, Bootle were not playing in the Football League when Watson played there.

Andrew Watson was born on 24 May 1856 in Georgetown British Guiana, His father Peter Miller Watson was a plantation manager and slave owner originally from Orkney, Scotland. His mother, Hannah Rose was a local British Guianese woman. As a child he moved to Britain with his father and sister Annetta leaving his mother behind.

His father died in 1869 and fortunately he left the children a decent inheritance. Andrew was educated at Heath Grammar School in Halifax, West Yorkshire and from 1871 at King's College School, in Wimbledon, London, where he excelled at sports including football.

In 1875 he went to the University of Glasgow to study though he left after a year, to become a partner in Watson, Miller, and Baird, a wholesale warehouse business in Glasgow.

He became a very good footballer playing for his first senior club Parkgrove, where he was also their match secretary, making him the first black administrator in football. At Parkgrove he played alongside another black player, Robert Walker and also took part in athletics competitions, winning the high jump on several occasions.

In November 1877 he married Jessie Nimmo Armour. They had a son Rupert Andrew who was born in 1878, and a daughter Agnes Maude born in 1880. The family moved to London in for his work. His wife died in the autumn of 1882 and their two children returned to Glasgow to live with their grandparents.

Within six years of playing he had established himself as one of the most talented and well-respected players, helping to develop the Scottish passing and running game which was seen as an early step in the football played today.

In April 1880 he signed for Queen's Park, which was Britain's largest football team. He also became their secretary in November 1881. He led the team to two consecutive Scottish Cup wins in 1881 and 1882, which made him the first black player to win a major competition.

He moved to London in 1882 where he played for Swifts and became the first black player to play in the English Cup. In 1883, he was the first foreign player to be invited to join Corinthians which was the leading amateur club in England, the Corinthians. The team's achievements included beating Blackburn Rovers 8-1 because they were the holders of the English Cup. He also played for other amateur English clubs, including Pilgrims, Brentwood, and London Caledonians.

Due to his inherited wealth, he could afford to move around at will. He regularly travelled to Glasgow to play for Queen's Park, mainly for charity games but also for the opening of the second Hampden Park. He came back for 1986 when the team won the Scottish Cup.

In February 1887 he got married for a second time, to Eliza Kate Tyler. She was the daughter of Joseph Tyler, an East India merchant. They had two children, a son called Henry Tyler born in 1888 and a daughter called Phyllis Kate born in 1891.

Later that year he moved to Liverpool, where he worked on ships for 20 years and sat exams to qualify as a marine engineer. He was also recruited by Bootle FC. At the time they were Everton's main rivals.

Bootle offered wages and signing-on fees to their players, and there is speculation as to whether Watson was paid as, if he was, then he would be the first black man to play football professionally. It is commonly thought that it was Arthur Wharton, who turned professional in 1889.

He won three international caps for Scotland. He captained the side for his first cap against England on 12 March 1881 in London. Scotland won 6-1on 12 March 1881, in which he captained the side. Scotland won 6–1, which was a record home defeat for England. A few days later, he again captained Scotland in their 5-1 win over Wales.

On 11 March 1882 he got his last cap for Scotland in a 5-1 victory over England in Glasgow. His move to London effectively ended his international career as the Scottish Football Association only picked players who were based in Scotland at the time.

After he retired around 1910, he moved with his family to Kew, west London.

On 8 March 1921 he died of pneumonia at 88 Forest Road on 8 March 1921, aged 64. He was buried in Richmond Cemetery.

His passing went unnoticed by the media and football establishment. His wife Eliza died in 1949.

After Watson, the next non-white person to receive a full international cap for Scotland was Paul Wilson in 1975. The next black person selected to play for Scotland after him was Nigel Quashie in 2004, 120 years later.

In 2020 a mural of him was painted on the side of a cafe in Shawlands, south Glasgow, and he also features prominently in the First Hampden Mural at Hampden Bowling Club.

First Black women's footballer in Britain

Emma Clarke – (1876-????)

Emma Clarke was a British footballer, considered to be the first known black women's footballer in Britain.

Emma Clarke was born in1876 in Bootle, Merseyside to parents William and Wilhelmina Clarke. She had a sister who also played football. She was one of 14 children

At the time, Bootle was a very hostile environment for Black people who were considered second-class citizens. There was very little harmony between the white and Black communities.

She developed her skills playing football in the neighbourhood streets. At the age of fifteen, she began working as a confectioner's apprentice. Her football skills were developed on the cobbled streets of her local neighbourhood. She played as an outfield player but also as a goalkeeper.

Her club football career began in 1895 when she made her debut for the British Ladies' Football Club, an early all-women's football club patronised by Lady Florence Dixie. There were a number of ladies called Clarke in the team so there are no precise details of her career with the British Ladies. However, there are photos of her lining up in the official team photo for the South team of the British Ladies in their inaugural exhibition match, which her team lost 7-1. The game was watched by more than 10,000 people at Crouch End, London. The game is recognised as the first proper women's game played under the football's founding association rules.

In 1896 she made her debut for Mrs Graham's XI. Mrs Graham aka Helen Graham Matthews was a British Suffragette and footballer. She lived a few streets away from the Clarkes. The team toured Scotland in1896 and the matches regularly attracted crowds in the thousands. Players were paid their expenses and an estimated sum of a shilling a week on the tour.

In 1897 she played for a team which was described as, The New Woman and Ten of Her Lady Friends, against Eleven Gentlemen. The ladies team won 3–1, though the game was described as grotesque, though it was noted that the ladies distinguished themselves in the second half. The general tone, obviously from men, was that football simply was not for men. It is thought that her sister played in the match.

Her career as a footballer continued until at least 1903 and not much is known of her life after that.

For decades, Clarke and her contribution to the game was mistaken for goalkeeper Carrie Boustead, once described by a journalist as, a coloured lady of Dutch build, who was later confirmed to be white. Clarke was rediscovered by artist Stuart Gibbs only when a photo of the team that toured Scotland was discovered. He then identified that the player in question was Clarke, not Boustead.

However there is additional controversy to this tale. Apparently there was another Emma Clarke with a sister called Florence, who was born in Plumstead in south London on the 2 December 1871. Her parents were called John and Caroline Clarke.

Caroline Clarke was born in Ceylon (modern-day Sri Lanka), the daughter of a relationship between a British national residing in southern Ceylon and a dark-skinned local. Caroline was accepted as the daughter of Mr and Mrs Bogg, Emma's grandparents, and taken back to England, where she grew up in mid-19th century London.

She later married John Clarke and they had ten children, seven of whom were girls with Emma being the fifth child. Florence, one her younger sisters, was also a very talented footballer, and along with Emma also played for British Ladies FC.

In 1949 the Kentish Independent newspaper published an article to mark the golden wedding of Florence. It stated the footballing sisters were from Plumstead and that before her marriage, Florence had been gaining a name in soccer circles as a member of the British Ladies football team, playing inside right. The team toured England, Ireland, Scotland and Wales, and in the north played a number of men's teams. A family descendant recalled that his grandmother told him a story of an affair which led to a mixed race child. He was told that this heritage showed in the footballing sisters' generation and particularly in Emma.

After a few years the football club disbanded and the Clarke sisters settled down to domesticity. In 1899 Emma married Thomas Porter, a labourer with the local council, and they had two children, Ethel and Charlie.

Sadly in 1925, this Emma died aged 53 of carcinoma of the uterus and asthenia.

In 1899, Florence married George Carver who was a footballer playing for Woolwich Arsenal, which become Arsenal FC. They lived in Plumstead until Florence died in 1955.

In 2019 the Nubian Jak Community Trust unveiled a blue heritage plaque commemorating Emma Clarke at Campsbourne School, Hornsey, which is the site of her team, the former Crouch End FC.

The fact is that a person called Emma Clarke who was black did exist and she did play football. There are pictures and reports which confirm this, but sadly there are no conclusive details of her life. Sadly, there was little regard paid to her as a black woman, so full details are hard to come by.

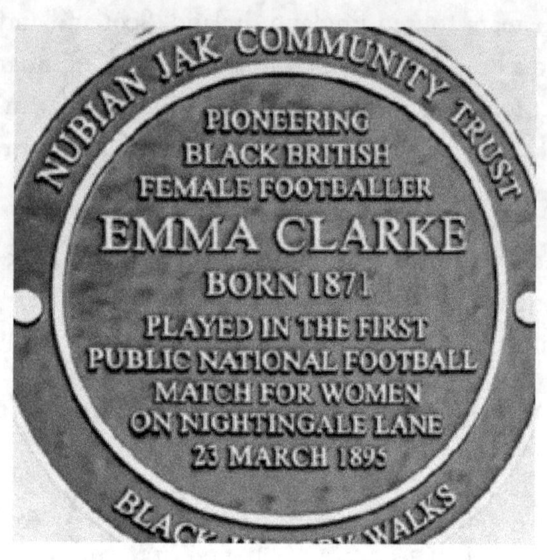

First Black professional footballer

Arthur Kwame Wharton — (1865-1930)

Arthur Wharton is considered to be the first black professional footballer in the world. Though not the first black player outright as amateurs Robert Walker, of Queen's Park, and Scotland international player, Andrew Watson, predate him. Watson was possibly a professional for Bootle F.C. in 1887, before him. Wharton may have been the first black professional and the first to play in the Football League.

Arthur Kwame Wharton was born on 28 October 1865 in Jamestown, Gold Coast, which is now Accra, Ghana. His father Henry Wharton was Grenadian, while his mother, Annie Florence Egyriba was a member of the Fante Ghanaian royalty. In 1882, he moved to England aged 19 to train as a Methodist missionary. He soon abandoned this in favour of becoming a full-time athlete.

He was a good all-round sportsman. In 1886 he became the first man in the world to run 100 yards in ten seconds, setting a record which lasted for 30 years. He dabbled in professional cricket and set a record time cycling between Blackburn and Preston.

He started his football career as an amateur playing in goal for Darlington. He was spotted by Preston North End after playing against them. He joined Darlington and was part of the team that reached FA Cup semi-finals in 1886–87. During the third-round victory against Renton, his performance in keeping a clean sheet, was described by Athletic News as "one of the best exhibitions of goalkeeping I have seen for a long time." He was part of the team known as The Invincibles in the 1880s, but he left the team in 1888 to concentrate on his running, which meant he was not part of the team that went on to win won the Double in 1888–89.

In 1889 he returned to football joining Rotherham Town as a professional, despite failing to impress at Sheffield Wednesday.

In 1890 he married Emma Lister, who lived from 1866 to 1944, in Rotherham, Yorkshire. By 1891 he was the landlord of the Albert Tavern in Rotherham.

In 1894 he moved to Sheffield United, though he was understudy to regular first-team goalkeeper William "Fatty" Foulke. During the 1894–1895 season, he only played three games for Sheffield United, against Leicester Fosse, Linfield and Sunderland. The match against Sunderland was a First Division game, which made him the first mixed-heritage player to play in the First Division.

In 1895 he left Sheffield United for Stalybridge Rovers but after falling out with the management he moved to Ashton North End in 1897, where he opened a tobacconist shop in Ashton-under-Lyne.

In 1899 Ashton North End went bankrupt, so he returned to Stalybridge Rovers, before ending his career playing for Stockport County in the Second Division in 1901–1902. In addition to playing in goal, he occasionally played outfield as a winger.

Sadly he developed a drinking problem and retired from football in 1902. He got a job as a colliery haulage worker at the Yorkshire Main Colliery in Edlington. By 1911 he was employed as a collier and living in Moor Thorpe, West Yorkshire, with his wife Emma.

With the outbreak of World War I in 1914, he joined the Volunteer Training Corps, which was the equivalent of the Home Guard in World War II defending Britain.

He died in 1930, following a long bout of syphilis and epithelioma, which is a form of cancer.

He was buried in an unmarked pauper's grave. In 1997 the grave was given a headstone after a campaign by anti-racism campaigners Football Unites, Racism Divides.

In 2003 he was inducted into the English Football Hall of Fame in recognition of the impact he made on the game. A campaign to have a statue erected in Darlington as well as in Rotherham to acknowledge his achievements has gained wide support within the professional game.

In 2012 a small statue of him was presented to Sepp Blatter at the headquarters of FIFA, where it will be on permanent display.

On 16 October 2014 a statue honouring him was unveiled at St George's Park National Football Centre.

In 2020 a mural was unveiled in Darlington on the 155th anniversary of his birth.

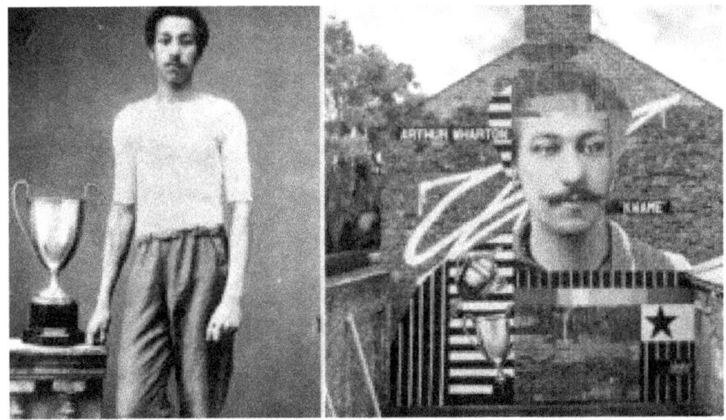

First Black British footballer to play for England

John Charles – (1944-2002)

John Charles was an English footballer who played for West Ham United as a defender. Nicknamed Charlo, he was the first black player to represent England at Under-18 and any level within the National team. He was also the first black player to play for a first division West Ham United side when he made his debut in 1963.

John William Charles was born on 9 September 9 1944 in Canning Town, London, to Moister, a Grenadian father who was a seaman and a white mother, Jessie, from East London. He was the eighth of nine children. He went to Clarkson Street School and Pretoria School in Canning Town, where he showed proficiency at football. He was also a skilful cricketer. There were few black children at the school so he stood out with his siblings.

While playing for his local side, West Ham Boys, he was spotted by Ernie Gregory who was a scout and former goalkeeper for West Ham United. Gregory recommended him to chief scout Wally St. Pier. As a result, in 1959, he was signed as a youth player.

On 20 May 1962 he was part of an England Under-18 side which beat Israel 3-1 in Tel Aviv, scoring a goal. The teams played again two days later and this time Israel won 2-1. A year later the UEFA Under-18 tournament was held in England. He played in the last group game against the Soviet Union, which England won 2-0. England went on to win this tournament for the next time in their history.

In 1963 when he turned 17, he signed as a professional and captained the West Ham team which won the Youth Cup against Liverpool. This made him the first black player to lead a first-class side to a major trophy.

The same year he made his debut for the first team against Blackburn Rovers at the age of 18. He was described as being a very good full-back, tough as old boots, well known for his tacking and not taking any prisoners.

1963 was a big year for him as he married his wife Carol on 6 July. The day was a celebration and there was no aggravation though this was an interracial marriage. The only downside was the fact that their wedding presents got stolen.

Unfortunately, he received injuries which prevented him from forming part of the West Ham teams which won the 1964 FA Cup Final and the 1965 UEFA Cup Winners' Cup Final.

He played most of his games alongside Bobby Moore. He made 142 appearances for West Ham in all competitions scoring two goals; one in a League Cup game against Grimsby Town, the other being the single West Ham goal in a Manchester United 6–1 victory at Upton Park in which Manchester United won the 1966-67 Football League cup.

Future football manager Harry Redknapp played alongside him in the 1963 youth side and rated him as a strong tackler and leader, who liked to enjoy himself and was liked by everyone at the club. At the time all members of the team came from within five miles of the football ground. His brother Clive also played for the club.

He played during an era where black football players were subject to torrents of constant racial abuse, with the authorities doing little or nothing to stop or control it. The abuse came from both supporters and opposing fans. It would be intensified if any black player dared to make a mistake. Players were expected to just shrug it off as being just part of the game, though racism and discrimination were obviously an issue outside the game.

From the autumn of 1969 until spring 1970 hamstring injuries restricted him to only five games. In 1971, he left West Ham and was offered a move to Leyton Orient which was managed by former West Ham player, Jimmy Bloomfield. However due to the recurring hamstring problems he retired from football aged only 26 to run the family's market greengrocers stall.

He was part of a strong drinking culture which existed at West Ham in the 1960s and admitted to becoming a borderline alcoholic when he finished playing football. However, following the end of his football career his business prospects improved. As a footballer at West Ham he got £30 per week and £2 for a goal. In his first weeks running a greengrocer's stall he earned £500. As a result he went on to open several grocers' stalls in Kent. However by the 1990s, big supermarkets were becoming more popular and his business began to fail.

He then decided to move to Terra Mitica in Benidorm with his wife Carol. They planned to stay for a few years, but after a year he was diagnosed with lung cancer. The hospitals in Spain were good, but they were very expensive, so they were advised to return home to Britain.

On 17 August 2002 he died aged 57. A few days later he was taken by horse and carriage to the crematorium in Plaistow via the Boleyn Ground.

He was survived by his wife, Carol and his three children, sons Keith and Butch and daughter, Lesley.

First Black British England football captain and first black British manager in England's top division

Paul Ince – (1967-)

Paul Ince began his journey as a professional player in 1982 and continued until 2007. Starting his career with West Ham United, he later played for prominent clubs such as Manchester United, Liverpool, and Middlesbrough, among others. In 1993, he made history as the first black player to captain the England football team against the United States and on June 2008 he was appointed manager of Blackburn Rovers and became the first black British manager in England's top division.

Paul Emerson Carlyle Ince was born on 21 October 1967 in Ilford, London to his father Carlyle Jones, and mother Peggy. He attended Goodmayes Primary School, Ilford and Mayfield Boys School, Goodmayes, growing up a West Ham United supporter. He had a troubled early life in and out of school.

At 12 he was spotted playing football by West Ham manager John Lyall and at 14 he signed for West Ham as a trainee. Lyall helped him through his troubled school times eventually signing him as a YTS trainee, on leaving school, in 1984.

He came through the West Ham youth team and made his debut in English football on 30 November 1986 against Newcastle United in the First Division He went on to become a regular in the 1987–88 season, proving himself to have all-round qualities of pace and stamina, and possessing uncompromising tackling and good passing ability. He also packed a powerful shot and was seen as a natural successor in West Ham's midfield for the veteran Billy Bonds, who retired at the end of the 1987–88 season. He also won England under-21 caps to go with England youth caps for playing as an apprentice.

In 1989 he joined Manchester United, where he enjoyed considerable success, winning the FA Cup in his debut year. He was also becoming established within the England setup. On 9 September 1992 he made his full England debut at the age of 24, featuring in a 1-0 defeat to Spain. He went on to make history when on 6 June 1993 he was given the captain's armband in just his seventh appearance, deputising in place of David Platt and Tony Adams against the United States. He became the first black man to captain the national team. He would captain the national side another six times during his career. England lost this match 2-0.

In June 1995 he was sold to Inter Milan with some success despite facing significant amounts of racial abuse. He continued to excel on the international stage, notably featuring in Euro '96 and the 1998 World Cup.

By 1997 he returned to Britain playing for various clubs, including Liverpool, Middlesbrough and Wolverhampton Wanderers, before transitioning into management.

In 2006 he became the player/coach of Swindon Town, then moved to player/manager with Macclesfield Town

In 2007 he achieved success as the manager of Milton Keynes Dons, winning the Football League Trophy in 2008. Milton Keynes Dons were also promoted to League One. He was named as League Two Manager of the Month in October and December 2007, and again in April 2008

As a result of his success at Milton Keynes Dons, on 22 June 2008 he was appointed manager of Blackburn Rovers and became the first black British manager in England's top division. However after a decent start he lost the support of the fans and after winning just three games out of 17, he was sacked on 16 December 2008 after six months in charge, one of the shortest reigns of a Premier League manager.

In 2022 he took on the role of interim manager at Reading, later being appointed permanently. However, his tenure ended in 2023 after a string of unfavourable results.

Throughout his career was celebrated for his energy, technical abilities, and leadership qualities. His legacy as a trailblazer for black footballers in England remains significant, paving the way for future generations.

First Black British England women's football captain

Mary Phillip – (1977-)

Mary Phillip is a former English international footballer and a football team manager who manages men's Kent County League team Peckham Town. A versatile player, she played in all four positions at the back and also in midfield. She captained England and was the first black player to captain an England women's international football team.

Mary Rose Phillip was born on 14 March 1977 in Peckham. Her father was a bus driver of Saint Lucian descent, and her mother was a primary school teacher of Irish origin. She was keen on football from childhood, but grew up being told that girls should not be playing football and she should set her sights on being a secretary. She was also exposed to racism, such as growing up seeing the signs saying, "No Blacks, No Dogs, No Irish".

As a 12 year old she began playing for Millwall Lionesses. During her time there she helped them win the FA Cup and Premier League Cup.

As an 18 year old she received an unexpected call-up to join the 1995 World Cup squad, after only a couple of training sessions. It turned out that she was pregnant at the time, she was not showing and was able to train. She won six caps then spent four years from 1998 to 2002 not playing any international games while she had her two sons. In 2000 she moved to Fulham who were the only team giving players professional contracts. She was one of a group of 16 ladies to become the first full-time female footballers. The pay was nothing like what the men were getting, but it was a start.

She was told that being a mum, having a child at 18 and another at 22, she would not be able to play football and definitely not play for England. Her courage and determination won through and she proved people wrong.

She subsequently became the club captain at Fulham due to her strength and composure at the heart of defence. In 2003 Fulham won the FA Women's

Cup in front of 10,000 fans at Selhurst Park and 1.9m viewers on BBC Television. The team went on to complete the treble in 2003, adding the FA Women's Premier League National Division, FA Women's Premier League Cup to the FA Women's Cup.

She won eight titles with Fulham. She left them in 2004 to join Arsenal. At Arsenal, she formed a strong defensive partnership with Faye White which helped the team achieve significant success domestically and in Europe. Over four years while she was there, they earned 12 titles, This included the quadruple-winning season of 2006-2007 when they won the Women's Premier League, Women's FA Cup, Premier League Cup and UEFA Women's Cup (now Champions League).

After the 2007-2008 season she left Arsenal to join Chelsea.

She returned to international duties in 2002, after she had given birth to her two sons. She subsequently captained England in two international friendly games against Sweden in February 2006 when Faye White had an ankle injury, and then again against France with Faye White this time suffering a cruciate ligament injury. She was the first black player to captain an England women's international side.

When she was named in the squad for the China World Cup, she became the first English player to feature in two World Cup squads. She won 65 caps for playing for England.

In October 2008 she retired from football at the age of 31. She went on to become a football coach. She had been coaching youth teams at her local club, Peckham Town, for a few years. She started her UEFA A Licence to get properly qualified, in 2016.

Having coached the Under-18s and then the senior squad, in 2019, she became the manager of the senior team. That season, in 2020 they won the London Senior Trophy, the club's first cup win. She became the first female manager to lead a men's side to cup success in England.

In 2017 as she was completing her A Licence, she learned that she had Multiple Sclerosis. She is receiving drug treatment for the illness, and using the same determination that saw her achieve so much as a player, she has not let it impact her work as a coach.

She has two sons and two daughters.

First Black player to play for the British England football team

Viv Anderson MBE – (1956-)

Vivian Anderson, MBE was an English former professional footballer and coach. He won five senior trophies including the 1977–78 Football League title, and both the 1978–79 European Cup and the 1979–80 European Cup playing for Brian Clough's Nottingham Forest. He later played for Arsenal, Manchester United, Sheffield Wednesday, Barnsley and Middlesbrough. He was the first black and second non-white footballer after Paul Reaney to play for the senior men's England national football team, in a friendly against Czechoslovakia in 1978. He went on to get 3 caps and 2 goals for England.

Vivian Alexander Anderson was born on 29 July 1956 in Clifton, Nottingham to his parents, Audley and Myrtle who were both from Jamaica as part of the Windrush generation.

Despite the racial tensions in society at the time, he has said that he did not really encounter discrimination as a child, presumably being shielded by his parents. He had a happy childhood only marred by his brother Donald being diagnosed with polio when he was five. He played street football and was liked at school though not academic getting three CSE's.

He was spotted aged 14 playing football on a beach to get a trial for Sheffield United, which turned into a trial for Manchester United. He spent a year as a schoolboy training at Old Trafford but disappointingly got released.

Upon leaving school he worked as a silkscreen printer for three weeks where he felt he was just a glorified tea boy and dogsbody. Fortunately he got an apprenticeship with Nottingham Forest making his debut in the youth team at 17. He eventually broke into the full team in 1974 and became a regular when Brian Clough became manager while Forest was in the Second Division. The team went on to get promoted to the First Division in 1977, winning the title and the League Cup, a year later.

He was one of the first black players to play for English clubs at the time, and regularly suffered racial abuse from fans of rival teams, and his own supporters. He was regularly pelted with bananas and targeted with racist chants. In 1977 his manager Brian Clough had sponsored the launch of the Anti-Nazi League, a campaign that opposed the growing threat of the National Front. Clough took him aside as a 19-year-old after he had been pelted with bananas and other fruit during a warm-up against Carlisle in the mid-1970s, and told him to focus, and if he let people dictate to him, he would never make it as a footballer. He decided to dismiss the racism and just get on with it.

Playing for a successful club raised his profile nationally and he made his debut for England in November 1978, in a friendly against Czechoslovakia. He became the first black and second non-white footballer to represent the men's senior England team after Paul Reaney who had first appeared for England in 1968. He was clearly in the team on merit playing well in a form team. He was a much-admired tackler and was also quick going forward and occasionally scoring vital goals.

His second cap came in June 1979 in a friendly against Sweden. His third was his first competitive international, defeating Bulgaria 2–0 at Wembley to qualify for the 1980 European Championships.

Forest continued their winning ways retaining the League Cup and winning successive European Cups in 1979 and 1980.

He made his World Cup debut in a qualifier for the 1982 competition in a 4–0 win over Norway.

After the 1980 European cup win, the Forest team began to decline, got older and begin to break up. His England appearances also began to decline. He eventually got his 11th cap, in April 1984, almost two years after his 10th.

In the same year, he moved to Arsenal for £250,000, and his international standing improved. He won six successive caps from 1984 and into 1985, including four qualifiers for the 1986 World Cup in Mexico. In the first match he scored the first of his two international goals in an 8–0 mauling of Turkey.

He won three caps at the end of 1986 during the qualifiers for the 1988 European Championships in Germany. In one of the qualifiers against Yugoslavia, he scored his second and final international goal.

In 1987 he enjoyed some club success for the first time in seven years with Arsenal when they beat Liverpool 2-1 in the League Cup Final.

Later the same year, after a tribunal agreed a £250,000 fee, he left Arsenal to become Alex Ferguson's first signing since taking over as manager of Manchester United.

Internationally he played his 30th and final cap for England playing against Colombia, having to make way for younger players.

At Manchester United he was part of the rebuilding of the team following a bad start to the 1986-1987 season. He helped them improve in the 1987–1988 season, as they finished second in the league but never really looked like overhauling Liverpool,

In the 1988-1989 season he was still the first-choice at right-back but the season was not successful with them ending 11th in the league. In the 1989-1990 season they finished 13th though they did win the FA Cup, though he was not in the squad for the final.

In the 1990-1991 season Alex Ferguson brought in Denis Irwin, a natural replacement, and he realised his time at Manchester United was coming to an end.

In January 1991 he joined Sheffield Wednesday on a free transfer. They got promoted from Second Division and won the League Cup final against Manchester United, though he could not play being cup-tied. He managed to get a regular position in the first team, captaining the side on many occasions.

In June 1993 he left Sheffield Wednesday to become player-manager of Barnsley. However, his first season at Oakwell was a disappointment as Barnsley narrowly avoided relegation to Division Two.

At the end of 1993–94 he quit Barnsley after just a year to become assistant manager of Middlesbrough under Bryan Robson his former Manchester United teammate.

Despite retiring from playing football in 1994, he was still officially registered as a player and following an injury crisis at Middlesbrough he played two games for the club in 1994–95 when they were promoted to the Premier League as Division One champions. After gaining promotion he finally hung up his playing boots.

The Middlesbrough team reached and lost both domestic cup finals in 1996–1997. However, they were relegated after being deducted three points for postponing a December fixture at late notice because many of their players were unable to play due to illness or injury.

However, Middlesbrough went on to win promotion at the first attempt and were League Cup runners-up once again. In June 2001 he finally left them with Bryan Robson when Terry Venables was brought in with the club facing relegation. Though they had never achieved anything higher than ninth place in the final table the duo had managed to establish Middlesbrough in the Premier League.

In the 2000 New Years Honours list he was awarded Member of the Order of the British Empire (MBE).

In 2004 he was inducted into the English Football Hall of Fame in recognition of his impact on the English league. He remains a keen supporter of the National Football Museum and regularly attends special events at the museum.

As of 2005 he ran a sports travel agency and also works as a goodwill ambassador for the Football Association. He appears as an occasional guest pundit on MUTV; Manchester United's official TV station.

He is CEO of Playonpro, an organisation that helps ex-players, sportsmen and women, come to terms with their new life when their sporting career comes to an end.

He lives in Manchester with his long-term partner, Nicole, and he has two sons Charlie and Freddie and daughter Ruby.

First Black woman to manage an England national football team

Hope Powell CBE – (1966-)

Hope Powell CBE is an English former international footballer. In 1998 the Football Association (FA) appointed her as England's first-ever full-time national coach. She led the team at the 2001, 2005, 2009 and 2013 editions of the UEFA Women's Championship. This made her the first Black woman to manage an England national football team.

Hope Patricia Powell was born on 8 December 1966 to Jamaican parents. She was raised in Lewisham, London with family. She was into football from an early age with posters of Kevin Keegan and Ray Wilkins on her bedroom wall. Her early life seems a bit like the film Bend it Like Beckham. Her family did not get her obsession with football as it was not perceived as the appropriate choice for her as a girl. She played against boys in the streets, proving herself to be better than most of them. All she ever wanted to be was a footballer.

She went to Abbey Wood School. She played alongside another girl called Jane Bartley in the school mixed football team, until they beat another school who complained about Abbey Wood playing two girls. The complaint reached the FA who banned them from playing. Three years later an unsuccessful appeal was made to the Equal Opportunities Commission. The irony was that by then Hope had played football for England and Jane Bartley had played for Wales, but they were not allowed to play for their own school

At the age of 11 she started attending training sessions, though not exactly with her mum's permission. In 1978 by the age of 12, she managed to convince her mum she could make it and her mum let her sign officially for Millwall, buying her first football boots for her.

At Millwall Lionesses she met Alan May, a senior manager with British Telecom, who became her coach and mentor. In addition to football he taught her how to manage people and inspired her throughout her career

She made her debut in the 1980-1981 season, but though she was skilful, she was lightweight and needed beefing up to play against women twice her age.

In 1983 she was selected for the England squad along with a talented player from Fulham called Brenda Sempare. They were the only black girls on the team and they faced some resentment as the new kids on the block.

In September 1983 she made her England debut coming on as a sub against the Republic of Ireland in a European qualifier. She was just 16 and England won 6-0.

The following year the England ladies got to the final of the European Competition for Women's football, the forerunner for the UEFA European Championships. They lost the first leg to Sweden 1-0 in Sweden. The return leg was held at Kenilworth Road, Luton in rain-swept muddy conditions because somewhat disgustingly, no London club, let alone Wembley were interested in holding the game. England was beaten by Sweden on penalties.

Back on the domestic scene, Millwall grew to be one of the most successful ladies team in England. In 1987 she left to join rivals Friends of Fulham. Her two year spell there culminated in an appearance at the 1989 Women's FA Cup final. She scored twice and had an exceptional game, but Fulham were beaten 3–2 by Leasowe Pacific. The match was played at Old Trafford where only 914 people turned up to watch, though it was also broadcast on Channel 4.

In 1989 she went back to Millwall Lionesses where she became the team's all-time record goal scorer. In 1991 they reached the Women's FA Cup final beating Doncaster Belles 1–0 at Prenton Park, winning the Cup for the first time. They also won the Greater London League to qualify for the inaugural National Division in 1991–1992.

In 1990 she graduated from Brunel University in London with a degree in Sport Science and History.

Despite all the success, the team broke up. She moved with teammate Sue Law to form a new club called Bromley Borough in 1991. The club started in the South East Counties League and quickly progressed through the divisions.

In 1992 she was joined by her England teammate Brenda Sempare, and Bromley Borough went on to win all 16 matches in the South East Counties League Division One, scoring 142 goals. The team also reached the semi-final of the Women's FA Cup losing 2–0 to treble-winning Arsenal.

In 1993–1994 Bromley Borough won the National League Division One South, securing promotion into the topflight of English women's football. Although they were beaten 10–1 by Doncaster Belles in the fifth round of the FA Women's Cup.

For the 1994–1995 season, the club partnered with Croydon FC and made Debbie Bampton, who was one of her England teammates, the manager. The strength of the squad at the club was demonstrated by the fact that she was one of six Croydon players who represented England at the 1995 FIFA Women's World Cup.

In the 1995-1996 season Croydon secured a domestic double winning the FA Woman's Cup and FA Woman's Premier League. She was captain and Bampton was player-manager. A somewhat farcical end of season fixture backlog saw Croydon having to play five games in ten days. They won four and drew one to erode Doncaster Belles' 13-point lead and win the National Premier Division on goal difference.

In the 1997–1998 season, Croydon lost both domestic Cup finals to Arsenal. They also lost the 1998 FA Women's Cup final 3–2, although she did score Croydon's second goal, Powell missed out on her third winners' medal.

This was her final season as a player and she retired to take over as England coach.

She had passed the FA's preliminary coaching award at the age of 19. During her later playing career she had worked as a development officer for Lewisham London Borough Council and in Crystal Palace FC's community outreach scheme. She had also been a volunteer coach at soccer camps in the United States. Ted Copeland, manager of the England team from 1993 to 1998, encouraged her to complete the FA's new female coach mentoring scheme and obtain her 'B' licence while she was still playing.

In 1998 the FA appointed her as England's first-ever full-time national coach in 1998. At 31 she became the youngest ever coach of any English national football team, as well as the first woman and the first black person to hold the office.

On 26 July 1998 she managed England for the first time in a friendly against Sweden at Victoria Road, Dagenham, which England lost 1-0. The next month she had her first competitive game in charge against Norway which the team lost 2-0. This meant they faced a relegation play-off against Romania which England won 6-2.

She led England at the 2001, 2005, 2009 and 2013 editions of the UEFA Women's Championship. After failing to qualify in 2003, she guided England to the quarterfinals of the FIFA Women's World Cup in 2007 and 2011. England's best results, reaching the final of the UEFA Women's Championship in 1984 and 2009, both featured her. She was a player at the former and coach at the latter.

As well as managing the England senior team, she oversaw the whole structure from Under-15s to the Under-23s, a coach mentoring scheme and The FA's National Player Development Centre at Loughborough University.

In the Queen's 2002 Birthday Honours list she was appointed Officer of the Order of the British Empire (OBE) for services to sport.

In 2003 she became the first woman to be awarded the UEFA Pro Licence the highest coaching qualification available, studying alongside Stuart Pearce.

It was speculated that she might become the first female manager in English men's football when she was linked with the vacant managerial role at Grimsby Town in October 2009. However caretaker manager Neil Woods was appointed on a permanent basis.

In May 2009 her administration implemented central contracts, to help players focus on full-time training and playing, without having to fit it around full-time employment. Initially 17 players signed contracts.

In the 2010 Queen's Birthday Honours list, she was awarded Commander of the Order of the British Empire (CBE).

At the 2011 FIFA Women's World Cup, England suffered a quarter-final penalty shootout defeat to France following a 1–1 draw. She controversially called players who had failed to volunteer to take a penalty, cowards.

Her last major tournament was at UEFA Women's Euro 2013 where England was knocked out in the group stages. As a result, there was a lot of noise for her to get sacked.

On 20 August 2013 she was sacked as manager of the England women's team.

In 2016 she published her autobiography, Hope: My Life in Football.

In July 2017 she became manager of Brighton and Hove Albion Women's first team. In four Women's Super League seasons, she led the club to two ninth place finishes, a seventh place and the club's best finish a sixth place in the 2020-2021 season.

On 31 October 2022 she stepped down as manager following an 8-0 defeat to Tottenham Hotspur.

In May 2023 she joined the England men's team as a technical advisor for the 2023 FIFA U20 World Cup in Argentina

In July 2023 she became the Women's Technical Director at Birmingham City Football Club.

First Black person to be a Football Association Director

Dame Heather Rabbatts DBE – (1955-)

Dame Heather Rabbatts DBE is a Jamaican-born British solicitor, businesswoman, and broadcaster, who rose to prominence as the Chief executive of the London Borough of Lambeth, the youngest council chief in the UK. She served as a Football Association director from 2011 to 2017 and was the first Black or ethnic minority person to do so. She was also the only woman on its board.

Heather Victoria Rabbatts was born in Kingston, Jamaica in 1955 to a white working-class father from Peckham and Jamaican mother. Her father became an army officer and then a draughtsman. She moved to England, aged 3. The family lived for a time in Chatham Kent, a predominantly white area. She left school with five O-levels and attended evening classes to study for A-levels. Through hard work and sheer determination she attended the London School of Economics and became a barrister in 1981, a job she loved, but family commitments forced a change in career.

In 1987 she moved to work in local government and worked her way up to becoming Deputy Chief Executive of Hammersmith and Fulham in 1989. She then became Chief Executive of Merton before being appointed to the post of Chief Executive of Lambeth in 1995. This made her the youngest council chief in the country. She helped to make significant improvements in housing, education, and council tax collection. She helped to eradicate the Loony Left image and combat the level of fraud and corruption.

From 1999 she was a Governor of the BBC but resigned in 2001 when she joined Channel 4 as the managing director of Channel 4's education programmes and business, 4Learning. She was a Governor at the London School of Economics, an Associate of The King's Fund and on the board of directors at the British Council.

In March 2000 she left Lambeth to set up a public sector consultancy company called iMPOWER. She was the Chief Executive and co-chair

In the 2000 New Years Honours list she was appointed Commander of the Order of the British Empire (CBE) for services to football and equality.

On 3 May 2006 she was appointed the new Executive Deputy Chair of Millwall F.C., and, on 27 October 2006, she was appointed the Executive Chairwoman of Millwall Holdings plc. This was an interesting appointment given the racism and football violence associated with the club, which the club wanted to change.

She felt her role was to challenge perceptions and encourage a more diverse and multiracial audience. She admitted she did not know much about football, the sport or business but did know how to make improvements. She had to spearhead the regeneration in the area, which she knew because her father came from Peckham; modernise a company which was listed on the stock market; and try and transform a football club with a challenging reputation.

She had challenges with the fans, who were suspicious of her. She also had issues with the old boys club of football where there were very few female executives.

In 2010 she became a Trustee of Malaria No More UK and later took over as the Chair of Trustees.

On 22 December 2011 she became the first woman to be appointed as a director of The Football Association. This was in response to criticism of the exclusive white, male, middle-class nature of the Association and an attempt to include more diversity. She was the first Black or ethnic minority person to do so

In October 2013 she criticised the make-up of the Football Association's commission to improve the national team as being all-white and all-male; ironic, given her appointment in 2011. Rio Ferdinand was subsequently added to the commission.

In February 2013 she was considered to be one of the 100 most powerful women in the United Kingdom by Woman's Hour on BBC Radio 4.

On 1 June 2015 she resigned from FIFA's anti-discrimination taskforce following Sepp Blatter's re-election as president. She found it unacceptable that little had been done to reform FIFA and re-electing Blatter just undermined the credibility of the taskforce.

In the 2016 New Years Honours list she became a Commander of the Order of the British Empire (DBE) for services to football and equality

In June 2017 she decided to step down from the board of the FA feeling that some progress had been made but there was still a lot to be done. The FA should lead by example regarding black and non-white coaches and managers. She felt, not enough was being done within the England team's set-up and that a generation of black and non-white coaches would be lost to the game unless changes are made.

She has also held major positions in media roles such as Chair of Shed Media, Managing Director of Cove Pictures, a TV/Film Production company, and was a non-executive board member for Arts Alliance, a major film/digital investment fund, and Chair of Soho Theatre. Board member of Into Film which supports Film Clubs in schools and runs programmes for specific groups of young people, such as those experiencing mental health difficulties in film making. She has held non-executive roles, including Grosvenor Estates GBI and the Royal Opera House, Bank of England, London School of Economics. She has served on the Board of Crossrail, the Supervisory Board of the Foreign and Commonwealth Office.

In January 2024 she was appointed a non-executive director to the board of M&C Saachi which describes itself as a creative company that connects specialist expertise, fuelled by data and technology, to help clients Navigate, Create and Lead Meaningful Change.

She was married to Mike Lee OBE, a former communications expert. They both had sons from former marriages. Sadly, Mike Lee died from a heart attack in September 2018.

First Player to top both the Premier League's goal scoring and assist charts in the same season

Andrew Cole- (1971-)

Andrew Cole is a former football striker, playing from 1988 to 2008. He is the fourth-highest goal scorer in Premier League history with 187 goals, and used to hold the Premier League records for most goals scored in a 42-game season, 34. He was the fastest player to score 50 goals, in 65 matches, and he was the first player to top both the Premier League's goal scoring and assist charts in the same season, 1993–94.

Andrew Alexander "Andy" Cole was born on 15 October 1971, Nottingham. His father, Lincoln, came to the UK from Jamaica in 1957 and worked as a coal miner in Gedling, Nottinghamshire.

Andy Cole began his football career as a youth player for Arsenal when he left school in 1988. He became a professional in 1989. He made his only appearance for Arsenal, at 19, in a First Division game as a substitute against Sheffield United at Highbury on December 29 1990, which Arsenal won 4-1. He was also a substitute in a drawn Charity Shield match against Tottenham Hotspur in 1991.

The next season, he was loaned to Fulham in the Third Division, scoring three goals in 13 matches. In 1992 he joined Second Division Bristol City on loan before signing a £500,000 permanent deal.

In February 1993 Division One leaders Newcastle United broke their transfer record paying £1.75 million for him. He then scored 12 goals in 12 league matches as Newcastle won the Division One title winning promotion to the Premier League. He went on to be prolific as a striker.

He scored 34 goals in 40 matches during Newcastle's first Premier League season as they finished third, qualifying for the UEFA Cup for the first time since the 1970s. He scored 41 total goals in all competitions, breaking the club's goal scoring record which had been set by Hughie Gallacher nearly 70 years earlier. He scored in 26 games in 1993–94, which is a season record in the competition by a player. He went on to be voted PFA Young Player of the Year for that season.

He scored 9 goals in 18 Premier League matches for Newcastle after the start of the 1994–95 season, and also scored a hat-trick against Royal Antwerp in the UEFA Cup. He scored 68 goals in 84 matches for Newcastle.

On 10 January 1995, in a shock deal he was sold to Manchester United for a deal worth £7 million, £6 million cash plus £1 million-rated Keith Gillespie going in the opposite direction, setting a new record for the most expensive British transfer. Newcastle fans were annoyed with manager Kevin Keegan for selling him, leading to Keegan publicly confronting fans citing his drop in form and enthusiasm as the reason.

He managed to score 12 goals in just 18 Premier League matches for United. This included 5 goals in the 9–0 rout of Ipswich Town, making him the first player to score five goals in a Premier League match.

He continued to be a prolific striker with Manchester United though his position was challenged by other players such as Eric Cantona, Ole Gunnar Solskjaer, Teddy Sheringham and Dwight Yorke.

In the 1996–97 season he suffered two broken legs following a tackle by Neil Ruddock in a reserve match against Liverpool, which restricted his first-team chances.

Despite this he continued to set records. In the 1998-99 season he scored his 100th Premier League goal and the next season his 100th goal for Manchester United, helping the club win Premier League, FA Cup and UEFA Champions League titles. He became the club's record European goal scorer beating the 30 year record set by Dennis Law.

However, he faced competition from fellow strikers Ruud van Nistelrooy, Dwight Yorke, Ole Gunnar Solskjær and Paul Scholes. As a result he was sold to Blackburn Rovers for £8 million in December 2001 and within two months he received a League Cup winner's medal. This meant that within seven seasons, he had won all four domestic trophies plus a European trophy. He ended the season with a total of 18 goals in all competitions, 5 for Manchester United and 13 in just 20 matches for Blackburn.

In July 2002 he married his long-time girlfriend Shirley Dewar. Their son, Devante, is also a professional footballer playing forward for Barnsley.

By the 2003-04 Blackburn were in decline and his relationship with manager Graeme Souness was not good after Cole reported him to the Professional Footballers' Association accusing him of unfair treatment.

He left Blackburn joining a number of clubs, Fulham, Manchester City, Birmingham City, Portsmouth, Sunderland and Nottingham Forest.

In November 2008 he announced his retirement from football, ending a 19-year career.

Despite all his club achievements, his international career did not take off. He was first capped for England in 1995 and earned only 15 caps by the time he retired. He scored once against Albania Cole in a World Cup qualifier.

He went on to coach at Milton Keynes Dons and Huddersfield Town

In June 2014 he suffered from kidney failure, undergoing a kidney transplant in April 2017 with his nephew Alexander as a donor. Getting up and walking was a chore. His weight shot up to about 18 stone, with all the water retention he was holding. Having been a footballer and fit all his life, this random illness changed his whole life. He has since set up the Andy Cole Fund to raise money for Kidney Research UK

He has condemned racial incidents in football on various occasions. He felt that football authorities are not doing enough to fight racism in the sport and are content to sweep it under the carpet. He condemned incidents involving Real Madrid's Vinicius Jr. where a fan racially abused the player. He considered that the comments from the head of La Liga, suggested a permissive attitude towards racism.

First Black chairman of the Professional Footballers' Association

Garth Crooks OBE – (1958-)

Garth Crooks, OBE is an English football pundit and former professional player, playing from 1976 to 1990, for Stoke City, Tottenham Hotspur, Manchester United, West Bromwich Albion and Charlton Athletic. Throughout his career he was an active member of the Professional Footballers' Association and was elected the first black chairman in 1988.

Garth Anthony Crooks was born on 10 March 1958 in Bucknall, Stoke-on-Trent, to Jamaican parents. He developed a love for football. He progressed through the youth ranks at his local team, Stoke City before signing on as a professional in March 1976. He made his debut in April in a home game against Coventry City becoming the first black player to play for Stoke since Roy Brown in the 1940s.

He quickly made an impact by becoming the team's top scorer. Despite facing significant racial abuse, he persevered and excelled on the field. In 1980, he transferred to Tottenham Hotspur, where he helped the team win the FA Cup in 1981 and 1982 and the UEFA Cup in 1984.

In 1983 he went on loan to Manchester United and In 1985 he went on loan to West Bromwich Albion.

That same year he began taking advantage of a tuition-reimbursement benefit offered by the Professional Footballers' Association (PFA), the players' union for soccer athletes. He started with classes at the College of North East London, earning a degree in political science from North London Poly. He later went to Kings College London to study Sports Law.

In 1988 he was loaned to Charlton Athletic. This year he was also elected chairman of the 4,000-member PFA, which is the world's oldest professional athletes' association. He was the first black player ever to lead the PFA, and supported a clean-up campaign in British soccer to help end some of the racism and hooliganism in and around the game. It led to a law being passed in 1991 prohibiting the chanting of racial slurs at soccer games and giving law-enforcement officials the power to arrest offending fans. This was a major milestone for all players who have suffered years of abuse just for playing their sport.

In 1990 he was forced to retire from football due to a knee injury. As a result he gave up his role as PFA chairman. He was invited by HRH Prince Philip to chair the Institute of Professional Sport

In 1995 he was appointed to the English Sports Council by the Secretary of State.

In the 1999 Queens Birthday Honours, he was appointed an Officer of the Order of the British Empire (OBE) for his services to football punditry,

In 2003 he joined the Foreign and Commonwealth Office Caribbean Board.

In 2019 he stepped down as a trustee with Kick it Out which was a campaign started in1993 to essentially kick racism out of football in protest at the appointment of Sanjay Bhandari, a lawyer, instead of ex-footballer Brendon Batson. He felt the campaign should be more player-led at a time when footballers are being racially abused on and off the pitch.

He has been a special advisor to the renamed European Human Rights Commission, formerly known as the CRE, He has addressed the European Parliament, European Commission and UEFA on racial discrimination in football.

He chaired the Football Foundation Grass Roots Advisory Panel for 5 years and was instrumental in creating the biggest and most successful football charity in the world. He is a Member of Sport England and serves on the Sports Lottery Panel.

Since retiring from football, he has developed a successful career as a football pundit with the BBC.

First Black footballer to be transferred for a fee of £1 million

Justin Fashanu – (1961-1998)

Justin Fashanu was an English footballer who played for a variety of clubs between 1978 and 1997. In 1981 he transferred to Nottingham Forest from Norwich City, becoming the first black footballer to be transferred for a fee of £1 million.

Justinius Soni (Justin) Fashanu was born on February 19, 1961, in Hackney, London. His father, Patrick Fashanu, was a Nigerian barrister, and his mother, Pearl Lawrence, a nurse from Guyana. However the couple separated and Justin and his younger brother John were placed in a care home and later fostered by Alf and Betty Jackson in Norfolk.

As a youth, he excelled in boxing and football, attending Attleborough High School, where he was scouted by Norwich City. He turned professional in December 1978 and made a name for himself with Norwich City, scoring 40 goals in 103 appearances and winning the BBC Goal of the Season award.

His name became linked with bigger clubs and in August 1981 he signed for Nottingham Forest, becoming Britain's first £1 million black footballer.

Despite his talent, he faced severe racial abuse and, after transferring to Nottingham Forest, he also encountered challenges related to his sexuality. His relationship with manager Brian Clough soured after Clough discovered his homosexuality, leading to him being barred from training and his performance declining.

He came out publically as gay in 1990, becoming the first prominent professional footballer in England to do so. This decision brought him significant media attention, both positive and negative. He faced homophobic abuse from fans and discrimination within the sport, which significantly affected his career.

After a series of transfers, injuries, and brief stints with various clubs, his career waned. In 1998, facing an accusation of sexual assault in the US, he fled to England and tragically took his own life on May 3, 1998, at the age of 37. In his suicide note, he denied the charges and expressed his despair over the treatment he received due to his sexuality.

His legacy lives on through efforts to combat homophobia in football. The Justin Campaign, founded in his memory, works to promote inclusivity in sports. His life and career have been honoured in various ways, including a documentary film and induction into the National Football Museum Hall of Fame. A mural in Norwich also commemorates his impact on football and his pioneering role as an openly gay athlete.

First Black British player to sign for Real Madrid

Laurie Cunningham – (1956-1989)

Laurence Cunningham was an English professional footballer. A left winger, he notably played in England, France and Spain, where he became the first ever British player to sign for Real Madrid.

Laurie Paul Cunningham was born on March 8, 1956, in Archway, London, to Jamaican parents who were part of the Windrush Generation. He developed a passion for football and dancing during his youth in the 1970s. His father, Elias, was a former Jamaican race-horse jockey.

He began his football career by signing a schoolboy contract with Arsenal in 1970, but he was released in 1972. He then joined Leyton Orient in 1974, scoring 15 goals in 86 league appearances over three years.

In 1977 he transferred to West Bromwich Albion for £110,000, where he played alongside Cyrille Regis and later Brendon Batson. The trio became known as "The Three Degrees," reflecting their significant presence as black players in top-flight English football.

He made history by becoming the second black player to represent England at any level, playing for the U21 team in 1977 and later earning six caps for the senior England team between 1979 and 1980.

In 1979 he made history by becoming the first British player to transfer to Real Madrid, for a fee of £950,000. On his debut he scored twice, helping Real Madrid win the league and cup double. Despite his success, injuries and competition limited his appearances for both club and country.

Throughout the 1980s, his career took him to several clubs including Manchester United, Sporting Gijón, Marseille, Leicester City, Rayo Vallecano, Charleroi, and Wimbledon. He was part of the Wimbledon team that won the 1988 FA Cup Final against Liverpool.

His life tragically ended on July 15, 1989, when he died in a car crash in Madrid at the age of 33. He left behind his wife, Silvia Sendin-Soria, and their son, Sergio. His legacy endures, with numerous honours recognizing his impact on football.

In 2004, he was named one of West Bromwich Albion's 16 greatest players, and in 2017, statues commemorating his contributions were unveiled in both Leyton and West Bromwich.

Blue plaques in his honour have also been placed at significant locations, celebrating his contributions to the sport and his role in breaking racial barriers in football.

First Black referee to officiate in the Premier League

Uriah Rennie – (1959-2025)

Uriah Rennie is a former football referee. He progressed through the ranks and on 23 August 1997 he officiated at a Premiership game between Leeds United and Crystal Palace at Elland Road becoming the first Black man to referee a Premier League game.

Uriah Rennie was born on October 23, 1959, in Wybourn, Sheffield to Jamaican parents. He developed a passion for football, alongside his interests in kick-boxing and aikido. He started his refereeing career in 1979, working in local leagues before moving up to the Northern Premier League and eventually joining the Football League List of referees in 1994.

The journey to becoming a top-level referee is challenging, involving years of experience, fitness tests, written exams, and regular assessments. Referees start at the grassroots level and gradually move up through the ranks, with each promotion typically taking a season. Even at the highest levels of non-league football, referees earn less than £300 per match, making dedication essential.

On August 23, 1997, he made history by officiating a Premier League game between Leeds United and Crystal Palace, becoming the first black man to referee at this level. His rise was marked by significant scrutiny and criticism, but also by acclaim and admiration from football fans. Known for his bold and confident officiating style, he was not afraid to make controversial calls, such as sending off Newcastle legend Alan Shearer in his 100th game for the club.

Despite facing challenges, including a temporary demotion, his determination saw him return to the Premier League. In 2000, he became a FIFA referee, officiating at international matches until his retirement from the FIFA list in 2004. He refereed 345 official games from 1997 to 2008, issuing 984 yellow and 70 red cards. He ended his career by overseeing Liverpool's 2-0 victory over Tottenham Hotspur on May 11, 2008.

Beyond football, he earned an MBA from Sheffield Hallam University and worked for Sheffield City Trust for over 30 years. He served as a magistrate, an ambassador for The Children's Hospital Charity, a trustee of Voluntary Action Sheffield, and a patron of Weston Park Hospital Cancer Charity and St Luke's Hospice. In 2010, he became president of Hallam FC, and in 2023, he received an honorary doctorate from Sheffield Hallam University for his community work.

He supported education and sport in South Yorkshire, exemplifying how sports can transform lives.

Sadly he suffered a rare condition which left him hospitalised and paralysed from the waist down. He was also suffering from cancer and died on 8 June 2025.

Despite progress, the refereeing and football management sectors lack diversity. In the 2021-22 season, only 2% of referees in the top seven divisions were Black or Asian. Financial hurdles and systemic biases in the assessment process hinder the advancement of referees from diverse backgrounds. Efforts to promote diversity are ongoing, but progress is slow.

In 2023, Sam Allison became the second black referee in the Premier League, 15 years after Rennie made his debute. His story highlights the challenges and triumphs of breaking barriers in sports and serves as an inspiration for future generations.

First Black Woman to debut at number 1 in the Billboard blues chart and be nominated for a Grammy in the blues category

Joan Armatrading – (1950-)

Joan Armatrading is a British singer-songwriter, notable as the first Black woman in the UK to gain prominence for performing her own songs. She has built a loyal following since the 1970s, making significant strides in the music industry. In 2007, she became the first British female artist to debut at number 1 on the Billboard Blues Chart and the first female UK artist nominated for a Grammy in the blues category. Over her career, she has received three Grammy nominations, two Brit Award nominations, and an Ivor Novello Award for Outstanding Contemporary Song Collection.

Joan Anita Barbara Armatrading was born on December 9, 1950, in Basseterre, St. Kitts. She moved to Birmingham, England, at the age of seven, the third of six children. Her father, a former band member, forbade his children from touching his guitar, but she began song writing at 14 using a piano her mother bought. She taught herself guitar on a pawn shop purchase and left school at 15 to support her family, though she lost her first job for playing her guitar during breaks.

At 16, she performed her own songs at Birmingham University and local clubs. Her music spans rock, folk, jazz, blues, soul, and reggae. In 1968, she joined a touring production of the musical Hair and later collaborated with Pam Nestor on her debut album Whatever's for Us, in 1972.

After overcoming challenges with her record label, she signed with A&M Records, releasing successful albums such as Back to the Night in 1975 and Joan Armatrading in 1976 , which included the hit Love and Affection. She continued to produce hits through the late 1970s and 1980s, with albums, Me Myself I, in 1980 and, Walk Under Ladders, in 1981.

She has maintained her artistic integrity throughout her career, consistently receiving critical acclaim for her distinctive voice and musicianship.

In 1996 she received an Ivor Novello Award for Outstanding Contemporary Song Collection.

In the 2001 Birthday Honours list she was appointed Member of the Order of the British Empire (MBE) for services to music, charity and equal rights.

In addition to her music career, in 2001, after five years of studying, she earned a BA degree in history from the Open University, of which she became a trustee.

In 2007 she released album Into the Blues, which debuted at No. 1 on the US Billboard Blues Chart, making her the first UK female artist to earn that distinction. Into the Blues was also nominated for a Grammy Award, making her the first female UK artist to be nominated in the Grammy Blues category. The album remained at No 1 for 12 consecutive weeks. She toured the world in support of it and also released a deluxe edition of CD with DVD which showed her at her very best, live, on stage, performing music from across her career.

In October 2011 she was presented with a BASCA Gold Badge Award in recognition of her contribution to music. In May 2012, before her concert at Uttoxeter, as part of the 2012 Acoustic Festival of Britain, she was presented with a Lifetime Achievement Award.

In 2014 and 2015, she embarked on her last major tour, the Me Myself I Tour, the first to feature her solo on stage. The tour covered an incredible 235 dates with most selling out as soon as they went on sale. She made it clear that she was not leaving the road for good just withdrawing from yearlong tour. An accompanying CD/DVD album, entitled Me Myself I World Tour, was released in 2016.

In April 2016 she was presented with a Lifetime Achievement Award at the BBC Radio 2 Folk Awards in recognition of her influence on a generation of singer-songwriters as one of the outstanding voices in British music since the 1970s.

In the 2020 Birthday Honours list she was appointed Commander of the Order of the British Empire (CBE) for services to music, charity and equal rights.

In 2023 she was a guest at the Coronation of King Charles III and Camilla.

Her musical influence extends to various genres, and she continues to inspire with her innovative music and dedication to her craft. She remains a respected figure in the music industry, known for her deeply personal and emotionally resonant songs. Despite her success, she values privacy, focusing on her music and the love and pain it portrays rather than her personal life. She lives in Surrey, where she has a recording studio, and continues to produce and perform music, leaving an indelible mark on the world of music.

First video containing Black artists played on MTV

Musical Youth – (1982-2001)

In the early 1980s, the group Musical Youth scored a hit with their single Pass the Dutchie which was a reworking of the Mighty Diamonds Pass the Kouchie, with revised lyrics to make it more suitable for a younger audience. It quickly soared to the top of the charts in various countries, including the UK, Ireland, Australia, and Canada, and gained significant airplay on MTV, marking a milestone as the first video by black artists to receive such attention on the channel.

Musical Youth's success was part of a broader narrative concerning representation in the music industry. During MTV's infancy, there was a notable absence of music videos from black artists in heavy rotation. While Michael Jackson's Billie Jean is often credited as the first black artist video to receive heavy rotation, it was actually Prince who achieved this milestone first. Nevertheless, the early years of MTV were criticized for a perceived bias towards white artists, reflecting historical patterns of racial segregation in the music business.

The story of Musical Youth begins in Birmingham, England, where the group was formed by Freddie Waite and the Grant brothers, Kelvin and Michael. They honed their musical talents at a young age, drawing inspiration from reggae icons like Sugar Minott and Gregory Isaacs. After gaining attention with their early performances and radio appearances, they were signed to MCA Records and released their debut album, The Youth of Today, in 1982. The album enjoyed moderate success, propelled by hit singles Pass the Dutchie and Youth of Today.

Despite their initial success, they faced challenges in sustaining their career. Lineup changes and personal struggles led to a decline in their popularity by the mid-1980s. Despite attempts at a comeback, including a reunion in the early 2000s, the band never regained its former prominence.

Tragically, the band experienced personal losses, including the untimely deaths of Patrick Waite in 1993 and Freddie "Junior" Waite in 2022. Junior's passing, in particular, brought attention to the issue of mental health within the music industry.

While Musical Youth's journey had its highs and lows, their impact on music history remains significant. Their contribution to reggae-infused pop and their breakthrough on MTV paved the way for future generations of black artists in the mainstream music scene.

First Black British woman to headline the Pyramid Stage, Glastonbury

Skin from Skunk Anansie / Deborah Anne Dyer OBE – (1967-)

Skunk Anansie is a British rock band formed in 1994, known for their powerful sound and impactful presence. The band's members include Skin (lead vocals, guitar), Cass (bass, guitar, backing vocals), Ace (guitar, backing vocals), and Mark Richardson (drums and percussion). The name Skunk Anansie combines elements from Akan folk tales from Ghana with Skunk added as a twist, reflecting their edgy style.

When Skunk Anansie took to The Pyramid Stage at Glastonbary on the Sunday night of June 27, 1999, they made history. Front woman Skin became the first Black British headliner of the festival, something that would not be repeated for 20 years when Stormzy graced the stage with his iconic bulletproof vest. They were the last band of the 20th Century to headline the Glastonbury Festival closing the Pyramid Stage.

Skunk Anansie's music stands out in the Britrock scene for its hard-hitting sound, distinct from the lighter tones of Britpop. Despite facing challenges, including racial biases in the music industry, the band has remained steadfast in their identity and message. They widespread recognition for their dynamic performances and chart-topping hits

Lead vocalist Skin, born Deborah Ann Dyer, was born on August 3 1967 in Brixton, London to Jamaican parents. She overcame adversity to pursue her passion for music. Despite facing violence and prejudice, she channelled her experiences into her art, becoming known for her powerful voice and unique style.

The band toured globally, released three studio albums, and disbanded in 2001. Skin pursued a solo career, releasing albums and performing across Europe.

After a hiatus, they reunited in 2009 to the excitement of fans worldwide. They continued to release successful albums and captivate audiences with their electrifying live shows. They earned accolades such as the Kerrang! Hall of Fame Award in 2019.

Outside of music, Skin has made significant contributions to various causes and communities. She has been vocal about social and political issues, advocating against racism and Brexit's negative impacts.

In January 2021 Skin assumed the role of Chancellor at Leeds Arts University in Leeds, England.

In the Queen's 2021 Birthday Honours list, she was appointed Officer of the Order of the British Empire (OBE) for services to music. It was actually presented by King Charles in 2023.

Skunk Anansie's influence extends beyond music, inspiring generations with their resilience, talent, and unwavering commitment to their craft.

First Black British solo artist to headline the Glastonbury Festival

Stormzy – (1993-)

Stormzy is a British rapper, singer and songwriter. He was named Best Grime Act at the 2014 and 2015 MOBO Awards and an artist to look out for in the BBC's Sound of 2015 list. His debut 2017 album, Gang Signs & Prayer, was the first grime album to reach number one on the UK Albums Chart and won British Album of the Year at the 2018 Brit Awards. In 2019, he achieved his first UK number-one single with Vossi Bop and became the first black British solo artist rapper to headline the Glastonbury Festival, where he wore a Union Jack stab vest designed by artist Banksy, to highlight the rise in knife crime in London.

Stormzy, born Michael Ebenezer Kwadjo Omari Owuo Jr on 26 July 1993, in Croydon, London, is a renowned British rapper, singer, and songwriter. He grew up in South Norwood, London, with Ghanaian heritage. He attended Stanley Technical High School in South Norwood.. Despite a rebellious streak as a youngster, he excelled academically, achieving impressive grades in his GCSEs and pursuing an apprenticeship after school.

His journey into the music scene began at a young age, honing his skills in rap battles at his local youth club. He gained attention by posting freestyle videos online and releasing his debut EP, Dreamers Disease, in July 2014. His freestyle tune, Shut Up! garnered significant attention, marking his breakthrough as an artist.

His rise to prominence continued with accolades such as winning Best Grime Act at the MOBO Awards and becoming the first unsigned rapper to perform on the BBC programme, Later... with Jools Holland. He released his debut album, Gang Signs & Prayer, in 2017, which made history as the first grime album to top the UK Albums Chart and won British Album of the Year at the Brit Awards.

Throughout his career, he has used his platform to address social issues and advocate for change. He has been vocal about political matters, endorsing Labour Party leader Jeremy Corbyn and criticizing government responses to events like the Grenfell Tower fire.

He has been a staunch supporter of racial equality and justice, pledging significant donations to related causes and launching initiatives such as the Stormzy Scholarship for Black UK Students at the University of Cambridge.

Beyond music, his influence extends into various ventures, including literature with his #Merky Books imprint and philanthropy through charitable donations. He has also ventured into gaming and sports, appearing in video games and participating in community initiatives like acquiring assets for his childhood football club, AFC Croydon Athletic.

His journey exemplifies not only his musical prowess but also his commitment to social impact and community empowerment, making him a prominent figure in both the entertainment industry and activism. He has grown from a rapper to becoming a local, national, international icon, dedicated to giving back to the community whenever possible. He spends most of his money contributing to charitable donations that give back to the community.

Timeline of the Black Firsts

1774 - First Black person to vote in a general election - Charles Sancho

1831 - First Black woman to publish and write an autobiography in the UK - Mary Prince

1835 - First Black police Officer in Britain - John Kent

1838 - First Black police officer to join the London Metropolitan Police - Robert Branford

1855 - First Black nurse practitioner - Mary Seacole

1865 - First Black British MP in Scotland - Peter McLagan

1881 - First Black person to play football at international level - Andrew Watson

1883 - First Black British barrister and first graduate of the University of Oxford - Christian Cole

1889 - First Black professional footballer - Arthur Wharton

1889 - First Black person to be knighted in Britain - Sir William Conrad Reeves

1895 - First Black women's footballer in Britain - Emma Clarke

1904 - First Black Mayor of a British Town - Allan Glaisyer Minns

1906 - First Black man to play rugby for England - James Peters

1908 - First black British Olympian born in Scotland - Louis Bruce

1910 - First Black Bus Driver - Joe Clough

1913 - First Black mayor in London - John Archer

1917 - First Black British Army Officer - Walter Tull

1917 - First Black British Pilot - William Robinson Clarke

1920 - First Black British Olympian - Harry Edward

1939 - First Black singer to feature on BBC Radio - Evelyn Dove

1939 - First Black Special Constable in Devon - Cecil Wilberforce Rodgers

1941 - First Black woman in the British Armed Forces - Lilian Bader

1941 - First Black Woman to be employed by the BBC - Una Marson

1948 - First Black fighter to win a British boxing title - Dick Turpin

1951- First Black British actor leading a film - Earl Cameron CBE

1954 - First Black person to have a number-one hit in the UK Singles Chart - Winifred Atwell

1955 - First Black British fireman - Frank Bailey

1958 - Founder of Britain's first major black newspaper - Claudia Jones

1960 - First Black teacher employed by the Liverpool Education Authority - Norman Beaton

1960 - First Black female book publisher - Margaret Busby CBE, Hon. FRSL

1962 - First Black British Train Driver - Wilston Samuel Jackson

1962 - First Black Magistrate - Eric Irons OBE

1963 - First Black British footballer to play for England - John Charles

1964 - First Black Special Police Officer in Gloucestershire - Astley Lloyd Blair

1966 - First Black Guard at Euston Station - Asquith Xavier

1966 - Founder New Beacon Books, the first specialist Caribbean publishing company in Britain - John La Rose

1967 - First Black police officer to join the London Metropolitan Police - Norwell Roberts QPM

1968 - First Black woman police officer in Britain - Fay Allen

1968 - First Black head of a major Barristers Chambers. First Black Deputy Circuit Judge in the UK – Tunji Sowande

1968 - First Black head teacher in London - Beryl Gilroy

1968 - First Black British Femle Olympian - Anita Neil

1968 - First Black person to be an on-camera reporter and interviewer on British Television - Barbara Blake-Hannah

1969 - First Black Headteacher in Britain - Yvonne Conolly CBE

1969 - First Black UK peer - Baron Learie Constantine, Kt, MBE

1970 - First Black well-known Stand-up Comedian - Charlie Williams

1970 - First Black head teacher in Wales - Betty Campbell

1972 - First Black captain for Great Britain in any sport - Clive Sullivan MBE

1973 - First Black woman to be awarded the MBE - Sybil Phoenix OBE

1973 - First Black British News Reporter - Sir Trevor McDonald

1974 - First Black Daily Radio Show / First National Black Newspaper - Alex Pascall OBE

1978 - First Black player to play for the England football team - Viv Anderson MBE

1979 - First sickle-cell and thalassemia nurse specialist - Dame Elizabeth Anionwu OM DBE FRCN

1979 - First Black British player to sign for Real Madrid - Laurie Cunningham

1981 - First Black woman to be a governor of the BBC - Dame Jocelyn Barrow DBE

1981 - First Black female newsreader on British television - Moira Stuart CBE

1981 - First Black footballer to command a seven-figure fee - Justin Fashanu

1982 - First Black Women's theatre company - Theatre of Black Women

1982 - First video containing Black artists played on MTV - Musical Youth

1983 - First Black mayor of Southwark - Sam Beaver King MBE

1984 - First Black British woman to win an Olympic gold medal - Tessa Sanderson CBE

1985 - First Black male bishop in the Church of Englan - Wilfred Wood KA

1987 - First Black British MP – One of 3 - Bernie Grant

1987 - First Black woman elected to Parliament - Diane Abbott

1988 - First Black Chief Executive of the Inner London Education Authority - Baron Herman Ousley

1988 - First Black man to become a Queen's Counsel in England and Wales – Dr John Anthony Roberts QC CBE

1988 - First Black model to appear on the front cover of Time, French Vogue, Russian Vogue and American Vogue - Naomi Campbell

1988 - First Black chairman of the Professional Footballers' Association - Garth Crooks OBE

1989 - First Black Director of Education and Leisure Services in Britain - Gus John

1989 - First Black Professor in Scotland - Sir Godfrey Palmer Kt OBE CD

1990 - First Black presenter of the children's television programme Blue Peter - Diane-Louise Jordan

1991 - First British comedy troupe consisting entirely of Black actresses - Bibi Crew

1992 - First Black leader of a major British trade union - Baron William Morris of Handsworth

1992 - First Black presenter of a TV cooking show - Ainsley Harriot MBE

1993 - First British man to win 100 metres gold at the Olympic Games, World Championships, European Championships and Commonwealth Games - Linford Christie OBE

1993 - First player to top the Premier League's goalscoring and assist charts in the same season - Andrew Cole

1993 - First Black British England football captain - Paul Ince

1997 - First Black British Football Referee - Uriah Rennie

1998 - First Black woman to manage an England national football team - Hope Powell

1999 - First Black British woman to headline the Pyramid Stage, Glastonbury - Skin from Skunk Anansie / Debbie Ann Dyer OBE

2000 - First Black British Female standup to sell out a West End theatre - Angie Le Mar

2000 First Black British boxer to win Olympic gold at super-heavyweight division - Audley Harrison MBE

2001 - First Black British boxer to reach the final of the World Amateur Boxing Championships - David Haye

2002 - First Black British Cabinet Minister - Baron Paul Boateng CVO PC DL

2002 - First Black Chief Executive of the Inner London Education Authority - Caroline Newman

2002 - First Black living poet to be published in the Penguin Modern Classics series - Linton Kwesi Johnson

2003 - First Black woman to become a Cabinet Minister - Baroness Valerie Amos LG CH PC

2004 - First Black chief constable in the United Kingdom - Michael Fuller

2004 - First Black person to be appointed to the senior judiciary of England and Wales - Dame Linda Dobbs DBE

2005 - First Black archbishop in the Church of England - Baron John Sentamu PC

2006 - First Black British England women's football captain - Mary Phillip

2007 - First Black woman to be appointed a Queen's Council - Baroness Patricia Scotland of Asthal

2007 - First Black female UK artist to be nominated for a Grammy in the blues category - Joan Armatrading CBE

2008 - First Black British F1 Grand Prix World Champion - Sir Lewis Hamilton MBE Hon FREng

2008 - First Black British Premiership football manager - Paul Ince

2011 - First Black Studies professor in the UK - Kehinde Andrews

2011 - First Black person to be a Football Association Director - Dame Heather Rabbatts DBE

2012 - First British athlete to win two gold medals at the same world championship - Sir Mohamed Farah CBE OLY

2013 - First Black person to become a Permanent Secretary at the Treasury - Dame Sharon White, Lady Chote DBE

2013 - First Black Children's Laureate - Malorie Blackman OBE

2013 - First Black filmmaker to win Academy Award for best picture - Sir Steve McQueen CBE

2015 - First professional orchestra made up of majority Black, Asian and ethnically diverse musicians - Chinekei Orchestra

2016 - First Black musician to win the BBC Young Musician Award - Sheku Kanneh-Mason MBE

2018 - First Black woman to be appointed to a professorial chair in History in the United Kingdom - Olivette Otele FRHists FLSW

2019 - First Black female bishop in the Church of England - Rose Hudson-Wilkin CD MBE KHC

2019 - First Black Chief Midwifery Officer - Jacqueline Dunkley-Bent OBE

2019 - First Black British model for Victoria's Secret Angel - Leomie Anderson

2019 - First Black British person to win the Booker Prize - Bernardine Evaristo OBE FRSL FRSA

2019 - First Black British solo artist to headline Glastonbury Festival – Stormzy

2020 - First Black writer to reach number one in the UK paperback fiction charts - Bernardine Evaristo OBE FRSL FRSA

2020 - First Black woman to win the Book of the Year award for her novel Queenie - Candice Carty-Williams

2020 - First Black woman to win a gold medal in the Physics News Award - Margaret Aderin-Pocock MBE

2021 - First Black British actor to win an Oscar - Daniel Kaluuya

2021 - First Black chair of the Rugby Football Union - Tom Ilube CBE

2024 – First Black woman leader of the Conservative Party – Kemi Badenoch

Reflection

This has been about identifying the first Black pioneers in particular areas and I know there are a lot of other firsts out there at all levels of British society, which I have not captured. However, just as important are the second and subsequent black people in positions. One person achieving is no guarantee that others will be deemed acceptable regardless of their ability or capability.

www.ingramcontent.com/pod-product-compliance
Lightning Source LLC
Chambersburg PA
CBHW070501160726

48003CB00004B/1375